*Understanding
The
Short Story*

UNDERSTANDING THE SHORT STORY

Annelle S. Houk
Carlotta L. Bogart

THE ODYSSEY PRESS, NEW YORK

Copyright © 1969 by Western Publishing Company, Inc.
Published by The Odyssey Press, a division of
Western Publishing Company, Inc.

All rights reserved

Printed in the United States

Library of Congress Catalog Card Number: 68-55259

A 0 9 8 7 6 5 4 3 2 1

ACKNOWLEDGMENTS

The authors are grateful to the following publishers and literary agents for permission to use the materials listed below.

THE BODLEY HEAD. For "The Schartz-Metterklume Method" from *The Bodley Head Saki* by H. H. Munro. Reprinted with the permission of The Bodley Head.

J. M. DENT & SONS LTD. For "The Crumbs of One Man's Year" from *Quite Early One Morning* by Dylan Thomas. Reprinted with the permission of J. M. Dent & Sons Ltd. and the Trustees for the Copyrights of the late Dylan Thomas. For "The Secret Sharer" by Joseph Conrad. Reprinted with permission of J. M. Dent & Sons Ltd. and the Trustees of the Joseph Conrad Estate.

ALFRED A. KNOPF, INC. For "The Other Side of the Hedge" *(The Celestial Omnibus)* by E. M. Forster. From *The Collected Tales of E. M. Forster*. Published in 1947 by Alfred A. Knopf, Inc. Reprinted by permission of the publisher.

NEW DIRECTIONS PUBLISHING CORPORATION. For "The Crumbs of One Man's Year" from *Quite Early One Morning* by Dylan Thomas. Copyright 1954 by New Directions. Reprinted by permission of the publisher, New Directions Publishing Corporation.

ACKNOWLEDGMENTS

SCHOCKEN BOOKS INC. For "A Country Doctor" from *The Penal Colony* by Franz Kafka. Copyright 1948 by Schocken Books Inc., New York. Translated by Willa and Edwin Muir. For "Couriers" from *Parables and Paradoxes* by Franz Kafka. Copyright 1945, 1958 by Schocken Books Inc., New York. Reprinted by permission of the publisher.

CHARLES SCRIBNER'S SONS. "The Beggar" is reprinted with the permission of Charles Scribner's Sons from *Stories of Russian Life* by Anton Chekov, translated by Marian Fell. Copyright 1914 Charles Scribner's Sons; renewal copyright 1942 Olivia Fell Vans Agnew.

SIDGWICK & JACKSON LTD. For "The Other Side of the Hedge" by E. M. Forster. From *The Collected Tales of E. M. Forster*. Reprinted by permission of the Author's Representatives and of the Publishers Sidgwick & Jackson Ltd.

MRS. HELEN THURBER. For "The Unicorn in the Garden" by James Thurber. Copr. © 1940 James Thurber. From *Fables For Our Time,* published by Harper and Row. Originally printed in *The New Yorker*. Reprinted by permission of Mrs. Helen Thurber.

THE VIKING PRESS, INC. For "The Schartz-Metterklume Method" by H. H. Munro, from *The Complete Short Stories of Saki* by H. H. Munro. All Rights Reserved. Reprinted by permission of The Viking Press, Inc.

A. WATKINS, INC. For "The Champion of the World" by Roald Dahl. Copyright 1959 Roald Dahl, first published in the *New Yorker* magazine.

To the Reader

We believe two things about you: you already read with enjoyment short stories that you understand, and you are willing to understand more difficult stories if you are shown how.

Therefore, we have chosen stories that we hope you will enjoy, though some may puzzle you at first, and that we are confident you can learn to read in greater depth. Because we are convinced that every effective story can be understood by anyone who can read its details intelligently, we will show you how to recognize significant detail, how to ask questions of interpretation, how to arrange detail to answer those questions, and how then to develop these subjects for papers.

At times we write at length about our understanding of a story. Never accept that interpretation or any other until you have understood it, tested it, and honestly agreed with it. Cling stubbornly to your right to be puzzled. That dissatisfied, genuine "I don't understand *why*" is your greatest natural asset as a critical reader. Because our techniques for reading detail will help answer your questions, you may simply adopt them directly. We hope that some of you will use them to develop far better techniques of your own.

Your most rewarding approach to reading is alert openness to all that an author may attempt to convey. Hence, every story should be read without deciding ahead why or if you should like it and with no anticipation of problems to be solved. For you and every reader, the understanding of a story should be as creative an art as the writing of it was for the author. This means bringing such close attention to the information that the author provides that by the time major action begins you are anticipating the range of possibilities in that time and that place for those people. For you, then, a short story is a discovery, and what the author creates on a page you recreate in your mind. As a consequence, though you can never know positively the intention of an author, you can discover his method and much of his meaning quite precisely. Relax, read, and enjoy—then study to extend that enjoyment.

A. S. H.
C. L. B.

Contents

Introduction	1
THE SCHARTZ-METTERKLUME METHOD	5
Saki (H. H. Munro)	
HOP-FROG	21
Edgar Allan Poe	
THE UNICORN IN THE GARDEN	42
James Thurber	
THE BEGGAR	53
Anton Chekov	
BARTLEBY	77
Herman Melville	
THE HOLLOW OF THE THREE HILLS	134
Nathaniel Hawthorne	
THE SECRET SHARER	149
Joseph Conrad	
THE CHAMPION OF THE WORLD	203
Roald Dahl	

CONTENTS

The Crumbs of One Man's Year   232
    Dylan Thomas

Fable, Parable, and Allegory   252

The Prodigal Son   257
    Luke 15: 11–32

Couriers   263
    Franz Kafka

The Other Side of the Hedge   266
    E. M. Forster

A Country Doctor   277
    Franz Kafka

Index   319

*Understanding
The
Short Story*

Introduction

The short story is essentially a brief prose fictional narrative. However, only the word *fictional* applies constantly to all works currently called short stories: all are artistic representations of truth rather than factual, literal presentations of reality. To present artistically even the most realistic story, the author must select his characters and their conflict, choose complicating actions to bring the conflict to a climax, and decide on a resolution—all for the purpose of conveying through fiction some comment of his own about the nature of man or of man's place in the universe. Since what authors do with the short story actually determines its definition, any broad definition must be modified greatly to include the tremendous variety of short stories.

Each work calls for an individual analysis to discover what qualifies it to be called a short story. As Edgar Allan Poe and most critics since have demanded, the majority of short stories are of a length to be read at a single sitting. However, there is now plentiful brief fiction that takes longer. Even the definition of prose when applied to narrative fiction is changing as authors more and more frequently use the highly figurative, symbolic, and rhythmic language of poetry. Also, the concept of narrative as the telling of a story with a beginning, middle, and end now has to be modified to permit discussion of the loosely knit tale, the sketch with an emphasis rather than a story line, and the single episode examined at length for a restricted purpose, like the illumination of character. The stories in this book have been deliberately chosen to show as much as possible of this evolved diversity in length, language, and form.

The very diversity of the short story makes futile any argument that one kind of short story is greater or better than another. Each story teller reflects the concerns and uses the forms of his day so long as they express what he wants to say. Major innovations occur only in those periods when the concerns change so much that the existing forms and the traditional uses of language no longer seem adequate to express them. When fiction is in transition in form or style, its quality is often so uneven that readers and critics dismiss the new in favor of the sustained quality of the old although they will later applaud these same innovations when some author finally perfects them. Therefore, the most recent form evolved need not be the best, though it may be the most interesting for the contemporary reader.

Despite all the modifications of the short story's definition, certain limitations—set primarily by length—do distinguish from the novel and the drama almost all short stories of whatever period. In brief fiction an author usually has room to develop only one character to any marked extent, and he has many problems in making a major change in that character believable. To make a change credible, the major character almost always must be presented at some critical moment of his life when a conflict, usually of long standing, is about to be brought to a climax and resolved in a way that will change his life or his character or both. Since the action begins, then, in the middle of things, what can be shown chronologically in any short story is usually a matter of hours or days, with whatever has happened in the past presented in flashbacks justified by their relevance to the present action of the major character. The limitation to a concern with a single character also tends to minimize the minor conflicts that in the novel and drama often elaborate the central conflict. Therefore, minor characters exist in part for themselves but primarily to sharpen the major characterization by contrast of motives, actions, and attitudes.

While the length of the story restricts the development of character and conflict, it often encourages authors to use diction, symbols,

INTRODUCTION

and structure with the compactness of narrative poetry. The modern preference for dramatic form is also a prime cause for the multiplication of symbols in the short story. Particularly for the presentation of character, the modern writers depend more upon the person's actions and conversations to disclose his character and less upon the narrator's assertions or extensive descriptions of the person's state of mind. In a sense, then, the short story has moved in narrative technique toward the drama and poetry, and away from the novel. Therefore, the short story increasingly demands the same close attention that too often is reserved solely for reading poetry.

This extended definition of the short story is of no use to the reader unless it can make a difference in his understanding when he reads. All of these definitions and terms now must be translated into techniques of study applicable to the reader's personal experience of fiction. Because the majority of short stories are formal—even the majority of stories that reflect contemporary concerns—techniques taught here will assist the reader in understanding form. When he begins the study of the psychological story, the reader still will find these tools necessary. In the modern symbolic story, he will find them crucial.

Understanding a story involves understanding several levels of meaning. The simplest of these is the factual level of who did what. The far more important question, why, draws the reader into a consideration of the deepest nature of the fictional characters and, on a universal level, into a consideration of the nature of man. If the simplest factual understanding of the story is not absolutely clear, almost inevitably a reader makes serious misjudgments of character and meaning when he attempts interpretation. Particularly if a reader, as a student, is to write papers about his reading, he must be positive of precisely which details lead him to intuit the ideas of an author or to form his opinion of a character. This book focuses on the recognition of significant details, the gathering of them, and the appropriate use of them to back critical opinion.

It is the method of this book to introduce literary terms where they can be applied to a specific piece of fiction, to reinforce their introduction with practice in a second story, and to keep applying them while adding new techniques to assist in reading increasingly difficult literature. Discussion, explanation, and suggestions for further study follow each story. Because these study materials are cumulative, what is learned from the first story will be needed and used throughout the book. The materials following every story increase the reader's skill and add some essential step for understanding later stories. Therefore, the stories should be studied in order.

The Schartz-Metterklume Method
BY "SAKI" (H. H. MUNRO)

Lady Carlotta stepped out on to the platform of the small wayside station and took a turn or two up and down its uninteresting length, to kill time till the train should be pleased to proceed on its way. Then, in the roadway beyond, she saw a horse struggling with a more than ample load, and a carter of the sort that seems to bear a sullen hatred against the animal that helps him to earn a living. Lady Carlotta promptly betook her to the roadway, and put rather a different complexion on the struggle. Certain of her acquaintances were wont to give her plentiful admonition as to the undesirability of interfering on behalf of a distressed animal, such interference being "none of her business." Only once had she put the doctrine of non-interference into practice, when one of its most eloquent exponents had been besieged for nearly three hours in a small and extremely uncomfortable maytree by an angry boar-pig, while Lady Carlotta, on the other side of the fence, had proceeded with the water-colour sketch she was engaged on, and refused to interfere between the boar and his prisoner. It is to be feared that she lost the friendship of the ultimately rescued lady. On this occasion she merely lost the train, which gave way to the first sign of impatience it had shown throughout the journey, and steamed off without her. She bore the desertion with philosophical indifference; her friends and relations were thoroughly well used to the fact of her luggage arriving without her. She wired a vague noncommittal message to her destination to say that she was coming on "by another train." Before she had time to think what her next move might be she was confronted by an imposingly attired lady, who seemed to be taking a prolonged mental inventory of her clothes and looks.

"You must be Miss Hope, the governess I've come to meet," said the apparition, in a tone that admitted of very little argument.

"Very well, if I must I must," said Lady Carlotta to herself with dangerous meekness.

"I am Mrs. Quabarl," continued the lady; "and where, pray, is your luggage?"

"It's gone astray," said the alleged governess, falling in with the excellent rule of life that the absent are always to blame; the luggage had, in point of fact, behaved with perfect correctitude. "I've just telegraphed about it," she added, with a nearer approach to truth.

"How provoking," said Mrs. Quabarl; "these railway companies are so careless. However, my maid can lend you things for the night," and she led the way to her car.

During the drive to the Quabarl mansion Lady Carlotta was impressively introduced to the nature of the charge that had been thrust upon her; she learned that Claude and Wilfred were delicate, sensitive young people, that Irene had the artistic temperament highly developed, and that Viola was something or other else of a mould usually commonplace among children of that class and type in the twentieth century.

"I wish them not only to be *taught*," said Mrs. Quabarl, "but *interested* in what they learn. In their history lessons, for instance, you must try to make them feel that they are being introduced to the life-stories of men and women who really lived, not merely committing a mass of names and dates to memory. French, of course, I shall expect you to talk at mealtimes several days in the week."

"I shall talk French four days of the week and Russian in the remaining three."

"Russian? My dear Miss Hope, no one in the house speaks or understands Russian."

"That will not embarrass me in the least," said Lady Carlotta coldly.

Mrs. Quabarl, to use a colloquial expression, was knocked off her perch. She was one of those imperfectly self-assured individuals who are magnificent and autocratic as long as they are not seriously opposed. The least show of unexpected resistance goes a long way towards rendering them cowed and apologetic. When the new governess failed to express wondering admiration of the large newly purchased and expensive car, and lightly alluded to the superior advantages of one or two makes which had just been put on the market, the discomfiture of her patroness became almost abject. Her feelings were those which might have animated a general of ancient warfaring days, on beholding his heaviest battle-elephant ignominiously driven off the field by slingers and javelin throwers.

At dinner that evening, although reinforced by her husband, who usually duplicated her opinions and lent her moral support generally, Mrs. Quabarl regained none of her lost ground. The governess not only helped herself well and truly to wine, but held forth with considerable show of critical knowledge on various vintage matters, concerning which the Quabarls were in no wise able to pose as authorities. Previous governesses had limited their conversation on the wine topic to a respectful and doubtless sincere expression of a preference for water. When this one went as far as to recommend a wine firm in whose hands you could not go very far wrong Mrs. Quabarl thought it time to turn the conversation into more usual channels.

"We got very satisfactory references about you from Canon Teep," she observed; "a very estimable man, I should think."

"Drinks like a fish and beats his wife, otherwise a very lovable character," said the governess imperturbably.

"My *dear* Miss Hope! I trust you are exaggerating," exclaimed the Quabarls in unison.

"One must in justice admit that there is some provocation," continued the romancer. "Mrs. Teep is quite the most irritating bridge-player that I have ever sat down with; her leads and declarations would condone a certain amount of brutality in her partner, but to souse her with the contents of the only soda-water syphon in the house on a Sunday afternoon, when one couldn't get another, argues an indifference to the comfort of others which I cannot altogether overlook. You may think me hasty in my judgments, but it was practically on account of the syphon incident that I left."

"We will talk of this some other time," said Mrs. Quabarl hastily.

"I shall never allude to it again," said the governess with decision.

Mr. Quabarl made a welcome diversion by asking what studies the new instructress proposed to inaugurate on the morrow.

"History to begin with," she informed him.

"Ah, history," he observed sagely; "now, in teaching them history you must take care to interest them in what they learn. You must make them feel that they are being introduced to the life-stories of men and women who really lived—"

"I've told her all that," interposed Mrs. Quabarl.

"I teach history on the Schartz-Metterklume method," said the governess loftily.

"Ah, yes," said her listeners, thinking it expedient to assume an acquaintance at least with the name.

"What are you children doing out here?" demanded Mrs. Quabarl the next morning, on finding Irene sitting rather glumly at the head of the stairs, while her sister was perched in an attitude of depressed discomfort on the window-seat behind her, with a wolf-skin rug almost covering her.

"We are having a history lesson," came the unexpected reply. "I am supposed to be Rome, and Viola up there is the she-wolf; not a real wolf, but the figure of one that the Romans used to set store by—I forget why. Claude and Wilfred have gone to fetch the shabby women."

"The shabby women?"

"Yes, they've got to carry them off. They didn't want to, but Miss Hope got one of father's fives-bats and said she'd give them a number nine spanking if they didn't, so they've gone to do it."

A loud, angry screaming from the direction of the lawn drew Mrs. Quabarl thither in hot haste, fearful lest the threatened castigation might even now be in process of infliction. The outcry, however, came principally from the two small daughters of the lodge-keeper, who were being hauled and pushed towards the house by the panting and dishevelled Claude and Wilfred, whose task was rendered even more arduous by the incessant, if not very effectual, attacks of the captured maidens' small brother. The governess, fives-bat in hand, sat negligently on the stone balustrade, presiding over the scene with the cold impartiality of a Goddess of Battles. A furious and repeated chorus of "I'll tell muvver" rose from the lodge children, but the lodge-mother, who was hard of hearing, was for the moment immersed in the preoccupation of her washtub. After an apprehensive glance in the direction of the lodge (the good woman was gifted with the highly militant temper which is sometimes the privilege of deafness) Mrs. Quabarl flew indignantly to the rescue of the struggling captives.

"Wilfred! Claude! Let those children go at once. Miss Hope, what on earth is the meaning of this scene?"

"Early Roman history; the Sabine women, don't you know? It's the Schartz-Metterklume method to make children understand history by acting it themselves; fixes it in their memory, you know. Of course, if, thanks to your interference, your boys go through life thinking that the Sabine women ultimately escaped, I really cannot be held responsible."

"You may be very clever and modern, Miss Hope," said Mrs. Quabarl firmly, "but I should like you to leave here by the next train. Your luggage will be sent after you as soon as it arrives."

"I'm not certain exactly where I shall be for the next few days," said the dismissed instructress of youth; "you might keep my luggage till I wire my address. There are only a couple of trunks and some golfclubs and a leopard cub."

"A leopard cub!" gasped Mrs. Quabarl. Even in her departure this extraordinary person seemed destined to leave a trail of embarrassment behind her.

"Well, it's rather left off being a cub; it's more than half-grown, you know. A fowl every day and a rabbit on Sundays is what it usually gets. Raw beef makes it too excitable. Don't trouble about getting the car for me, I'm rather inclined for a walk."

And Lady Carlotta strode out of the Quabarl horizon.

The advent of the genuine Miss Hope, who had made a mistake as to the day on which she was due to arrive, caused a turmoil which that good lady was quite unused to inspiring. Obviously the Quabarl family had been woefully befooled, but a certain amount of relief came with the knowledge.

"How tiresome for you, dear Carlotta," said her hostess, when the overdue guest ultimately arrived; "how very tiresome losing your train and having to stop overnight in a strange place."

"Oh, dear, no," said Lady Carlotta; "not at all tiresome—for me."

The Objective Summary

If a reader is to understand a story thoroughly, he must develop some technique for looking objectively at it, and he must repeatedly check to see if his feelings interfere with his recognition or handling of fact. A simple but effective test is for the reader to require himself to write a one or two sentence **objective summary** of a story as soon as he completes his first reading of it. Suppose he writes of "The Schartz-Metterklume Method":

> An English noblewoman stranded in a small town amuses herself for a day at the expense of local pompous, social-climbing fakes by pretending to be a governess.

There are three main tests for a reader's objectivity:

1. **Are his facts accurate?** Lady Carlotta is an English noblewoman. She does impersonate a governess in a house in a small town.
2. **Has he interpreted rather than recorded actions?** An objective summary calls for a simple statement of what Lady Carlotta does, not why she does it. Although she certainly does amuse herself at

the Quabarls' expense, the statement is an interpretation, not an objective record.

3. **Has he attitudes toward the characters that may color his view of the facts?** If he thinks of the Quabarls as "pompous, social-climbing fakes," he may substitute his own opinions for the facts that Saki gives to make these characters individuals. If this substitution occurs, the reader will be in constant danger of oversimplifying his characters and hence of responding shallowly to what the author has to say about what people are like.

Because the Quabarls were interpreted rather than identified and because Lady Carlotta's action was explained rather than illustrated, the sample summary fails to establish clearly the basic facts of the story.

An objective single sentence summary of any story can be set up on a rather precise formula:

1. the major characters must be named and further identified by nouns (often written as appositives) that state facts about occupation, rank, or training;

2. the subject of the sentence is almost inevitably the major character;

3. the verb or verbs of the sentence—in the active voice—are a summary, in order, of the major actions of the story.

An adequate objective summary of "The Schartz-Metterklume Method" written according to this formula would be:

> Lady Carlotta, an English noblewoman, loses her train at a small wayside station, decides that if she "must be" governess she will be, acts as governess until she is fired, and continues her journey.

Two things are clear from this sentence: despite its accuracy, this is emphatically *not* what the story is about, and, secondly, it does not reflect at all the flavor of the story. Why then bother to write such a sentence? First, as he struggled to condense the story, the reader should have become aware that there were many things about it that he did not know precisely. Second, he should have recognized that the objective level of the story consists primarily of action, and that there are really not a great many major actions. (Action is seldom what a story is about but is almost always the essential framework on which the reader's understanding depends.) Third, if he has successfully removed his opinions from the sentence, he has forced himself to identify them clearly. After such an exercise, he should be more able and willing to find and examine facts, and he should be able to avoid letting his opinions warp his study. Probably the best thing that can happen to a reader is that he will realize the impossibility of writing an adequate objective summary of a story until after studying it thoroughly.

The Action Line

The simplest technique for examining action in a short story is the making of an **action line**—a summary list of all major actions in chronological order. The list begins in this story with the first action, Lady Carlotta's leaving the train, and it ends with her arriving at her destination.

Listed in this fashion, each of the major events of the story can be evaluated for its purpose and effect; and the action line can serve as an accurate index to details needed for study in greater depth. The action included is limited to major movements or speeches of persons. What is omitted is description, interpretation, and internal action (thoughts and decisions). That is not to say that Mrs. Quabarl thinks nothing, for example, when Lady Carlotta "strode out of the Quabarl horizon" leaving her anticipating the arrival of luggage and a leopard. In other words, though what a character thinks is critically important to the understanding of a story, all that appears in an action line summary is the outward result of that thought. In this case, the turmoil inspired by the arrival of the real Miss Hope is represented on the action line simply as "Miss Hope arrives." The reader must supply, from his own mind, what goes on in the minds of the Quabarls. Understood in this way, an action line is nothing more than an ascending chronological list of the major outward

"SAKI": *The Schartz-Metterklume Method*

                Lady Carlotta arrives at original destination
                Miss Hope arrives
                      strides out of the Quabarls' horizon
          Lady Carlotta explains about luggage and leopard
                    says she will send luggage
            Mrs. Quabarl fires Miss Hope
        Lady Carlotta places blame for wrecked history on
                          Mrs. Quabarl
                asks meaning of scene
                  orders Lady Carlotta to stop
            Mrs. Quabarl discovers history in action
         Quabarls say "Ah, yes," indicating acquaintance with
                          Method
        Lady Carlotta announces the Schartz-Metterklume
                          Method
      Mr. Quabarl changes subject to how to teach history
     Lady Carlotta says she will never discuss it again
    Mrs. Quabarl says they will discuss it later
   Lady Carlotta discredits her "former employers"
  Mrs. Quabarl changes the subject to Miss Hope's references
        drinks and gives advice about wines
 Lady Carlotta says she won't be embarrassed by that
  Mrs. Quabarl squelches with "no one speaks Russian"
Lady Carlotta announces she will speak Russian as well as French
 Mrs. Quabarl orders French spoken
  Lady Carlotta replies, "If I must, I must"
 Mrs. Quabarl says "You must be Miss Hope"
       wires about luggage
      loses train
     interferes with carter
Lady Carlotta leaves train

events in a short story. It excludes all thoughts but records acts that result from decisions. The action line is thus a summary of major events only—the expository actions that introduce a character in a particular setting and prepare for a conflict, and the actions that initiate, complicate, bring to a climax, and resolve a conflict.

The initial problem in learning to make action lines is deciding what to include. If one includes too little, his list will be boringly general and perhaps capable of summarizing a number of different stories. Including too much is not so serious an error because major points that are obscured can always be dug back out again. Certainly the long list assures that one story can never be mistaken for another. Nevertheless, every reader needs a criterion for telling a major from a minor action. That criterion is an understanding of the meaning of conflict.

Conflict

A **conflict** is a sharp disagreement or a collision of interests, ideas, and so forth. Its use as a literary term differs from the popular use only in that its emphasis is not only on the process of conflict but also on its resolution. There are four basic general conflicts possible: (1) man against himself; (2) man against another man; (3) man against society; (4) man against nature and/or the supernatural. Of course, sometimes society and nature are personified in some way, and even the gods act as persons. In "The Schartz-Metterklume Method" the conflict is man-against-man: Lady Carlotta against Mrs. Quabarl. Although the conflict could be discussed as a study of the individual (Lady Carlotta) against the superficial conventions of society (Mrs. Quabarl), the better decision is to deal with a conflict in its simplest terms.

Since a conflict does involve opposing forces, and since an action line is a chronological summary of the major development in that conflict, logically the action line is also a summary of the external evidence of a conflict. In every short story, hence in every action summary, there must be some action that sets in motion the conflict —a conflict that is potential, however, in the nature of the major character from the beginning of the story. Here Lady Carlotta is the **protagonist** (the major actor), and Mrs. Quabarl is her opponent (the **antagonist**). This first essential action is called the inciting action precisely because it stimulates the protagonist to respond in some manner.

The Inciting Action

The **inciting action** has several characteristics that identify it, even in a story more difficult than "The Schartz-Metterklume Method":

1. a character or a force other than the protagonist performs an action not expected by the protagonist;

2. that act forces or provokes the protagonist to action;

3. the protagonist responds in accordance with his nature but without time to think deeply (usually his response is dual: an immediate emotional action followed almost instantly by a second action that represents the way that the protagonist deliberately handles that emotion);

4. his responses define the precise nature of his opposition to the antagonist and make inevitable his particular conflict (given an inciting action, and the particular response of the protagonist, the reader should not be able to imagine a conflict different from that presented by the author).

The inciting action is the point that marks the beginning of the actions of the conflict. In almost no story can it be the first action because the author must have an opportunity to introduce his characters, at least hint at their natures, and set them in a precise time and place. This necessary information is considered to be expository (explanatory); therefore, this part of the story is called the **exposition.** The **expository actions** that occur before the inciting action should be listed on the action line. They can easily be differentiated from the inciting action because they do not define but only prepare for the conflict. Obviously, it is essential that Lady Carlotta get off the train, so that action should be included in the action line. Equally obviously, however, her leaving the train is not the inciting action because any number of different stories could develop from that fact alone (she could board the train again, break a leg on the platform, be run over by the train, etc.). Seeing the horse and interfering with its driver can be seen as important in revealing her character. These actions are even necessary for the story (hence the action line) since her interference keeps her from catching her train again. However, the action, though necessary, does not "make inevitable this particular story" because the carter certainly is not her antagonist throughout the story—nor for that matter, is the horse. In contrast, the whole incident of her placidly painting while her friend begged to be rescued from the boar has no place on an action line because nothing but present action goes on the action line. However, it serves as an excellent example of **antecedent action:** action that occurs before a story but that bears directly either on the nature of a character or on the outcome of the action. Surely her willingness to lose a friend by following her advice prepares the reader to believe that she is quite capable of impulsively imitating a governess. Telegraphing friends about her delayed arrival can go into the action line also, but only because it frees her to respond as she wishes to the inciting action.

Apply the four tests for the inciting action to the next possible action:

1. **Does a character other than the protagonist (Lady Carlotta) act unexpectedly?** Has Lady Carlotta any reason to expect a person like Mrs. Quabarl to appear at all, and much less to decide, after examining the dress of Lady Carlotta, that a noblewoman is her expected governess?
2. **Does the antagonist's (Mrs. Quabarl's) action force or provoke the protagonist to action? (Remember that speech is an action, especially a speech that reflects a decision.)** If Mrs. Quabarl had not acted and spoken as she did, would Lady Carlotta have been likely to pretend to be the governess?
3. **Does the protagonist respond in accordance with her nature but without time to think deeply?** Given that Lady Carlotta would leave a friend in a tree three hours simply to demonstrate to her the error of her advice never to interfere with animals, can you believe that, confronted by "an apparition" whose "tone

... admitted of very little argument," Lady Carlotta would impersonate a governess?
4. **Does the protagonist's response define the precise nature of her opposition to the antagonist, and does it make inevitable this particular story?** Does the dangerously meek acceptance by Lady Carlotta of her role as governess hired by a woman whose tone admits of little argument make you believe that all the rest happened as Saki says? Does the whole story grow believably from the natures of the two women?

After answering these questions, it is clear that Mrs. Quabarl's saying "You must be Miss Hope" is the inciting action and that Lady Carlotta's reply, "If I must, I must," is the protagonist's response.

Complication of the Conflict

Once the inciting action by someone other than the protagonist has provoked the protagonist's response, the complication of the conflict follows. The **complication** is that part of the story described in the cliche "the plot thickens." Technically, the complication is the series of actions which intensifies the conflict by bringing the protagonist and the antagonist closer and closer to a collision. Quite frequently, at points in the story the protagonist and the antagonist meet. If the meeting is for neither character a last straw, however, other complications will follow until the continuation of the conflict becomes intolerable for the antagonist.

In "The Schartz-Metterklume Method," the basic conflict between Lady Carlotta and Mrs. Quabarl clearly develops through a series of meetings that finally become intolerable for Mrs. Quabarl. The reader's understanding of the word "complication" should help him to select from the story the major actions of Lady Carlotta and Mrs. Quabarl toward each other that should be included in an action summary.

An excellent example of a major action is Lady Carlotta's saying that she will speak Russian three days a week without the least embarrassment, despite Mrs. Quabarl's intended squelch that "no one in the house speaks or understands Russian." It is major because, with Mrs. Quabarl unprepared to hear her authority challenged, Lady Carlotta's pronouncement forces Mrs. Quabarl to attempt to put her in her place. Even a minor incident like the comments about the car should be included in a paper about the ladies' power struggle, but it can be omitted from the action line because Mrs. Quabarl makes no active response to it.

The narrator gives away the beginning of the second major action in the complication by stating that "At dinner that evening . . . Mrs. Quabarl regained none of her lost ground." Her only hope is to make Lady Carlotta remember her subordinate social position as governess. Just as Mrs. Quabarl intended her protest about Russian to mean "You will not speak Russian," only to have Lady Carlotta ignore her intention, so Lady Carlotta thwarts Mrs. Quabarl's efforts to shift from the subject of wine to one she deems more proper: the question of Lady Carlotta's dependence for her position on references from her former employers. In each episode, the reader needs to find first an authoritative pronouncment by Mrs. Quabarl that would have silenced if not shattered a real Miss Hope, and second an immediate, delightfully unexpected but instantly believeable squelch by Lady Carlotta. The reader can identify two such exchanges that occur before the practical application of the Schartz-Metterklume Method to the history of the Sabine women.

Crisis, Climax, and Resolution

At the end of the history lesson, Lady Carlotta's failure, again, to bow properly to Mrs. Quabarl's authority is a final affront. This crisis for Mrs. Quabarl causes her to perform the final action which is the climax of the conflict: the firing of Miss Hope. Mrs. Quabarl's action as the antagonist provokes Lady Carlotta to the speeches and actions that actually resolve the conflict.

At the end of a conflict, a crisis, a climax, and a resolution always occur. Two of these must be recorded in the action line. The **crisis** cannot be recorded because it is not an action at all but a point of tension in the antagonist rather than in the protagonist. The crisis is the moment when the antagonist finds the conflict absolutely intolerable. The crisis causes him to act directly (or to provoke the action of some other minor character or some force) to confront the protagonist. This is the **climax.** The protagonist then resolves the conflict. That response of the protagonist to the climax will be an action, a speech, a change of character, or any combination of these. The **resolution** of this conflict by the protagonist need not mean necessarily that he defeats the antagonist in the external action. In tragic stories—in which the protagonist misjudges himself, his antagonist, and/or the nature of their conflict—the tragic protagonist usually makes a decision that gives him a moral victory, but he often dies by the action of the antagonist.

A Tool for Criticism

Now it should be possible to write a clear objective sentence summary. Yet, such a statement should be even less satisfying to a reader than it was after a first reading of the story. A rereading of the complete action line on page 13 should make several things apparent:

1. an action summary recalls vividly to mind the important details of the entire action;

2. the actions recorded at each step in the conflict reveal in greater and greater depth the aspects of the basic natures of the characters that made their conflict inevitable once they were in contact.

By the time a reader has analyzed a story carefully enough to prepare an action line and has determined who performs the inciting action, whose is the crisis, what action is the climax, and how the protagonist responds to the climax—by that time, the reader actually commands a very good factual understanding of the story. He has had to define for himself, at least tentatively, the basic characteristics of the protagonist and the antagonist; and, in seeing clearly their conflict, he has prepared himself, perhaps unconsciously, to deal with the author's understanding of the nature of man. In other words, what began as, and might have remained, an objective study clearly has become, also, a tool for criticism.

Questions for Discussion and Writing

1. How objective is the narrator of "The Schartz-Metterklume Method" in the first paragraph?

2. What actions in the action line are the results of decisions? How do you know?

3. In what way is "The Schartz-Metterklume Method" a conflict between the individual and the superficial conventions of society?

4. What precise facts about Lady Carlotta's beliefs can be proved from the incident when she leaves her friend treed by the boar?

5. In what ways are the inciting action and the protagonist's response unexpected?

6. Is there a similarity between Lady Carlotta's friend in the may-tree and Mrs. Quabarl?

7. Does Mrs. Quabarl deserve Lady Carlotta's response that she will speak Russian three days a week?

8. Why is it so especially funny that Lady Carlotta chooses Sunday as the day for her imagined bridge game and soda-water squirting?

9. What speech by Mrs. Quabarl, echoed by her husband, makes appropriate Lady Carlotta's teaching history as her first exhibition of the Schartz-Metterklume Method?

10. Why does the reader feel no pity for Mrs. Quabarl as she awaits the arrival of Lady Carlotta's leopard cub?

11. What qualifies "The Schartz-Metterklume Method" to be called a short story?

12. What is the conflict in "The Schartz-Metterklume Method"?

Hop-Frog

EDGAR ALLAN POE

I never knew any one so keenly alive to a joke as the king was. He seemed to live only for joking. To tell a good story of the joke kind, and to tell it well, was the surest road to his favor. Thus it happened that his seven ministers were all noted for their accomplishments as jokers. They all took after the king, too, in being large, corpulent, oily men, as well as inimitable jokers. Whether people grow fat by joking, or whether there is something in fat itself which predisposes to a joke, I have never been quite able to determine; but certain it is that a lean joker is a *rara avis in terris*.[1]

About the refinements, or, as he called them, the "ghosts" of wit, the king troubled himself very little. He had an especial admiration for *breadth* in a jest, and would often put up with *length,* for the sake of it. Over-niceties wearied him. He would have preferred Rabelais's *Gargantua,* to the *Zadig* of Voltaire:[2] and, upon the whole, practical jokes suited his taste far better than verbal ones.

At the date of my narrative, professing jesters had not altogether gone out of fashion at court. Several of the great continental "powers" still retained their "fools," who wore motley, with caps and bells, and who were expected to be always ready with sharp witticisms, at a moment's notice, in consideration of the crumbs that fell from the royal table.

---

[1] In Latin, literally "a strange bird on earth"; a rarity.
[2] Both satires, but the humor in *Gargantua* is exaggerated and coarse while that in *Zadig* is subtle and witty.

Our king, as a matter of course, retained his "fool." The fact is, he *required* something in the way of folly—if only to counterbalance the heavy wisdom of the seven wise men who were his ministers—not to mention himself.

His fool, or professional jester, was not *only* a fool, however. His value was trebled in the eyes of the king, by the fact of his being also a dwarf and a cripple. Dwarfs were as common at court, in those days, as fools; and many monarchs would have found it difficult to get through their days (days are rather longer at court than elsewhere) without both a jester to laugh *with,* and a dwarf to laugh *at.* But, as I have already observed, your jesters, in ninety-nine cases out of a hundred, are fat, round and unwieldy—so that it was no small source of self-gratulation with our king that, in Hop-Frog (this was the fool's name), he possessed a triplicate treasure in one person.

I believe the name "Hop-Frog" was *not* that given to the dwarf by his sponsors at baptism, but it was conferred upon him, by general consent of the seven ministers, on account of his inability to walk as other men do. In fact, Hop-Frog could only get along by a sort of interjectional gait—something between a leap and a wriggle—a movement that afforded illimitable amusement, and of course consolation, to the king, for (notwithstanding the protuberance of his stomach and a constitutional swelling of the head) the king, by his whole court, was accounted a capital figure.

But although Hop-Frog, through the distortion of his legs, could move only with great pain and difficulty along a road or floor, the prodigious muscular power which nature seemed to have bestowed upon his arms, by way of compensation for deficiency in the lower limbs, enabled him to perform many feats of wonderful dexterity, where trees or ropes were in question, or anything else to climb. At such exercises he certainly much more resembled a squirrel, or a small monkey, than a frog.

I am not able to say, with precision, from what country Hop-Frog originally came. It was from some barbarous region, however, that no person ever heard of—a vast distance from the court of our king. Hop-Frog, and a young girl very little less dwarfish than himself (although of exquisite proportions, and a marvellous dancer), had been forcibly carried off from their respective homes in adjoining provinces, and sent as presents to the king, by one of his ever-victorious generals.

Under these circumstances, it is not to be wondered at that a close intimacy arose between the two little captives. Indeed, they soon became sworn friends. Hop-Frog, who, although he made a great deal of sport, was by no means popular, had it not in his power to render Trippetta many services; but *she,* on account of her grace and exquisite beauty (although a dwarf) was universally admired and petted: so she possessed much influence; and never failed to use it, whenever she could, for the benefit of Hop-Frog.

On some grand state occasion—I forget what—the king determined to have a masquerade; and whenever a masquerade, or anything of that kind, occurred at our court, then the talents both of Hop-Frog and Trippetta were sure to be called in play. Hop-Frog, in especial, was so inventive in the way of getting up pageants, suggesting novel characters, and arranging costumes, for masked balls, that nothing could be done, it seems, without his assistance.

The night appointed for the fete had arrived. A gorgeous hall had been fitted up, under Trippetta's eye, with every kind of device which could possibly give éclat to a masquerade. The whole court was in a fever of expectation. As for costumes and characters, it might well be supposed that everybody had come to a decision on such points. Many had made up their minds (as to what roles they should assume) a week, or even a month, in advance; and, in fact, there was not a particle of indecision anywhere—except in the case of the king and his seven ministers. Why *they* hesitated I never could tell, unless they did it by way of a joke. More probably, they found it difficult, on account of being so fat, to make up their minds. At all events, time flew; and, as a last resource, they sent for Trippetta and Hop-Frog.

When the two little friends obeyed the summons of the king, they found him sitting at his wine with the seven members of his cabinet council; but the monarch appeared to be in a very ill humor. He knew that Hop-Frog was not fond of wine; for it excited the poor cripple almost to madness; and madness is no comfortable feeling. But the king loved his practical jokes, and took pleasure in forcing Hop-Frog to drink and (as the king called it) "to be merry."

"Come here, Hop-Frog," said he, as the jester and his friend entered the room: "swallow this bumper to the health of your absent friends (here Hop-Frog sighed), and then let us have the benefit of your invention. We want characters—*characters,* man—something novel—out of the way. We are wearied with this everlasting sameness. Come, drink! the wine will brighten your wits."

Hop-Frog endeavored, as usual, to get up a jest in reply to these advances from the king; but the effort was too much. It happened to be the poor dwarf's birthday, and the command to drink to his "absent friends" forced the tears to his eyes. Many large, bitter drops fell into the goblet as he took it, humbly, from the hand of the tyrant.

"Ah! ha! ha! ha!" roared the latter, as the dwarf reluctantly drained the beaker. "See what a glass of good wine can do! Why, your eyes are shining already!"

Poor fellow! his large eyes *gleamed,* rather than shone; for the effect of wine on his excitable brain was not more powerful than instantaneous. He placed the goblet nervously on the table, and looked round upon the company with a half-insane stare. They all seemed highly amused at the success of the king's *"joke."*

"And now to business," said the prime minister, a *very* fat man.

"Yes," said the king; "come, Hop-Frog, lend us your assistance. Characters, my fine fellow; we stand in need of characters—all of us—ha! ha! ha!" and as this was seriously meant for a joke, his laugh was chorused by the seven.

Hop-Frog also laughed, although feebly and somewhat vacantly.

"Come, come," said the king, impatiently, "have you nothing to suggest?"

"I am endeavoring to think of something *novel,*" replied the dwarf, abstractedly, for he was quite bewildered by the wine.

"Endeavoring!" cried the tyrant, fiercely; "what do you mean by *that?* Ah, I perceive. You are sulky, and want more wine. Here, drink this!" and he poured out another goblet full and offered it to the cripple, who merely gazed at it, gasping for breath.

"Drink, I say!" shouted the monster, "or by the fiends—"

The dwarf hesitated. The king grew purple with rage. The courtiers smirked. Trippetta, pale as a corpse, advanced to the monarch's seat, and, falling on her knees before him, implored him to spare her friend.

The tyrant regarded her, for some moments, in evident wonder at her audacity. He seemed quite at a loss what to do or say—how most becomingly to express his indignation. At last, without uttering a syllable, he pushed her violently from him, and threw the contents of the brimming goblet in her face.

The poor girl got up as best she could, and, not daring even to sigh, resumed her position at the foot of the table.

There was a dead silence for about half a minute, during which the falling of a leaf, or of a feather might have been heard. It was interrupted by a low, but harsh and protracted *grating* sound which seemed to come at once from every corner of the room.

"What—what—*what* are you making that noise for?" demanded the king, turning furiously to the dwarf.

The latter seemed to have recovered, in great measure, from his intoxication, and looking fixedly but quietly into the tyrant's face, merely ejaculated:

"I—I? How could it have been me?"

"The sound appeared to come from without," observed one of the courtiers. "I fancy it was the parrot at the window, whetting his bill upon his cage-wires."

"True," replied the monarch, as if much relieved by the suggestion; "but, on the honor of a knight, I could have sworn that it was the gritting of this vagabond's teeth."

Hereupon the dwarf laughed (the king was too confirmed a joker to object to any one's laughing), and displayed a set of large, powerful, and very repulsive teeth. Moreover, he avowed his perfect willingness to swallow as much wine as desired. The monarch was pacified; and having drained another bumper with no very perceptible ill effect, Hop-Frog entered at once, and with spirit, into the plans for the masquerade.

"I cannot tell what was the association of idea," observed he, very tranquilly, and as if he had never tasted wine in his life, "but *just after* your majesty had struck the girl and thrown the wine in her face—*just after* your majesty had done this, and while the parrot was making that odd noise outside the window, there came into my mind a capital diversion—one of my own country frolics—often enacted among us, at our masquerades: but here it will be new altogether. Unfortunately, however, it requires a company of eight persons, and—"

"Here we *are!*" cried the king, laughing at his acute discovery of the coincidence; "eight to a fraction—I and my seven ministers. Come! what is the diversion?"

"We call it," replied the cripple, "the Eight Chained Ourang-Outangs, and it really is excellent sport if well enacted."

"*We* will enact it," remarked the king, drawing himself up, and lowering his eyelids.

"The beauty of the game," continued Hop-Frog, "lies in the fright it occasions among the women."

"Capital!" roared in chorus the monarch and his ministry.

"*I* will equip you as ourang-outangs," proceeded the dwarf; "leave all that to me. The resemblance shall be so striking, that the company of masqueraders will take you for real beasts—and, of course, they will be as much terrified as astonished."

"O, this is exquisite!" exclaimed the king. "Hop-Frog! I will make a man of you."

"The chains are for the purpose of increasing the confusion by their jangling. You are supposed to have escaped, en masse, from your keepers. Your majesty cannot conceive the *effect* produced at a masquerade, by eight chained ourang-outangs, imagined to be real ones by most of the company; and rushing in with savage cries, among the crowd of delicately and gorgeously clothed men and women. The *contrast* is inimitable."

"It *must* be," said the king: and the council arose hurriedly (as it was growing late), to put in execution the scheme of Hop-Frog.

His mode of equipping the party as ourang-outangs was very simple, but effective enough for his purposes. The animals in question had, at the epoch of my story, very rarely been seen in any part of the civilized world; and as the imitations made by the dwarf were sufficiently beast-like and more than sufficiently hideous, their truthfulness to nature was thus thought to be secured.

The king and his ministers were first encased in tightfitting stockinet shirts and drawers. They were then saturated with tar. At this stage of the process, some one of the party suggested feathers; but the suggestion was at once overruled by the dwarf, who soon convinced the eight, by visual demonstration, that the hair of such a brute as the ourang-outang was much more efficiently represented by *flax*. A thick coating of the latter was accordingly plastered upon the coating of tar. A long chain was now procured. First, it was passed about the waist of the king, *and tied;* then about another of the party, and also tied; then about all successively, in the same manner. When this chaining arrangement was complete, and the party stood as far apart from each other as possible, they formed a circle; and to make all things appear natural, Hop-Frog passed the residue of the chain, in two diameters, at right angles, across the circle, after the fashion adopted, at the present day, by those who capture chimpanzees, or other large apes, in Borneo.

The grand saloon in which the masquerade was to take place, was a circular room, very lofty, and receiving the light of the sun only through a single window at top. At night (the season for which the apartment was especially designed) it was illuminated principally by a large chandelier, depending by a chain from the centre of the sky-light, and lowered, or elevated, by means of a counter-balance as usual; but (in order not to look unsightly) this latter passed outside the cupola and over the roof.

The arrangements of the room had been left to Trippetta's superintendence; but, in some particulars, it seems, she had been guided by the calmer judgment of her friend the dwarf. At his suggestion it was that, on this occasion, the chandelier was removed. Its waxen drippings (which, in weather so warm, it was quite impossible to prevent) would have been seriously detrimental to the rich dresses of the guests, who, on account of the crowded state of the saloon, could not *all* be expected to keep from out its centre—that is to say, from the chandelier. Additional sconces were set in various parts of the hall, out of the way; and a flambeau, emitting sweet odor, was placed in the right hand of each of the Caryatides[3] that stood against the wall—some fifty or sixty altogether.

The eight ourang-outangs, taking Hop-Frog's advice, waited patiently until midnight (when the room was thoroughly filled with masqueraders) before making their appearance. No sooner had the clock ceased striking, however, than they rushed, or rather rolled in, all together—for the impediment of their chains caused most of the party to fall, and all to stumble as they entered.

The excitement among the masqueraders was prodigious, and filled the heart of the king with glee. As had been anticipated, there were not a few of the guests who supposed the ferocious-looking creatures to be beasts of *some* kind in reality, if not precisely ourang-outangs. Many of the women swooned with affright; and had not the king taken the precaution to exclude all weapons from the saloon, his party might soon have expiated their frolic in their blood. As it was, a general rush was made for the doors, but the king had ordered them to be locked immediately upon his entrance; and, at the dwarf's suggestion, the keys had been deposited with *him*.

While the tumult was at its height, and each masquerader attentive only to his own safety—(for, in fact, there was much *real* danger from the pressure of the excited crowd.)—the chain by which the chandelier ordinarily hung, and which had been drawn up on its removal, might have been seen very gradually to descend, until its hooked extremity came within three feet of the floor.

Soon after this, the king and his seven friends, having reeled about the hall in all directions, found themselves, at length, in its centre, and, of course, in immediate contact with the chain. While they were thus situated, the dwarf, who had followed closely at their heels, in-

[3]Figures of Greek women in costume used as columns.

citing them to keep up the commotion, took hold of their own chain at the intersection of the two portions which crossed the circle diametrically and at right angles. Here, with the rapidity of thought, he inserted the hook from which the chandelier had been wont to depend; and, in an instant, by some unseen agency, the chandelier-chain was drawn so far upward as to take the hook out of reach, and, as an inevitable consequence, to drag the ourang-outangs together in close connection, and face to face.

The masqueraders, by this time, had recovered, in some measure, from their alarm; and, beginning to regard the whole matter as a well-contrived pleasantry, set up a loud shout of laughter at the predicament of the apes.

"Leave them to *me!*" now screamed Hop-Frog, his shrill voice making itself easily heard through all the din. "Leave them to *me*. I fancy *I* know them. If I can only get a good look at them, *I* can soon tell who they are."

Here, scrambling over the heads of the crowd, he managed to get to the wall; when, seizing a flambeau from one of the Caryatides, he returned, as he went, to the centre of the room—leaped, with the agility of a monkey, upon the king's head—and thence clambered a few feet up the chain—holding down the torch to examine the group of ourang-outangs, and still screaming, "*I* shall soon find out who they are!"

And now, while the whole assembly (the apes included) were convulsed with laughter, the jester suddenly uttered a shrill whistle; when the chain flew violently up for about thirty feet—dragging with it the dismayed and struggling ourang-outangs, and leaving them suspended in mid-air between the sky-light and the floor. Hop-Frog, clinging to the chain as it rose, still maintained his relative position in respect to the eight maskers, and still (as if nothing were the matter) continued to thrust his torch down towards them, as though endeavoring to discover who they were.

So thoroughly astonished were the whole company at this ascent, that a dead silence, of about a minute's duration, ensued. It was broken by just such a low, harsh, *grating* sound, as had before attracted the attention of the king and his councillors, when the former threw the wine in the face of Trippetta. But, on the present occasion, there could be no question as to *whence* the sound issued. It came from the fang-like teeth of the dwarf, who ground them and gnashed them as he foamed at the mouth, and glared, with an expression of maniacal rage, into the upturned countenances of the king and his seven companions.

"Ah, ha!" said at length the infuriated jester. "Ah, ha! I begin to see who these people *are*, now!" Here, pretending to scrutinize the king more closely, he held the flambeau to the flaxen coat which enveloped him, and which instantly burst into a sheet of vivid flame. In less than half a minute the whole eight ourang-outangs were blazing fiercely, amid the shrieks of the multitude who gazed at them from below, horror-stricken, and without the power to render them the slightest assistance.

At length the flames, suddenly increasing in virulence, forced the jester to climb higher up the chain, to be out of their reach, and, as he made this movement, the crowd again sank for a brief instant, into silence. The dwarf seized his opportunity, and once more spoke:

"I now see *distinctly*," he said, "what manner of people these maskers are. They are a great king and his seven privy-councillors —a king who does not scruple to strike a defenceless girl, and his seven councillors who abet him in the outrage. As for myself, I am simply Hop-Frog, the jester—and *this is my last jest*."

Owing to the high combustibility of both the flax and the tar to which it adhered, the dwarf had scarcely made an end of his brief speech before the work of vengeance was complete. The eight corpses swung in their chains, a fetid, blackened, hideous, and indistinguishable mass. The cripple hurled his torch at them, clambered leisurely to the ceiling, and disappeared through the sky-light.

It is supposed that Trippetta, stationed on the roof of the saloon, had been the accomplice of her friend in his fiery revenge, and that, together, they effected their escape to their own country: for neither was seen again.

Character

The action line is a tool for understanding the story at its first level: who does what. If the reader has carefully prepared the materials of the action line, he now understands the objective level of the conflict in Poe's "Hop-Frog" in considerable detail. Conflict, the primary term for choosing major actions to appear in the action summary, also points the reader toward the second level of understanding: *why* the king and Hop-Frog are in conflict. The answer must come from a study of their characters—a study that demands even closer attention to detail than does the making of an action summary.

The very definition of fiction contains the key to character. Because an author creates his characters to express his concern with a splinter of life, every physical detail, every decision, every action should have a detectable effect on the outcome of the story. Also, because in fiction the character is seen deciding and acting at critical moments, most of his actions stem from emotions or from deep thought and hence reveal his basic nature more than does his routine behavior. Actions, even the vital ones of the action line, are not the sole indicators of character, however.

Five Basic Traits

Details of character can most effectively be identified in terms of **traits**—the unique marks or distinctive features of appearance, nature, personality, and action that distinguish one individual from another. The five basic traits of a character are biological, physical, natural or habitual, emotional, and deliberative.

Because biological and physical traits are observable, external characteristics, a narrator usually asserts them. A character's **biological trait** answers only the question of the character's sex. **Physical traits** concern size, shape, weight, dress, gesture, and facial expression. Although in real life a man's physical features may have no relationship to his nature, in fiction the author designs physical traits to emphasize deeper qualities that prepare the reader for significant actions.

Rather than being asserted, **natural and habitual traits** usually are presented dramatically. That is, given only what a character says or does before the conflict begins, the reader must determine what kinds of actions and speeches are to be expected from that character whenever he is not under stress.

Natural traits and habitual traits frequently cannot be distinguished from one another because the reader's understanding of a character's nature is almost always an interpretation of a character's habits. If it is a character's nature to be happy, it will be his habit to smile. If a character habitually carries an umbrella, it is probably his nature to be cautious. The basic distinction is that those traits that are natural are spontaneous and often unlearned and are identifiable as a disposition or an attitude. Habits are almost always expected actions that express a character's nature, but they are almost always learned rather than spontaneous.

Emotional traits are essentially a catalogue of the emotions that the character feels and the objects of those emotions. What are his desires, his needs, his wishes? What does he love, or what does he hate? If a character can satisfy his emotions immediately, he will have no awareness of conflict and will never deliberate (think deeply). If a man never thinks, he must always have got what he wanted or needed, and he either fears nothing or has always successfully overpowered what he feared.

The term **deliberation** describes deeply serious thought rather than the sort needed for routine action or minor decision. It is reserved for how a character thinks when the active expression of his emotions is blocked. In this sense, only a frustrated man ever thinks. Two primary **deliberative traits** determine the quality of decision of which a character is capable. If he is concerned with ways and means of getting what he wants or removing what he fears, then his deliberation is *expedient*. If he concerns himself with whether or not acting in response to his emotions is right or wrong, his deliberation is *moral*.

However, moral deliberation need not result in a "right" action. Moral deliberation simply describes the concern of the thinking character with whether or not an action is right or wrong. The most significant characters are those whose decisions follow moral deliberation because they attempt to evaluate and control their emotions rather than simply to fulfill them.

Traits Revealed by Expected, Unexpected, and Deliberative Actions

In the majority of short stories, the actions of a character reveal far more of his most important traits than a narrator presents statically through description or assertion. Though in the traditional formal short story, such as Poe wrote, the reader is told a good deal directly by the narrator, in the modern psychological or symbolic story characters are presented almost completely by dramatic means—that is, through action. As may be anticipated, different kinds of action reveal different character traits. **Expected actions** reveal physical, natural, or habitual traits. Hop-Frog's action of walking with "an interjectional gait" derives from the physical trait of crippled legs. The king's laughing at Hop-Frog's tears when he drinks to his absent friends betrays the king's habitual trait of laughing at everything—an habitual action that stems from his selfish nature.

In a short story, most of the expository action will be habitual or natural (hence expected) while most of the significant action in the conflict itself will be either unexpected or deliberative. However, the reader should watch closely for an occasional, seemingly insignificant, unexpected action to occur immediately before the inciting action. Hop-Frog's weeping, for example, is not an expected action. Such **unexpected actions** signal emotional traits and prepare for the inciting action which generally expresses some strong emotional need, usually the antagonist's. The response of the protagonist to the inciting action is an act equally revealing of his key emotional traits. Generally speaking, the whole conflict is a process of heightening the emotional tension, and tension is heightened by postponing a character's expression of emotion. In fact, the crisis can now be recognized as the point at which the character must express directly some frustrated emotion regardless of the cost to him or to anyone else. Mrs. Quabarl's firing "Miss Hope" is such an expression; at a far greater degree of intensity, the king and his councillors burst into flames after the king's crisis: the moment he realizes he is impotent in the face of Hop-Frog's blind animal fury.

The usefulness of the action line as an index to important details of character should be increasingly clear since major actions reveal what elements of the natures of the opponents are in conflict. Because the complication is the process of increasingly frustrating at least one individual, the reader should be prepared to see the protagonist act deliberately. That is, he acts after he has thought deeply either about ways and means to end his frustration or about whether the way he wishes to act is morally right. Sometimes he deliberates both morally and expediently. The reader should remember that regardless of whether the character thinks morally or expediently, he will act to resolve the conflict when it reaches a climax. The response of a character to the climax of a conflict will reveal most completely the depth or the shallowness of his basic nature.

The Interpretation of Character: The Inciting Action

The interpretation of character begins in almost every story with some details in the first paragraph, so the reader knows the characters' natures well before the conflict begins. Regardless of how adept a reader is at interpreting detail in a first reading, to see clearly the characters' emotional traits he must look closely at the inciting action and the action surrounding it. If a reader assures himself what precise qualities of the characters are in conflict there, he will know exactly what sort of detail to look for elsewhere in the story.

When the king indignantly pushes Trippetta and flings wine in her face, Hop-Frog gnashes his teeth. For these facts of action to reveal all they can about characters requires that the reader ask himself the right questions. Since the inciting action and the response to it are both unexpected actions, they reveal emotional traits. Therefore, the reader must identify the specific wishes or needs or desires that drive the characters to act as they do.

Why did the king strike Trippetta? Because she tried to intervene while the king was attempting to force Hop-Frog to drink a second glass of wine. What did the king wish or need so badly that her request would have made him indignant? Why did the king push her and throw the wine and say nothing? Though most of the answers can be derived by logic, the narrator of this formal story provides very explicit answers to every one of these questions: "The tyrant regarded her ... in evident wonder at her audacity. He seemed quite at a loss ... how most becomingly to express his indignation." The major keys to his character are his "wonder at her audacity" and the limitation of his concern to seeing that his response is "becoming" to him. What sort of man is surprised that anyone would interfere with his least request? The narrator says "the tyrant," but the reader should keep exploring. What is that least request? " 'Drink, I say' shouted the monster." He is forcing Hop-Frog to drink despite the knowledge that wine "excited the poor cripple almost to madness." What sort of man can do that? If the reader has been identifying the traits of character that these actions reveal, he has seen that the king acts according to habit and satisfies his few emotions directly and immediately. In other words, the king has never had to deliberate either about what he wants or whether what he wants is right. Therefore, undoubtedly the reader will agree that the king is blind—blind to the way that he violates the human rights of others, blind to his own stupidity because he considers only his own image and his own desires when he acts, and blind to the possibility of a limit to his power. Once the reader has identified these emotional and habitual traits in the king, he can gather ample additional evidence of their existence.

The reader should always test his analysis of character by seeing how the major traits that he identifies affect the outcome of the conflict. Were the king not blind to the humanity of the dwarf, he might have recognized that his final affront to Trippetta was an intolerable act against the human being who was Hop-Frog. Had he not felt his power to be absolute he might have suspected that some day someone would tire of his practical jokes and seek vengeance. Were he not blind to his own stupidity, he surely could have recognized the implications of the plan of the dwarf. By using the inciting action as the key to character, the reader guarantees that he will find the major aspects of the king's character and that he will know what supporting detail to look for, particularly in the outcome of the story.

The reader will recall that Hop-Frog's response to the king's pushing Trippetta and flinging the wine in her face was "a low but harsh and protracted *grating* sound." Immediately Hop-Frog seems "to have recovered, in great measure, from his intoxication" and responds "quietly" to the king's furious *"what* are you making that noise for?" One of the courtiers thinks that the sound came from a parrot "whetting his bill upon cage wires." The king, much relieved, admits that he thought the sound to be "the gritting of this vagabond's teeth." Then, "the dwarf laughed," "displayed a set of large, powerful and repulsive teeth," and says that he is willing to drink as much wine as the king wishes. The understanding of Hop-Frog's nature must begin with the reader's understanding of all of the implications of that "protracted *grating* sound." What makes a man grind his teeth rather than say something? What part of a man is in control of his actions when he makes such primitive responses? Without question, Hop-Frog is inarticulate like an animal with the pent-up frustration of being always treated as if he were one, but he is inarticulate also because as a rational man he knows the limit of his power to resist the king. That Poe deliberately intended the reader to sense this dual nature of Hop-Frog can now easily be verified. What is this small dwarf's name? With what animals is he compared when performing "many feats of wonderful dexterity" using "the prodigious muscular power of his arms"? In fact, the idea of the parrot in the cage strongly implies that Hop-Frog's grating sound is a protest against his own invisible cage. However, though the king treats Hop-Frog as if he were an animal, what of Hop-Frog's abilities is valued most by the king? It is his rational ingenuity as a devisor of entertainments.

From Hop-Frog's two responses to the king's inciting action (grating his teeth and offering to drink as much wine as the king wishes), the reader becomes aware of the rational man-beast nature of Hop-Frog, and now he can ask himself the rest of the right questions for understanding Hop-Frog in the whole story.

The Interpretation of Character: The Additional Details

Since Hop-Frog did respond to the king's action against Trippetta, how does this action differ from those which he habitually accepts with not even a sound of protest? What does the king usually do, and what does Hop-Frog usually do in response? One example is extremely clear: "He knew that Hop-Frog was not fond of wine; ... But the king loved his practical jokes and took pleasure in forcing Hop-Frog to drink...." "Hop-Frog endeavored as usual to get up a jest in reply to these advances of the king...." The first break in the habitual activity of the court is Hop-Frog's inability to restrain his tears; yet, being made to drink to his absent friends on his birthday provokes him only to unexpected tears, not to conflict. Hop-Frog has a habit of action within which he can respond to this expected action (being asked to drink) by the king. However, the reader of detail will note that "his eyes *gleamed*" rather than shone in a "half-insane stare" produced by the "instantaneous effect of wine on his excitable brain." Although Hop-Frog wills himself to do what the king wishes, a repressed conflict of long standing is ready to emerge.

The unexpected inciting action of the king can cause Hop-Frog to respond in accordance with his nature but without time to think deeply. Once set in motion, this conflict will be complicated until it reaches a climax that is resolved in a way that will change radically Hop-Frog's life or his character or both. If the reader has sucessfully entered the mind of the crippled little man, stolen from his home and given as a present to a king who lives to play practical jokes, the reader needs no help to see that the king's abuse of the one person who saw Hop-Frog as a human being was the step that even a tyrant could not take with impunity.

A merely sympathetic reader feels pity for the dwarf and wishes him to repay the king not only for this one act but also for the abuses of a lifetime. The critical reader retains his objectivity as well as his sympathy. Such a reader watches a sensitive man pass through near-hysteria to a mad rationality characterized by deceptive calm and calculated control of speech, laughter, and agreeableness. The reader then can see that it is this mad creature who without the least human feeling takes successful advantage of the king's three most basic traits: his love of power, his faith in the infallibility of his judgment, and his inability to imagine the possibility of anyone's revolt. Such a reader stands back from Hop-Frog's vengeance because he sees that the king is without protection against the mind of the dwarf once his humanity is removed by wine. In other words, the reader instantly believes Hop-Frog's actions; he does not identify with them because he considers them irrational.

One major point of inquiry remains for the reader of character: an examination of the crisis, the climax, and the protagonist's response.

The Interpretation of Character: Crisis, Climax, and Resolution

The crisis is the point of highest tension in the antagonist though the protagonist may share the tension intensely, as Hop-Frog does here. It can be argued that the moment when Hop-Frog finds the conflict with the king absolutely intolerable is when the king insults Trippetta. This is true in the sense that the action makes Hop-Frog determined to confront the king at whatever cost to either of them. In the technical sense the final confrontation of Hop-Frog and the king does not occur until Hop-Frog, clinging to the chain above the orangutans and thrusting his torch almost into their faces, proclaims, "Ah, ha! I begin to see who these people *are* now!" His pretense of not knowing who they are and of holding the torch near them only for illumination cannot go on. Without question, this must be the moment of crisis for the king. However blind he may once have been, surely he now knows the limits of his power and the inevitability of his death. Under these circumstances it is reasonably inferred that for him the conflict is absolutely intolerable.

Without question, the climax of the story is the moment the eight men burst into flames. Hop-Frog responds to the climax in all three of the possible ways that a protagonist can resolve a conflict: (1) he delivers a speech about this being his last jest and why; (2) he performs an action: "He hurled his torch at them, clambered leisurely to the ceiling and disappeared through the skylight," and (3) he undergoes a change of character.

The reader should always remember that how the protagonist responds to the climax will reveal his deepest nature. Until Hop-Frog's whistle, "after which the chain flew violently up for about thirty feet," "the whole assembly, the apes included, were convulsed with laughter." In the minute's dead silence that followed the only sound was "a low harsh *grating* sound" that clearly "came from the fanglike teeth of the dwarf who ground them and gnashed them as he foamed at the mouth, and glared with an expression of maniacal rage into the upturned countenances of the king and his seven companions." Here is confrontation with a vengeance, but precisely who or what does confront the king? Is there any sign here of a man who could weep bitter tears for his absent friends? Does there remain even the coldly rational intelligence that deliberated expediently with such deadly effect? What then has happened to Hop-Frog? Was he, at the beginning of the story, more of a beast than a man? Why does Poe have him gnash his teeth, foam at the mouth, and "glare with maniacal rage" at the instant that he sets fire to the king? But which act is most revealing of the permanent character of Hop-Frog: the maniacal thrusting of the torch at the king or the contemptuous tossing of it at the spectators before he clambered leisurely up the chain and disappeared? The reader who attempts character analysis of Hop-Frog must be prepared to say with certainty what sort of man or beast leaves the king's castle. Here the reader must depend both on his close reading and his knowledge of people. The evidence is clear that Hop-Frog is insane.

Tormented for years as only an extremely intelligent and sensitive man could be, Hop-Frog has accepted all of the personal abuse that an unimaginative practical joker who had no respect for his mind could contrive. Driven almost mad by wine, he must stand helplessly by and watch the one person who cares for him be harmed for his sake. He responds to that abuse with a gnashing of teeth and a deceptive calm that allows him to speak of the incident as if it were merely a convenient point of reference in time. Immediately, he unfolds a superlative plan for an entertainment so complete that it includes even the protection of the king by disarming the guests, locking all exits to prevent the escape of the terror stricken, and removing the chandelier so that no hot wax will drip on any of the guests.

Clearly Hop-Frog's rational powers are at their sharpest, for he carefully contrives an inhumane death that permits his vengeance and guarantees his safe escape. Yet, not once in the course of his meticulous plans does he consider whether or not it is right that eight men die for the king's one blow and a single glass of wine. However, Hop-Frog actually ignites the king and his ministers not while he is rational but while he is in a blind animal fury. That act apparently returns him to rationality but not to sanity. It is Hop-Frog as rational beast, devoid of all human feeling, who climbs slightly above the flames to deliver his final explanatory speech, to toss aside the murder torch with total unconcern, and to make his leisurely way out into the world.

A reader who has studied "Hop-Frog" in this depth has begun at least half-consciously to involve himself in a study of the nature of man and to examine his own nature. If he has permitted himself involvement in the story on Poe's terms, the reader has experienced the powerful effect of the story because he recognizes that the wish for revenge that he shared with Hop-Frog has been fulfilled at the cost of Hop-Frog's humanity. This recognition by the reader of his personal capacity for violence and for consent to irrational retaliation produces the effect of horror of the tale.

EDGAR ALLAN POE: *Hop-Frog*

QUESTIONS FOR DISCUSSION AND WRITING

1. What in the natures of the king and Hop-Frog make their conflict inevitable?

2. Why are the physical traits of Hop-Frog appropriate to the protagonist's response to the inciting action, the crisis, the climax, and the resolution of "Hop-Frog"?

3. What are Hop-Frog's desires, needs, and wishes? What does he love? Hate?

4. What are the desires, needs, and wishes of the king? What does he love? Hate?

5. Why does the king not expect Trippetta's intervention on Hop-Frog's behalf?

6. Why does the king feel free to push Trippetta and fling wine in her face?

7. What is the difference between rational and reasonable? Why is Hop-Frog rational but not reasonable?

8. Why is Hop-Frog capable of vengeance for Trippetta when he has never taken it for himself?

9. When does the king first realize the limits of his power?

10. What is so especially effective about the narrator's statement that Hop-Frog "clambered leisurely to the ceiling and disappeared through the skylight"?

11. What is the basic nature of the king?

12. What has the simplicity of the king's nature to do with the outcome of the story?

13. In "The Schartz-Metterklume Method," what is the relation between the complexity of Lady Carlotta's character and her successful defeat of Mrs. Quabarl?

The Unicorn in the Garden

JAMES THURBER

Once upon a sunny morning a man who sat in a breakfast nook looked up from his scrambled eggs to see a white unicorn with a golden horn quietly cropping the roses in the garden. The man went up to the bedroom where his wife was still asleep and woke her. "There's a unicorn in the garden," he said. "Eating roses." She opened one unfriendly eye and looked at him. "The unicorn is a mythical beast," she said, and turned her back on him. The man walked slowly downstairs and out into the garden. The unicorn was still there; he was now browsing among the tulips. "Here, unicorn," said the man, and he pulled up a lily and gave it to him. The unicorn ate it gravely. With a high heart, because there was a unicorn in his garden, the man went upstairs and roused his wife again. "The unicorn," he said, "ate a lily." His wife sat up in bed and looked at him, coldly. "You are a booby," she said, "and I am going to have you put in the booby-hatch." The man, who had never liked the words "booby" and "booby-hatch," and who liked them even less on a shining morning when there was a unicorn in the garden, thought for a moment. "We'll see about that," he said. He walked over to the door. "He has a golden horn in the middle of his forehead," he told her. Then he went back to the garden to watch the unicorn; but the unicorn had gone away. The man sat down among the roses and went to sleep.

As soon as the husband had gone out of the house, the wife got up and dressed as fast as she could. She was very excited and there was a gloat in her eye. She telephoned the police and she telephoned a psychiatrist; she told them to hurry to her house and bring a strait-jacket. When the police and the psychiatrist arrived they sat down in chairs and looked at her, with great interest. "My husband," she said, "saw a unicorn this morning." The police looked at the psychiatrist and the psychiatrist looked at the police. "He told me it ate a lily," she said. The psychiatrist looked at the police and the police looked at the psychiatrist. "He told me it had a golden horn in the middle of its forehead," she said. At a solemn signal from the psychiatrist, the police leaped from their chairs and seized the wife. They had a hard time subduing her, for she put up a terrific struggle, but they finally subdued her. Just as they got her into the strait-jacket, the husband came back into the house.

"Did you tell your wife you saw a unicorn?" asked the police. "Of course not," said the husband. "The unicorn is a mythical beast." "That's all I wanted to know," said the psychiatrist. "Take her away. I'm sorry, sir, but your wife is as crazy as a jay bird." So they took her away, cursing and screaming, and shut her up in an institution. The husband lived happily ever after.

Moral: Don't count your boobies until they are hatched.

Organizing an Analysis

"The Unicorn in the Garden" is an exceptionally deceptive little story. Despite its being so short and seeming so simple, Thurber has sketched remarkably well the climax of a conflict clearly developed by expected, unexpected, and deliberate actions that identify the major habitual, natural, emotional, and deliberative traits of two characters.

Since the story is so brief, the reader will do well to include every action in his action line; otherwise, after only a first reading, he may overlook completely the inciting action and mistake the crisis for the climax. However, if the reader applies precisely the tests both for the inciting action and the protagonist's response, and for the crisis, climax, and resolution, he will have no difficulty in recognizing the precise nature of the conflict or its development. If he does not apply them, this apparently simple story can be bewildering when studied with close attention to the details of character, motivation, and the sources of humor.

For example, since the average reader has never seen a unicorn in his garden, much less fed him a lily, he may mistake the man's seeing the unicorn for an unexpected action. A closer look at the perfectly calm acceptance with which this very observant man watches the unicorn shows that he habitually sees all sorts of things not visible to persons bound by fact and logic. The reader must examine, too, for their place in habitual action such facts as that, despite the emphatic first rebuff by his wife, the husband goes a second time to attempt to report to her his further interesting observation of the unicorn. Almost every detail of the story needs to be evaluated that sharply.

One of the most effective techniques for reading any story is to ask, in the order of the action of the story, all of the questions that one can raise about character, relationships, and even definition of key words. Then the reader should jot down briefly, again in the order of this action, whatever answers come to mind. At first, the information may seem random or uselessly minute, and such careful interpretation of single details may appear to have no organization. However, if notes prepared in this way are reread at the end of his study, the reader usually will discover that he has a very thorough analysis of character, motive, and action that is structured by the story itself. He may unconsciously have asked a great many more questions about one subject than any others because of some particular personal interest or special knowledge. If he wishes to write a paper about a story, the reader will write with greater depth, greater perception, and greater effectiveness if he develops one of those questions in which he has shown unusual interest.

A large part of the study of "The Unicorn in the Garden" is designed to demonstrate the technique of organizing an analysis by asking sequential questions about actions and other details. The reader who wants seriously to test this technique should write down whatever answers he thinks of for each question given. Occasionally he may think of a number of potential answers, some of which seem stupidly obvious or distinctly irrelevant. Nevertheless, he should jot down notes about them all. Questions not asked here will occur to the reader. He always should include his own answers too in addition to, not in place of, the ones asked for.

Questions for Interpretation

There must never be a doubt that a real unicorn appears in the garden. (Coleridge calls the reader's acceptance of this sort of fact "the willing suspension of disbelief.") Therefore, the first question of interpretation is what is a unicorn. The wife is right: the unicorn is a mythical beast—an object of faith in which one sincerely believes regardless of how others may laugh at its lack of basis in fact. Who, then, is capable of seeing a mythical beast? If, by chance, one should see a unicorn in his own garden and find it friendly and lovely, what human need would demand expression? Every reader who as a small child ever carried a very special mud pie to an adult whom he loved has, in a sense, seen a unicorn and responded to that need. And if he was told to "get rid of that dirty mess" he knows how difficult it is to share any unicorn at all. Clearly the unicorn is not simply a beautiful white animal with a golden horn in its forehead. Precisely what more a symbol is will differ from reader to reader in terms of his own experience and his own needs. (Of all figurative devises, only the symbol offers this freedom of interpretation.) Whenever something in a story—occasionally a person, more often an animal or an object—is both itself and a representative of something more that is not named, that thing is a **symbol.** In this story, a great deal of the reader's insight into character comes from looking at the attitude of the man and of his wife toward the unicorn—toward the existence of mythical beasts, whatever they stand for. What differences in nature are shown by the ease with which the man both sees and accepts the unicorn and by his wife's immediate rejection of even the possibility of its existence?

After he determines fully what the unicorn symbolizes in this story, the reader must learn as much as he can both of the habits and of the natures of the two characters. What is the disposition or habit of a man who eats alone early and watches with interest whatever appears in his garden? What makes him capable of seeing a unicorn? What is the nature or habit of a woman who sleeps later than her husband and who wakes with "an unfriendly eye" to dismiss coldly his report on a mythical beast? Does the man expect his wife to believe that he has seen a unicorn, or does he merely hope? How do you know? Remember that a reader's personal experience is invaluable as confirmation of what he reads in a character. How frequently does this sort of exchange occur? How long has it taken this couple to develop this pattern? What in their natures makes them choose this way of avoiding direct conflict, or is this pattern set more by one of them than by the other? How do you know? Why is the pattern so frustrating to each of them? In what ways is it satisfactory? With what feelings does the husband return to the garden? Why is it appropriate to the nature of the man that the unicorn is still there? Why does his successful feeding of the unicorn send him "with a high heart" back upstairs to his wife? Is he used to her calling him a booby for seeing things like, but less spectacular than, unicorns? When his wife rebuffs him, what is his habitual response?

If the reader has answered each of these questions, he now has a good understanding of their natures, their conflict, and their habitual responses. How is the rest of their second exchange about the unicorn different from their usual pattern? When she says, "I am going to have you put in the booby hatch," is his response, "We'll see about that," expected or unexpected? How do you know? Why does he add what he must know is information that she will not care about: "He has a golden horn in the middle of his forehead"?

Now the characters go their separate ways to think their ways out of their frustration. Do they think morally or expediently? How do you know? When the husband returns to the garden, the unicorn is no longer there. Why? More specifically, what sort of attention is required for seeing a unicorn—what sort of attitude or interest in the world? Why does the man not have that attitude now? Why is he able to sit down among the roses and go to sleep? How well does he know his wife if he sleeps after her threat to put him in the booby hatch—a threat to which he responds, apparently not in the least threateningly, "We'll see about that"? In the light of the rest of the story, was his response also a threat? What power has he that could back a threat?

Meanwhile the wife dresses as fast as she can, is very excited, and has "a gloat in her eye." Why? What power relationship is almost always reflected by a person's gloating? What specific emotion does her particular "gloat" reveal? Does that desire begin now or has it existed for a long time? What is there about his report of seeing a unicorn that is different enough from his usual interruption of her sleep to make her resolve to put him away? Is this plan the decision of a moment or has she been waiting for an opportunity to take action that has long been contemplated, even if partly unconsciously? What outcome does she anticipate? Has she reason for anticipating success? (If she has no reason, why is the reader as surprised as she at what really happens?) What factors in her husband has she overlooked?

Only the final revelation of both characters remains. The primary question for the crisis, the climax, the resolution and any remaining action is: do the characters act in accordance with their basic natures? In other words, is the woman's manner of telling about her husband's report in keeping with her factual nature? What about her nature guarantees that she will not recognize the significance of the exchanges of glances by the psychiatrist and the police? Is it suitable that they have a hard time subduing her?

Now, for the husband: is his unexpected reply that "the unicorn is a mythical beast" prepared for in any way by what he has done or said in the past? How long has he known what he would answer when someone came to take him to the booby hatch? Why does he use his wife's words? Is he surprised at her reaction to being carried away? Can he live happily ever after?

If the notes answering these questions are reread, the reader should recognize readily any notes that actually are irrelevant. Also he should throw out all remarks that contradict the majority of his interpretations. However, when his interpretations seem to be contradictory he should not assume the majority to be right until he has checked each idea carefully against the facts of the action line for what they reveal in the natures of the characters.

Understanding the Effect of Analysis

What has happened to the effect of the story now that the reader understands the characters and their conflict so thoroughly? A first reaction may well be that the story has been ruined because it simply is not funny any more. If for the moment the reader has lost sight of the comic because he is so acutely aware of the pain of the couple's being unable to communicate, he needs especially to see how humor permits him to stand back with sufficient objectivity to recognize that the human condition is as much ridiculous as sad. Whenever, either because of a tragic or a comic view of the human condition, the reader becomes aware of the tremendous gap in human relationships between what ought to be and what is, he may be far more in a mood to cry than to laugh. What Thurber does in "The Unicorn in the Garden" is to restore the reader's dual perspective so that he can watch with some objectivity the behavior of these two characters when they attempt to close or to ignore that gap.

The Nature of Comedy

In comic stories the usually equal complexity of the characters and the consequent level at which the conflict is complicated almost assure the reader's objectivity. A comic protagonist and his antagonist almost always have equally satisfactory habits of action, equally strong emotional needs, and equal capacities for deliberation. Usually the protagonist has a slightly superior awareness of the conflict, but he seems to the reader to deserve his edge over the antagonist because the protagonist deliberates more often.

Since both characters can think effectively about ways and means of getting what they want, the reader's major focus is on their thinking rather than on their feelings. Therefore, the reader's involvement also is intellectual rather than emotional. No matter how serious the resolution might seem in real life, it gives the reader neither an emotional nor a moral reason to consider its seriousness in comedy.

Primarily, the comic spirit focuses on the ridiculous. Thurber first uses incongruity in putting together in a single story both one of the most ancient mythical figures—the unicorn—and one of the most modern breakfasts—scrambled eggs. He takes a cliche like "a bed of roses," says only the roses and then has a character literally fall asleep in the bed. Then he turns a verb like "to gloat" into something visible by echoing the biblical story of the man with the moat in his eye. However, the device that Thurber uses most effectively is the reversal of the reader's and the characters' expectations. Particularly, he has the two characters perform identical actions but with much more than opposite effect. While the husband looks at unicorns, his wife sleeps; while she rushes feverishly around to tell the police and the psychiatrist about the unicorn he has seen, he sleeps in the rose bed. He reports that there is a unicorn in the garden; she replies, "The unicorn is a mythical beast." The police and the psychiatrist ask if he saw a unicorn, and he replies, "The unicorn is a mythical beast." As a result, what she had planned for him happens to her: it is she who screams and curses when he lives happily ever after. Over and over things that look just alike have opposite results from the expected. These complete turns in the action are technically called **reversals.**

Despite his objective enjoyment even of the suffering of the characters, the reader usually learns from good comic writing. He probably will at least hesitate before he says again that someone's unicorn is a mythical beast, and he may be less hasty in deciding who is a booby and who is not. However, the reader of humor need not suffer, as he would in real life, from the knowledge that that poor sane woman is in an institution while that nut is out running around. Instead of having ruined the story, analysis should have permitted the reader both to enjoy the story in much greater depth than he could have at first and even to see, objectively enough to laugh, his own failures in communication, his own gloating, his own being caught in traps intended for others. Understanding a story is unimportant unless it contributes to understanding oneself and the human condition. The comic vision makes that understanding bearable.

Identifying the Major Character

By this time the reader is so thoroughly familiar with the story that he may not recognize that one technical problem remains. For this and several other stories in this collection, the reader needs to learn how to decide with assurance who is the major character. There are five principal tests:

1. **Who is the grammatical subject throughout most of the story, and who is the content subject of the majority of paragraphs?** A reader need check only a small part of a story to discover the approximate proportion. In "The Unicorn in the Garden" the vast majority of sentences have the subject "a man" or "he." In the first half of the story, even those sentences governed by the wife have as their subject "*his* wife," a subordination that is more than a social identification. Briefly and importantly she acts, however, to get him institutionalized. Even then, she reports more than she initiates action.
2. **Through whose mind is most of the watching or judging done?** The reader sees the unicorn because the man does, he feels the man's emotions when he is rejected, and he shows his intention to "see about that."
3. **Who is present when all major actions occur, particularly at the beginning and end of the story?** Obviously, only the man appears both at the beginning and the end of the story, and, though he is not present when his wife informs the police and psychiatrist that he has seen a unicorn, he is present in the crisis when she has been mistakenly seized and awaits his word to free her.

JAMES THURBER: *The Unicorn in the Garden*

4. **Whose is the conflict—that is, who is the protagonist?** The inciting action and the climax are the simplest points of a story to test. When she says, "I am going to put you in the booby hatch," he responds to her inciting action with, "We'll see about that." Also, it is his response to the climax—"Did you tell your wife you saw a unicorn?"—that guarantees that his life will be changed greatly from then on.

5. **Who is affected most by the resolution?** In many stories this question might be, "Whose need is most completely satisfied?" In others, where the protagonist is blind to the meaning of his experience, the question is, "Who should be most affected?" It would seem automatic that if someone died (or was put in a booby hatch) his life would be most affected. The careful reader will check further, however, to see if death or being institutionalized is a tremendous change from what life is like in the rest of the story. In "The Unicorn in the Garden" whose life is affected most? He will live without her. She, who has long been living with a booby, will still live with boobies, but in a booby hatch. His life is changed radically; hers is changed little.

QUESTIONS FOR DISCUSSION AND WRITING

1. What proves that the husband habitually sees all sorts of things not seen by people bound by fact and logic?

2. What does the unicorn symbolize in this story?

3. What are the natures of the man and his wife?

4. Why is the man able to fall asleep in the rose bed despite the threat of his wife to put him in a bobby hatch?

5. How long has the wife's desire to commit her husband existed?

6. What reason has the wife to expect that her husband will verify her report that he has seen a unicorn in the garden?

7. How does the unexpected association of objects contribute to the humor of "The Unicorn in the Garden"?

8. Why has the reader such enjoyment of the wife's being put into a strait jacket and taken to the booby hatch?

9. What does the moral at the end of "The Unicorn in the Garden" help the reader to learn painlessly about himself and the human condition?

10. Why is expedient rather than moral deliberation essential to the humor of both "The Schartz-Metterklume Method" and "The Unicorn in the Garden"?

12. What is the proof that Hop-Frog and not the king is the protagonist in "Hop-Frog"?

The Beggar

ANTON CHEKOV

Kind sir, have pity; turn your attention to a poor, hungry man! For three days I have had nothing to eat; I haven't five kopecks[1] for a lodging. I swear it before God. For eight years I was a village schoolteacher and then I lost my place through intrigues. I fell a victim to calumny. It is a year now since I have had anything to do—"

The advocate Skvortsoff looked at the ragged, fawn-colored overcoat of the applicant, at his dull, drunken eyes, at the red spot on either cheek, and it seemed to him as if he had seen this man somewhere before.

"I have now had an offer of a position in the province of Kaluga," the mendicant went on, "but I haven't the money to get there. Help me kindly; I am ashamed to ask, but—I am obliged to by circumstances."

Skvortsoff's eyes fell on the man's overshoes, one of which was high and the other low, and he suddenly remembered something.

"Look here, it seems to me I met you day before yesterday in Sadovaya Street," he said, "but you told me then that you were a student who had been expelled, and not a village schoolteacher. Do you remember?"

"No-no, that can't be so," mumbled the beggar, taken aback. "I am a village schoolteacher, and if you like I can show you my papers."

[1] Kopeck: a Russian coin worth less than one cent.

"Have done with lying! You called yourself a student and even told me what you had been expelled for. Don't you remember?"

Skvortsoff flushed and turned from the ragged creature with an expression of disgust.

"This is dishonesty, my dear sir!" he cried angrily. "This is swindling! I shall send the police for you, damn you! Even if you are poor and hungry, that does not give you any right to lie brazenly and shamelessly!"

The waif caught hold of the door handle and looked furtively round the antechamber, like a detected thief.

"I—I am not lying—" he muttered. "I can show you my papers."

"Who would believe you?" Skvortsoff continued indignantly. "Don't you know that it's a low, dirty trick to exploit the sympathy which society feels for village schoolteachers and students? It's revolting."

Skvortsoff lost his temper and began to berate the mendicant unmercifully. The impudent lying of the ragamuffin offended what he, Skvortsoff, most prized in himself: his kindness, his tender heart, his compassion for all unhappy things. That lie, an attempt to take advantage of the pity of its "subject," seemed to him to profane the charity which he liked to extend to the poor out of the purity of his heart. At first the waif continued to protest innocence, but soon he grew silent and hung his head in confusion.

"Sir!" he said, laying his hand on his heart, "the fact is I—was lying! I am neither a student nor a schoolteacher. All that was a fiction. Formerly I sang in a Russian choir and was sent away for drunkenness. But what else can I do? I can't get along without lying. No one will give me anything when I tell the truth. With truth a man would starve to death or die of cold for lack of a lodging. You reason justly, I understand you, but—what can I do?"

"What can you do? You ask what you can do?" cried Skvortsoff, coming close to him. "Work! That's what you can do! You must work!"

"Work—yes, I know that myself; but where can I find work?"

"Rot! You're young and healthy and strong; you could always

find work if you only wanted to, but you're lazy and spoiled and drunken! There's a smell about you like a taproom. You're rotten and false to the core, and all you can do is to lie. When you consent to lower yourself to work, you want a job in an office or in a choir or as a marker at billiards—any employment for which you can get money without doing anything! How would you like to try your hand at manual labor? No, you'd never be a porter or a factory hand; you're a man of pretentions, you are!"

"You judge harshly," cried the beggar with a bitter laugh. "Where can I find manual labor? It's too late for me to be a clerk because in trade one has to begin as a boy; no one would ever take me for a porter because they couldn't order me about; no factory would have me because for that one has to know a trade, and I know none."

"Nonsense! You always find some excuse! How would you like to chop wood for me?"

"I wouldn't refuse to do that, but in these days even skilled woodcutters find themselves sitting without bread."

"Huh! You loafers all talk that way. As soon as an offer is made you, you refuse it! Will you come and chop wood for me?"

"Yes, sir; I will."

"Very well; we'll soon find out. Splendid—we'll see—"

Skvortsoff hastened along, rubbing his hands, not without a feeling of malice, and called his cook out of the kitchen.

"Here, Olga," he said, "take this gentleman into the woodshed and let him chop wood."

The tatterdemalion scarecrow shrugged his shoulders as if in perplexity, and went irresolutely after the cook. It was obvious from his gait that he had not consented to go and chop wood because he was hungry and wanted work, but simply from pride and shame, because he had been trapped by his own words. It was obvious, too, that his strength had been undermined by vodka and that he was unhealthy and did not feel the slightest inclination for toil.

Skvortsoff hurried into the dining room. From its windows one could see the woodshed and everything that went on in the yard. Standing at the window, Skvortsoff saw the cook and the beggar come out into the yard by the back door and make their way across the dirty snow to the shed. Olga glared wrathfully at her companion, shoved him aside with her elbow, unlocked the shed, and angrily banged the door.

"We probably interrupted the woman over her coffee," thought Skvortsoff. "What an ill-tempered creature!"

Next he saw the pseudo teacher, pseudo student seat himself on a log and become lost in thought with his red cheeks resting on his fists. The woman flung down an ax at his feet, spat angrily, and judging from the expression of her lips, began to scold him. The beggar irresolutely pulled a billet of wood toward him, set it up between his feet, and tapped it feebly with the ax. The billet wavered and fell down. The beggar again pulled it to him, blew on his freezing hands, and tapped it with his ax cautiously, as if afraid of hitting his overshoe or of cutting off his finger. The stick of wood again fell to the ground.

Skvortsoff's anger had vanished and he now began to feel a little sorry and ashamed of himself for having set a spoiled, drunken, perchance sick man to work at menial labor in the cold.

"Well, never mind," he thought, going into his study from the dining room. "I did it for his own good."

An hour later Olga came in and announced that the wood had all been chopped.

"Good! Give him half a ruble,"[1] said Skvortsoff. "If he wants to he can come back and cut wood on the first day of each month. We can always find work for him."

On the first of the month the waif made his appearance again and earned half a ruble, although he could barely stand on his legs. From that day on he often appeared in the yard and every time work was found for him. Now he would shovel snow, now put the woodshed in order, now beat the dust out of rugs and mattresses. Every time he received from twenty to forty kopecks, and once, even a pair of old trousers were sent out to him.

---

[1] Ruble: worth a little over 50 cents.

ANTON CHEKOV: *The Beggar*

When Skvortsoff moved into another house he hired him to help in the packing and hauling of the furniture. This time the waif was sober, gloomy, and silent. He hardly touched the furniture, and walked behind the wagons hanging his head, not even making a pretense of appearing busy. He only shivered in the cold and became embarrassed when the carters jeered at him for his idleness, his feebleness, and his tattered, fancy overcoat. After the moving was over Skvortsoff sent for him.

"Well, I see that my words have taken effect," he said, handing him a ruble. "Here's for your pains. I see you are sober and have no objection to work. What is your name?"

"Lushkoff."

"Well, Lushkoff, I can now offer you some other, cleaner employment. Can you write?"

"I can."

"Then take this letter to a friend of mine tomorrow and you will be given some copying to do. Work hard, don't drink, and remember what I have said to you. Good-by!"

Pleased at having put a man on the right path, Skvortsoff tapped Lushkoff kindly on the shoulder and even gave him his hand at parting. Lushkoff took the letter, and from that day forth came no more to the yard for work.

Two years went by. Then one evening, as Skvortsoff was standing by the ticket window of a theater paying for his seat, he noticed a little man beside him with a coat collar of curly fur and a worn sealskin cap. This little individual timidly asked the ticket seller for a seat in the gallery and paid for it in copper coins.

"Lushkoff, is that you?" cried Skvortsoff, recognizing in the little man his former woodchopper. "How are you? What are you doing? How is everything with you?"

"All right. I am a notary now and get thirty-five rubles a month."

"Thank Heaven! That's fine! I am delighted for your sake. I am very, very glad, Lushkoff. You see, you are my godson, in a sense. I gave you a push along the right path, you know. Do you remember what a roasting I gave you, eh? I nearly had you sinking into the ground at my feet that day. Thank you, old man, for not forgetting my words."

"Thank you, too," said Lushkoff. "If I hadn't come to you then I might still have been calling myself a teacher or a student to this day. Yes, by flying to your protection I dragged myself out of a pit."

"I am very glad, indeed."

"Thank you for your kind words and deeds. You talked splendidly to me then. I am very grateful to you and to your cook. God bless that good and noble woman! You spoke finely then, and I shall be indebted to you to my dying day; but, strictly speaking, it was your cook, Olga, who saved me."

"How is that?"

"Like this. When I used to come to your house to chop wood she used to begin: 'Oh, you sot, you! Oh, you miserable creature! There's nothing for you but ruin.' And then she would sit down opposite me and grow sad, look into my face and weep. 'Oh, you unlucky man! There is no pleasure for you in this world and there will be none in the world to come. You drunkard! You will burn in hell. Oh, you unhappy one!' And so she would carry on, you know, in that strain. I can't tell you how much misery she suffered, how many tears she shed for my sake. But the chief thing was—she used to chop the wood for me. Do you know, sir, that I did not chop one single stick of wood for you? She did it all. Why this saved me, why I changed, why I stopped drinking at the sight of her I cannot explain. I only know that, owing to her words and noble deeds a change took place in my heart; she set me right and I shall never forget it. However, it is time to go now; there goes the bell."

Lushkoff bowed and departed to the gallery.

Conventions of Narration

Before the reader can study effectively either character or action in "The Beggar" he needs to understand some basic **conventions of narration** (unwritten agreements about form or practice in fiction). The major convention is that the author is not the person who tells the story. No matter how many of the facts in a work of fiction can be shown to be autobiographical, this convention holds. Otherwise, the author could be charged with all sorts of philosophical, ethical, or political opinions that need not be his even though they are quite definitely present in the story. What is even more important is that the narrator is a creation just as are the characters, the conflict, and the other story elements. The narrator is not the creator of the story: the author is. Therefore, the author must choose his narrator with care as deliberate as that with which he selects his characters and designs their actions. The reader's problem, then, is to determine, first, who tells the story and, second, what that narrator's abilities and limitations are.

There are six generally accepted different narrators of fiction that the reader must learn to distinguish if he is to understand stories in depth. Each of the six sees the story that he tells from a different point of view. The characteristics that distinguish these points of view are all conventions of narration. Three of the six narrators call themselves "I" and are hence considered narrators in the first person. Three use the third person: they talk about what happens but never are characters themselves.

Third-Person Narrators

In "The Schartz-Metterklume Method," the narrator is **omniscient.** That is, he knows everything—present, past, and future— including especially the thoughts of all of the characters. He is able to report that at some moment in the past Lady Carlotta stepped off the train, but he knows also what only she herself could know: that she got off to kill time. He was present when Lady Carlotta left her friend stranded in the maytree; he sits in on and interprets the dinner conversation of the Quabarls; and he sees the simultaneous arrivals of Miss Hope and Lady Carlotta in different parts of the country. Since no human being, not even an author, can be all-knowing and present in all places (including the minds of all characters), the reader simply must be willing to accept that some such omniscient, omnipresent being tells the story in the third person, in the past tense, and without mentioning himself at all. This is the convention of the omniscient narrator. He sees and knows all without regard to the limits of time or space and can give accurately the contents of the mind of any character. Also, any assertions that he makes about the character's attitude and ideas must be presumed to be true.

The second narrator who uses the third person—the limited-omniscient narrator—has the powers of the omniscient narrator but chooses to limit himself to the thoughts of a single character, though he keeps his ability to be present in all places at all times. It is he who narrates "The Beggar." He reports the exact words of both the beggar and Skvortsoff and he reports the thoughts of Skvortsoff, but he never enters the mind of the beggar. In other words, the narrator here also is omniscient because he can see and hear everything and furthermore can tell us the contents of Skvortsoff's mind. He has to be omniscient because, though most of the story is told from the viewpoint of Skvortsoff, a few omniscient objective passages provide information that, if Skvortsoff had known, certainly would have stopped him from giving Lushkoff a chance at a less arduous job. (The best example is the paragraph where Lushkoff is described following the movers to Skvortsoff's new house.) Therefore, the reader must conclude that the narrator is omniscient but for some reason chooses to limit his revelation of information to the mind of Skvortsoff. This convention of narration is called **the limited-omniscient narrator:** the narrator who can be in all times and places and know all, but who consistently enters only the mind of a single character, and who never himself participates in the action.

Once the reader knows the abilities of a narrator, he must determine what limitations the narrator has. The major conventional limitation—the author's decision that only the mind of Skvortsoff will be revealed and that much of the story will be narrated from his point of view—directs the reader's search for the narrator's human limitations. As a general rule, the convention of the limited-omniscient narrator is chosen by an author who wishes the reader to examine the mind of a character even more closely than he examines the story's action. With the fully omniscient narrator, the reader is assured that interpretations are accurate, that assertions are true, and that observations are correct. When information comes to the reader through the mind of a character like Skvortsoff, however, the reader can trust only the facts that are not colored by the narrator's human biases and abilities.

The third and final narrator who uses the third person is **the omnipresent narrator.** He does not know all, as the omniscient narrator does, but he can see all and hear all as if there were no walls and no barriers of time and place. Therefore, he can report conversations and record actions wherever they occur, and he can watch characters while they are alone. Interestingly, he can record what they think while they are alone only if they mutter to themselves. However, the omnipresent narrator does make the interpretations of actions that any intelligent observer might make. The linguistic clue to the omnipresent narrator's admission that he is inferring interpretation from what he hears is his frequent use of "as if" or "might" or "must have" or other qualifying comparisons. Although he presumably is human except for his ability to be omnipresent, all that can be known of him is that he is intelligent and sensitive enough that his observations and interpretations can be trusted. The omnipresent narrator is not represented here but is exemplified most effectively in many stories by Miss Eudora Welty, particularly "A Piece of News."

First-Person Narrators

The other conventions of narration involve three narrators in the first person. Any first-person narrator conventionally is presumed to make a story more believable because he either is a participant in it or was told as much about it as anyone could possibly know. Obviously, however, any first-person narrator has to be evaluated as a human being before anything that he says can be believed. If the village idiot attends a symphony concert, his judgment of the performance need not be accepted. If a lawyer's daughter is murdered, the lawyer should not represent the defense. In other words, a first-person narrator can have all of the strengths and all of the weaknesses that any single human being can have. He may be physically handicapped, and his disability may make him a better or a worse observer. He may have some emotional limitation—some love or some hate so strong that it blinds him to anything but what he wants to see. His education, his mentality, the breadth of his experience, his natural disposition—any of these characteristics may enhance or handicap his narration. Clearly then, a reader must study carefully the character of a first-person narrator.

If a **first-person narrator** is a **major character,** he has the advantage of being involved directly in the conflict. Therefore the reader often has a stronger sense of conflict and an even more dramatic participation in it than with another narrator. Such a narrator cannot present, however, the thoughts of any other than himself except by speculation—and speculation by a major character is almost always biased. The author who chooses to use a first-person major-character narrator often does so for the same reason that he might choose a limited-omniscient narrator in the third person: he wishes the reader to understand most deeply the nature of the character rather than the problems of the action. Therefore a first-person major-character narrator often narrates a story about an inner conflict dramatized in an outer one.

If a **first-person narrator** is a **minor character,** he has the advantage of seeing both sides of the conflict from a distance. If he is intelligent and uninvolved, his opinions about the conflict may add depth to the reader's understanding. Should he be either stupid or involved or both, the burden on the reader's powers of interpretation is increased, but this is always for some special purpose of the author that could not be achieved with another point of view.

The sixth possible narrator—**the first-person narrator** who tells the tale **at second-hand**—has less responsibility for the accuracy of the story than has any other narrator. Usually he is distant in time from the event and not affected by it; consequently, his being involved in the story at all is primarily a device to frame the tale that he tells. However, even the narrator of a tale may be a biased narrator. Every reader knows that a grandson who was seven when his grandfather died may not as a man recall accurately even the most familiar family story.

One other convention governs all first-person narrative whether the narrator is a first-person major character, or first-person minor character, or a first-person narrator at secondhand. The story is told either as it happens or in retrospect. If a person tells a story as it is in progress, he and the reader learn the facts simultaneously. Since the narrator is limited to recording things as they happen, he can do little interpreting. However, when a narrator looks back at an action completed in the past, he can add many touches to his story. Knowing at that distance from the event both the causes and effects of actions, he can foreshadow conclusions either obviously by remarking "little did I know . . ." or subtly by including detail, the significance of which he might not even have noticed if he were telling the story as it happened. The first-person narrator in the present tense quite frequently is an ironic narrator. That is, the author deliberately intends the reader to see much more clearly than the narrator precisely what the narrator reveals, particularly about himself. The first-person retrospective narrator is more often a philosopher who concerns himself at length with the significance of the things about which he tells. When an author chooses to have a retrospective narrator to tell about past events and to philosophize about them without himself seeing what his narrative shows—particularly about himself —the story will be far more subtly ironic than with any other point of view.

Point of View

Probably the simplest way to understand **point of view** as a term is to think of it literally as a position from which a person can see only what is before his physical eyes. The omniscient, limited-omniscient, and omnipresent narrators transcend that physical limitation in one or many ways. The narrators who are actual characters in the story that they narrate are subject to that physical restriction.

Planning Order of Study

With a number of techniques at hand, the reader may wonder how to start his study of "The Beggar." Having been told that its point of view is limited-omniscient, he knows that the story concerns internal more than external action and hence that character will be more important than action. Therefore, the reader may be tempted to jump into a listing of character traits and to skip making an action line. What is better is to establish a routine for gathering basic information about any story so that he will see clearly what information he does not have at the end of the application of each technique and can seek it by another method.

Separating Action from Interpretation

Almost without exception, the best first step in studying any story is writing the action summary. For "The Beggar" a reader needs to develop a minutely detailed action line that he scrupulously restricts to external action. The disproportion of external action to emotions, thoughts, and interpretations is itself overwhelming proof that internal, not external action is the prime interest of the author. In fact, the story told by the bare actions of even a paragraph and those actions as the narrator interprets them differ so dramatically that a reader may understand the narrator's internal conflict extremely well long before he identifies it methodically. If the bias of the narrator is stripped from the action that follows Skvortsoff's telling Olga to "take this gentleman into the woodshed and let him chop wood," the difference between action and interpretation is quite clear. To remove the narrator's emotional coloring from this scene's action, replace a slanted verb like "glared" with an emotionally neutral one like "looked." What remains of the scene is diagramed on page 65.

The discovery that Skvortsoff never actually sees the beggar chop a piece of wood proves how important separating action from interpre-

ANTON CHEKOV: *The Beggar*

                  announced that all the wood had been chopped
         Olga came in
     Skvortsoff went to his study
   The billet fell down
           tapped it with the ax
         blew on his hands
Lushkoff pulled it to him
The billet fell down
       tapped it with an ax
     set it between his feet
Lushkoff pulled the wood toward him
     spoke to him
    spat
Olga dropped the ax at his feet
       rested his cheeks on his fists
Lushkoff sat on a log
    shut the door
   unlocked the shed
      motioned him aside with her elbow
Olga looked at the beggar
They came out the back door and went to the shed
Skvortsoff saw the cook and the beggar
Skvortsoff hurried into the dining room
Lushkoff shrugged and went after Olga
Skvortsoff tells Olga to take Lushkoff and let him chop wood

tation is. So carefully prepared an action line will prove invaluable whenever the reader needs reliable evidence to test Skvortsoff's reactions, motives, and interpretations.

As a second routine step of analysis, the reader should determine who is the major character. Information easily obtained will answer the first three questions suggested on page 50. Despite the overwhelming evidence that Skvortsoff is the major character, however, the most important proof may be missing because the inciting action and Skvortsoff's response and the climax and resolution are not easy to find. That missing knowledge should direct the reader to identify the conflict precisely. Whenever that identification is difficult, the reader should study the end of the story, where the crisis, climax, and resolution have to be whether or not he can find them at first.

A third technique of study—precise questioning—should help the reader to define the conflict of Skvortsoff and Lushkoff. The story should end with a moment of crisis for Lushkoff as the antagonist after which he brings the conflict to a climax. Immediately, Skvortsoff should resolve it. Logic demands that the meeting of the two at the theater must contain these steps since a gap of two years separates that meeting from the rest of the story. The questions that the reader needs to ask are those that define crisis, conflict, and resolution. What does Skvortsoff say or do here that shows that a conflict continues? What statement by Skvortsoff antagonizes Lushkoff most? In what speech in the dialogue is it clear that Lushkoff wants the conflict settled once and for all? What of all that Lushkoff says is most unexpected by Skvortsoff? In what specific aspect of that speech does Lushkoff confront Skvortsoff most dramatically? How could Skvortsoff have been so very wrong in his expectations? What action of Lushkoff's is the climax—the action that says that regardless of the cost he intends not to go on in his old relationship to Skvortsoff? Is there a response by Skvortsoff? Why not? What action could Skvortsoff perform that would resolve anything with Lushkoff? For that matter, precisely what need have they both in common that makes them collide head-on here?

The Identity of Needs in the Inciting Action and the Climax

A need or desire or wish or fear deep in the nature of a man always moves him to whatever unexpected (nonhabitual) actions he performs. At the climax, the needs of Lushkoff as a human being are in direct conflict with those of Skvortsoff. Since the climax and the resolution identify the final clash between conflicting persons, the inciting action and protagonist's response mark a similar clash strong enough to commit them both to their external conflict. If the reader can state those opposing needs now, he can question closely every potential inciting action until he finds the one action by Lushkoff that provokes Skvortsoff to commit himself to the conflict identified in the climax. If familiar techniques do not yet yield all the information that he needs, the reader should consider what seems to make the analysis so difficult.

The most obvious difficulty is Skvortsoff himself. The fourth familiar technique—the simple listing of evidence of traits of a character—often will answer what questions remain. Applied here, however, its major usefulness is to help the reader to see what else he must do. From two pages of the story the reader can amass a considerable list of discoveries. Particularly he will see that Skvortsoff acts like a lawyer—with all that that occupation brings to the mind in the way of observing and interpreting details and examining witnesses. But the reader will see also the apparent paradox that Skvortsoff thinks of himself as kind, tender-hearted, and compassionate yet loses his temper and berates the beggar unmercifully. Soon the continuous difficulty of distinguishing fact from opinion will lead the reader to determine the reliability of the narrator before completing the character study.

Reliability of the Narrator

In stories narrated by omniscient or omnipresent narrators whose interpretations of character are always presumed to be accurate, most reaction is asserted and correct causes are ascribed to major actions. With all first-person narrators (except at rare times the narrator at second hand) and especially with the limited-omniscient narrator (the type who narrates "The Beggar"), the problem is quite different and more difficult. Because "The Beggar" has a narrator who uses the consciousness of Skvortsoff, who is violently involved in the conflict, the reliability of the evidence has to be assessed constantly.

The accepted convention is that an author will not permit a limited-omniscient narrator deliberately to lie unless the lie is clearly exposed in accurately reported conversation with another character whose reliability can be established. However, the convention permits a narrator constantly to interpret even accurate facts. His interpretation may be correct, partially wrong, or completely wrong. To complicate the problem, the reader can know that the other characters' speeches are recorded verbatim; but he has no evidence but that derived from character to help him to determine whether or not an accurately recorded speech is a lie, a distortion, or the truth. Even the evidence for character must be sifted from biased narration. Nevertheless, there are ample ways for the reader to check Skvortsoff's factual accuracy and his reliability as an interpreter.

Studying two major examples should make the reader confident of his ability to judge the reliability of Skvortsoff's report of facts of action. The first is a comparison of Lushkoff and Skvortsoff's interpretations of the same set of facts. What Skvortsoff observes from his dining room window when Olga takes the beggar to chop wood Lushkoff comments on in the theater scene. Nothing Lushkoff says in any way contradicts the facts in Skvortsoff's interpretation. However, he flatly contradicts Skvortsoff's understanding of them. The second example concerns Skvortsoff's opposite interpretations of Lushkoff's physical condition. At the beginning of the story, Skvortsoff responds to Lushkoff's asking where he can find work: "Rot! You're young and healthy and strong . . . ." Yet, just before Skvortsoff leaves the dining room window for his study, he "began to feel a little sorry and ashamed of himself for having set a spoiled, drunken, perchance sick man to work at menial labor in the cold." Clearly, if Skvortsoff makes opposite judgments of the same facts of Lushkoff's appearance, his judgments of the beggar's motives are even more suspect.

In real life, judging the precise motives of a human being from his actions is generally considered not merely impossible but even morally wrong because there is no accurate way of entering another person's mind. Such judgments in literature are not only possible but also necessary. If a story with even minor internal action is to be understood thoroughly, every detail of motive must be read as accurately as are details of action or of physical appearance. Besides, in well-written fiction, even with a limited narrator, all of the relevant facts can be known as they cannot in real life.

Evaluating Asserted Motives

The prime technique for the evaluation of motives is identifying bias in vocabulary by comparing assertions with the facts. A reader tests the statements of a narrator in exactly the same way that he tests the objectivity of his own summary of a story:
1. Are the narrator's facts accurate?
2. Has he interpreted rather than recorded actions?
3. Has his attitude toward the characters colored the facts?

Developing the ability to test a narrator's objectivity is made less difficult by the convention that the basic facts of his emotional reaction asserted by a character may be presumed to be true. Therefore, Skvortsoff can be believed to be angry or annoyed or pleased if he says that he is. The tests of objectivity are necessary because his explanation of causes for emotions cannot be trusted. Perhaps the most obvious example of colored narration begins: "Skvortsoff lost his temper and began to berate the mendicant unmercifully. The impudent lying of the ragamuffin offended what he, Skvortsoff, most prized in himself: his kindness, his tender heart, his compassion for all unhappy things." The reader must assume three facts: that Skvortsoff is indeed offended; that he believes sincerely that the offence is the beggar's lying in the face of his kindness, tenderness, and compassion; and that he loses his temper and is unmerciful in his verbal attack on the beggar.

The second technique for evaluating motives is the identification of contradictory statements. It is clearly impossible for Skvortsoff simultaneously to feel "compassion [mercy and pity] for all unhappy things"—of which Lushkoff is most obviously one—and by his own admission to be unmerciful [without mercy or pity] in his berating of the beggar. Equally, the kindness and tenderness "most prized in himself" scarcely suit his so quickly losing his temper. Furthermore, the prime impudence [insolence, boldness] of Lushkoff is his insistence that he is not lying even though Skvortsoff denounces him as a beggar that he had encountered before who also had mismatched galoshes but a different tale of woe. Skvortsoff's real motives have to be inferred from the nature of his actions. The beggar's insisting on his innocence offends Skvortsoff's pride—in his acuteness of observation, his memory for details, and his ability to argue convincingly from circumstantial evidence—not his compassion.

All sorts of additional verbal clues mark his bias against the beggar and in favor of himself. The beggar is a "mendicant," a "ragamuffin," and "a waif" who offends, lies impudently, takes advantage of, profanes, and protests until he hangs his head "in confusion." Skvortsoff prizes what he attributes to himself—kindness, a tender heart, compassion, pity, charity, and purity of heart. Clearly, both the violence of his attack on the beggar and the extent of his defense of himself are out of all proportion to any action by the beggar. Reading so carefully enables the reader to see that the beggar triggers a longstanding conflict within Skvortsoff many paragraphs before Skvortsoff actually commits himself to the conflict in the action.

Simple logic is a third tool for evaluating asserted motives. One excellent example of a vital judgment that needs to be tested against the facts is Skvortsoff's repeated assertions that Lushkoff is lying. Lushkoff insists from the beginning that he is not lying and can show papers to prove it. His anger overriding his occupational respect for evidence, Skvortsoff never asks to see them and responds, "Who would believe you?" Only after Skvortsoff berates him does Lushkoff state that: "The truth is I—was lying! ... No one will give me anything when I tell the truth." What are the facts? The one objective check that Skvortsoff could have made, he did not. Why? Because he prefers to rely on his judgment! Whether or not Lushkoff is the same beggar that Skvortsoff saw before becomes, then, a matter of Skvortsoff's word against Lushkoff's. Certainly if Lushkoff is not lying and Skvortsoff simply remembers inaccurately, it is true that no one will give the beggar anything when he tells the truth. Proof: Skvortsoff does not. Does Lushkoff lie, then, for the first time when he hesitates, then confesses that he was lying before?

Or is he lying again because his new lie is one more provocative of a satisfactory response from a man whose kindness, compassion, and tender heart have been affronted by his telling a story not worthy of those feelings? Because the reader gets all of his information about Lushkoff through the consciousness of Skvortsoff (except for one paragraph about Skvortsoff's move), it probably is impossible to prove conclusively that Lushkoff is at first telling the truth. However, the reader does know with certainty that Skvortsoff is most unreliable about his own motives. The possibility of his being more accurate about the motives of Lushkoff, whose mind he cannot enter, is even more remote. Though whether or not Lushkoff lies cannot be settled unequivocally, the reader must see the whole story with the possibility, even probability, constantly in mind that Lushkoff tells the truth except when he chooses to suit Skvortsoff. Perhaps the reader needs no cautioning that he gather a great deal of proof before he decides what the real motives of characters are. Skvortsoff was himself a lawyer trained to gather evidence and make logical deductions from it. Nevertheless, he gradually became so overly confident of his ability that his pride made him vulnerable to anyone who recognized his blindness to his own human fallibility.

Irony

When a reader is able to see far more than a character can see of himself, the story is said to be ironic. **Irony** designates a combination of circumstances or a result that is the opposite of what might be expected or what might be appropriate. If a character is aware of this gap between the ideal and reality or the expectation and the outcome, he may express this awareness in **verbal irony:** saying one thing and meaning another. Sometimes, a reader sees irony also because a character says almost nothing, as when Lushkoff hardly speaks in the scene where Skvortsoff gives him a letter for a better job. Once the reader becomes aware of the tremendous discrepancy between how Skvortsoff views himself and what Lushkoff knows that he really is, the reader will see that in the theater Lushkoff deliberately states his appreciation in a way that emphasizes Skvortsoff's moral inferiority to his cook. Nor will the reader miss the irony of Lushkoff's politely leaving the speechless Skvortsoff standing in the theater.

Internal and External Action

Because what happens in the action symbolizes Skvortsoff's blindness to his internal conflict, it is appropriate that there is no resolution in the action. There can be none unless Skvortsoff recognizes and by moral decision deliberately overcomes the split between what he thinks his actions represent and the reality of his motives. To trace the development of both conflicts so that he can assess the likelihood of Skvortsoff's ever recognizing or resolving his internal conflict, the reader needs a new technique that will permit him to see simultaneously the relationships among an action by the antagonist, the response that the antagonist expects from the protagonist, the actual response by the protagonist, the motive the protagonist believes he has, and (what the reader supplies) the protagonist's probable real motive. If the reader wishes, he may also consider the beggar's motives. How Lushkoff reacts to Skvortsoff and what he expects from him show Lushkoff's motivation. His motives are particularly clear once Skvortsoff's responses become exactly what Lushkoff expects.

"The Beggar" begins with an appeal by Lushkoff to Skvortsoff for his pity and his attention and, more specifically, for the means to eat and sleep. Skvortsoff's reaction is to examine with extremely close attention items of Lushkoff's appearance and to interpret those details as familiar to him. Clearly Lushkoff expects sympathy translated into money. Instead he gets examined head to toe. In his second speech he asks directly for funds. This time his appeal should either be accepted or rejected. However, Skvortsoff keeps looking curiously at him and suddenly reacts not to his words so much as to his overshoes and to his own supposed recollection. The lists that follow carry the five points for analysis through the inciting action. The reader should finish the story for himself before he presumes to understand it fully.

When the reader completes this analysis, he will not only command the story but also will have details organized to answer all of the questions left open by other kinds of analysis. For example, by tracing the differences between what the beggar expects and what Skvortsoff does, the reader can pinpoint the speech in which Skvortsoff becomes so emotionally involved that he no longer even thinks about the beggar's request. That speech marks the beginning of Skvortsoff's internal conflict. Skvortsoff's emotional involvement can be proven even more emphatically by examining each motive Skvortsoff claims. Had he felt the emotions that he asserted, his actions probably would have been those expected by the beggar. Losing his temper is his admission that Lushkoff's protests of innocence engage his emotions directly. With the help of that insight, the reader can find abundant evidence that Skvortsoff's attention is not on Lushkoff's begging at all. Instead, Skvortsoff uses the occasion for a performance—an act intended to evoke responses from Lushkoff which will prove to Skvortsoff the moral superiority of his observations and deliberations.

With close analysis, the reader will also see the irony that Lushkoff's recognition that he is being abused for Skvortsoff's emotional needs enables him to involve Skvortsoff in a major conflict where the beggar had intended originally only a brief encounter. That recognition is even more clearly illustrated in the climax when Lushkoff, with deliberate irony, lets Skvortsoff know that he too can serve the emotional needs of another.

Questions for Discussion and Writing

1. What is the major proof that the action in "The Beggar" is internal, not external?
2. Who is the major character?
3. What is the inciting action, the protagonist's response, the crisis, and the climax?
4. Why is there no resolution?
5. What is the significance of there being no physical traits of Skvortsoff whatsoever?

Antagonist's Action	Probable Response Expected	Protagonist's Response	Asserted Motive	Probable Motive
Lushkoff asks pity, attention, money for food, lodging	pity, money for food, lodging	Skvortsoff looked him over	sympathy	suspicion, pride in memory for detail, faces
tells of a new job, asks money for travel	money or a refusal	replies that he has seen him before, asks if he remembers		display of memory, pride in sophistication
offers to show papers as proof	examination of papers or money	calls him a liar, dishonest, threatens police, swears at him	disgust, anger	self-righteousness
says he is not lying, offers papers again	check papers, send for police, turn him away	asks who would believe him, accuses him of exploiting sympathy, loses temper, berates beggar	indignation, revulsion, kindness, tender heartedness, compassion, pity, charity, purity of heart	offended pride

ANTON CHEKOV: *The Beggar*

Inciting Action	Probable Response Expected	Protagonist's Response	Asserted Motive	Probable Motive
continues to protest innocence, grows silent, hangs his head, lays hand on heart, says he was lying, asks what he can do	"work" (not starve, tell better lies, go to prison)	tells him to work	charity from purity of heart	self-righteousness
asks where he can find work	manual labor	accuses him of laziness, rottenness, drunkenness, disparages his probable desire to do gentlemanly work	kindness	self-righteousness
explains that he knows no trade	suggestion of some menial job universally available	suggests manual labor, asks if he would "like" to chop wood for him	tender-heartedness, compassion	self-righteousness
INCITING ACTION	**PROBABLE RESPONSE EXPECTED**	**PROTAGONIST'S RESPONSE**	**ASSERTED MOTIVE**	**PROBABLE MOTIVE**
says he would not refuse accepts job	offer of job	asks if he will chop wood	pity	malice
		calls cook. sends him to chop wood	malice	malice
shrugs, goes with cook		watches them, goes to study	regret, shame	shame

6. Does the narrator of "The Beggar" ever lie? If so, when? Why? If not, why not?

7. If in a court of law Skvortsoff attempted to prove that Lushkoff was the same beggar whom he had seen before, how might the defense prove that all of his evidence was circumstantial?

8. What are the limitations of the narrator of "The Beggar"?

9. At what point in the beginning of the story does Skvortsoff become so emotionally involved that he no longer thinks about the question of Lushkoff's begging? What is he thinking about instead?

10. Beginning with Lushkoff's statement that "I—was lying," show how Lushkoff, by anticipating Skvortsoff's responses, forces Skvortsoff to give him a job.

11. How does what Lushkoff says in the climax show Skvortsoff that Lushkoff had taken advantage of him?

12. How does Skvortsoff's view of himself as kind and tenderhearted help prevent his involvement with the beggar?

13. Can Skvortsoff, after the scene at the theater, see the discrepancy between why he believed he acted and why he really acted?

14. If the irony of his life is clear to Skvortsoff, what can he do to resolve his internal conflict?

15. If he does not see the irony of his life, how will Skvortsoff be likely to resolve the external conflict?

16. Why is the realization of the irony of Skvortsoff's life more the reader's than the narrator's?

17. What is the irony of Hop-Frog's saying just before the climax, as he holds the torch toward the king and the ministers, "I begin to see who these people *are* now"?

18. What irony in Mrs. Quabarl's saying "You must be Miss Hope" makes the reader delight in Lady Carlotta's response?

Bartleby

HERMAN MELVILLE

I am a rather elderly man. The nature of my avocations, for the last thirty years, has brought me into more than ordinary contact with what would seem an interesting and somewhat singular set of men, of whom, as yet, nothing, that I know of, has ever been written—I mean the law-copyists, or scriveners. I have known very many of them, professionally and privately, and, if I pleased, could relate divers histories, at which goodnatured gentlemen might smile, and sentimental souls might weep. But I waive the biographies of all other scriveners, for a few passages in the life of Bartleby, who was a scrivener, the strangest I ever saw, or heard of. While, of other law-copyists, I might write the complete life, of Bartleby nothing of that sort can be done. I believe that no materials exist for a full and satisfactory biography of this man. It is an irreparable loss to literature. Bartleby was one of those beings of whom nothing is ascertainable, except from the original sources, and, in his case, those are very small. What my own astonished eyes saw of Bartleby, that is all I know of him, except, indeed, one vague report, which will appear in the sequel.

Ere introducing the scrivener, as he first appeared to me, it is fit I make some mention of myself, my employees, my business, my chambers, and general surroundings, because some such description is indispensable to an adequate understanding of the chief character about to be presented. Imprimis: I am a man who, from his youth upward, has been filled with a profound conviction that the easiest way of life is the best. Hence, though I belong to a profession proverbially energetic and nervous, even to turbulence, at times, yet nothing of that sort have I ever suffered to invade my peace. I am one of those unambitious lawyers who never address a jury, or in any way draw down public applause; but, in the cool tranquillity of a snug retreat, do a snug business among rich men's bonds, and mortgages, and titledeeds. All who know me consider me an eminently safe man. The late John Jacob Astor, a personage little given to poetic enthusiasm, had no hesitation in pronouncing my first grand point to be prudence; my next, method. I do not speak it in vanity, but simply record the fact, that I was not unemployed in my profession by the late John Jacob Astor; a name which, I admit, I love to repeat; for it hath a rounded and orbicular sound to it, and rings like unto bullion. I will freely add that I was not insensible to the late John Jacob Astor's good opinion.

Some time prior to the period at which this little history begins, my avocations had been largely increased. The good old office, now extinct in the State of New York, of a Master in Chancery had been conferred upon me. It was not a very arduous office, but very pleasantly remunerative. I seldom lose my temper; much more seldom indulge in dangerous indignation at wrongs and outrages; but I must be permitted to be rash here and declare that I consider the sudden and violent abrogation of the office of Master in Chancery, by the new Constitution, as a——premature act; inasmuch as I had counted upon a life-lease of the profits, whereas I only received those of a few short years. But this is by the way.

My chambers were up stairs, at No. — Wall Street. At one end, they looked upon the white wall of the interior of a spacious skylight shaft, penetrating the building from top to bottom.

This view might have been considered rather tame than otherwise, deficient in what landscape painters call "life." But, if so, the view from the other end of my chambers offered, at least, a contrast, if nothing more. In that direction, my windows commanded an unobstructed view of a lofty brick wall, black by age and everlasting shade; which wall required no spy-glass to bring out its lurking beauties, but, for the benefit of all near-sighted spectators, was pushed up to within ten feet of my window-panes. Owing to the great height of the surrounding buildings, and my chambers being on the second floor, the interval between this wall and mine not a little resembled a huge square cistern.

At the period just preceding the advent of Bartleby, I had two persons as copyists in my employment, and a promising lad as an office-boy. First, Turkey; second, Nippers; third, Ginger Nut. These may seem names the like of which are not usually found in the Directory. In truth, they were nicknames, mutually conferred upon each other by my three clerks, and were deemed expressive of their respective persons or characters. Turkey was a short, pursy Englishman, of about my own age—that is, somewhere not far from sixty. In the morning, one might say, his face was of a fine florid hue, but after twelve o'clock, meridian—his dinner hour—it blazed like a grate full of Christmas coals, and continued blazing—but, as it were, with a gradual wane—till six o'clock, P.M., or thereabouts; after which, I saw no more of the proprietor of the face, which, gaining its meridian with the sun, seemed to set with it, to rise, culminate, and decline the following day, with the like regularity and undiminished glory. There are many singular coincidences I have known in the course of my life, not the least among which was the fact, that, exactly when Turkey displayed his fullest beams from his red and radiant countenance, just then, too, at that critical moment, began the daily period when I considered his business capacities as seriously disturbed for the remainder of the twenty-four hours. Not that he was absolutely idle, or averse to business then; far from it. The difficulty was, he was apt to be altogether too energetic. There was a strange, inflamed, flurried, flighty recklessness of activity about him. He would be incautious in dipping his pen into his inkstand. All his blots upon my documents were dropped there after twelve o'clock, meridian. Indeed, not only would he be reckless and sadly given to making blots in the afternoon, but, some days, he went further, and was rather noisy. At such times, too, his face flamed with augmented blazonry, as if cannel coal had been heaped on anthracite. He made an unpleasant racket with his chair, spilled his sand-box; in mending his pens, impatiently split them all to pieces, and threw them on the floor in a sudden passion; stood up, and leaned over his table, boxing his papers about in a most indecorous manner, very sad to behold in an elderly man like him. Nevertheless, as he was in many ways a most valuable person to me, and all the time before twelve o'clock, meridian, was the quickest, steadiest creature, too, accomplishing a great deal of work in a style not easily to be matched—for these reasons, I was willing to overlook his eccentricities, though, indeed, occasionally, I remonstrated with him. I did this very gently, however, because, though the civilest, nay, the blandest and most reverential of men in the morning, yet, in the afternoon, he was disposed, upon provocation, to be slightly rash with his tongue—in fact, insolent. Now, valuing his morning services as I did, and resolved not to lose them—yet, at the same time, made uncomfortable by his inflamed ways after twelve o'clock—and being a man of peace, unwilling by my admonitions to call forth unseemly retorts from him, I took upon me, one Saturday noon (he was always worse on Saturdays) to hint to him, very kindly, that, perhaps, now that he was growing old, it might be well to abridge his labors; in short, he need not come to my chambers after twelve o'clock, but, dinner over, had best go home to his lodgings, and rest himself till tea-time. But no; he insisted upon his afternoon devotions. His countenance became intolerably fervid, as he oratorically assured me—gesticulating with a long ruler at the other end of the room—that if his services in the morning were useful, how indispensable, then, in the afternoon?

"With submission, sir," said Turkey, on this occasion, "I consider myself your right-hand man. In the morning I but marshal and deploy my columns; but in the afternoon I put myself at their head, and gallantly charge the foe, thus"—and he made a violent thrust with the ruler.

"But the blots, Turkey," intimated I.

"True; but, with submission, sir, behold these hairs! I am getting old. Surely, sir, a blot or two of a warm afternoon is not to be severely urged against gray hairs. Old age—even if it blot the page—is honorable. With submission, sir, we both are getting old."

This appeal to my fellow-feeling was hardly to be resisted. At all events, I saw that go he would not. So I made up my mind to let him stay, resolving, nevertheless, to see to it that, during the afternoon, he had to do with my less important papers.

Nippers, the second on my list, was a whiskered, sallow, and, upon the whole, rather piratical-looking young man, of about five-and-twenty. I always deemed him the victim of two evil powers—ambition and indigestion. The ambition was evinced by a certain impatience of the duties of a mere copyist, an unwarranted usurpation of strictly professional affairs, such as the original drawing up of legal documents. The indigestion seemed betokened in an occasional nervous testiness and grinning irritability, causing the teeth to audibly grind together over mistakes committed in copying; unnecessary maledictions, hissed, rather than spoken, in the heat of business; and especially by a continual discontent with the height of the table where he worked. Though of a very ingenious mechanical turn, Nippers could never get this table to suit him. He put chips under it, blocks of various sorts, bits of pasteboard, and at last went so far as to attempt an exquisite adjustment, by final pieces of folded blotting-paper. But no invention would answer. If, for the sake of easing his back, he brought the table-lid at a sharp angle well up toward his chin, and wrote there like a man using the steep roof of a Dutch house for his desk, then he declared that it stopped the circulation in his arms. If now he lowered the table to his waistbands, and stooped over it in writing, then there was a sore aching in his back. In short, the truth of the matter was, Nippers knew not what he wanted. Or, if he wanted anything, it was to be rid of a scrivener's table altogether. Among the manifestations of his diseased ambition was a fondness he had for receiving visits from certain ambiguous-looking fellows in seedy coats, whom he called his clients. Indeed, I was aware that not only was he, at times, considerable of a ward-politician, but he occasionally did a little business at the Justices' courts, and was not unknown on the steps of the Tombs. I have good reason to believe, however, that one individual who called upon him at my chambers, and who, with a grand air, he insisted was his client, was no other than a dun, and the alleged title-deed, a bill. But, with all his failings, and the annoyances he caused me, Nippers, like his compatriot Turkey, was a very useful man to me; wrote a neat, swift hand; and, when he chose, was not deficient in a gentlemanly sort of deportment. Added to this, he always dressed in a gentlemanly sort of way; and so, incidentally, reflected credit upon my chambers. Whereas, with respect to Turkey, I had much ado to keep him from being a reproach to me. His clothes were apt to look oily, and smell of eating-houses. He wore his pantaloons very loose and baggy in summer. His coats were execrable; his hat not to be handled. But while the hat was a thing of indifference to me, inasmuch as his natural civility and deference, as a dependent Englishman, always led him to doff it the moment he entered the room, yet his coat was another matter. Concerning his coats, I reasoned with him, but with no effect. The truth was, I suppose, that a man with so small an income could not afford to sport such a lustrous face and a lustrous coat at one and the same time. As Nippers once observed, Turkey's money went chiefly for red ink. One winter day, I presented Turkey with a highly respectable-looking coat of my own—a padded gray coat, of a most comfortable warmth, and which buttoned straight up from the knee to the neck. I thought Turkey would appreciate the favor, and abate his rashness and obstreperousness of afternoons. But no; I verily believe that buttoning himself up in so downy and blanket-like a coat had a pernicious effect upon him—upon the same principle that too much oats are bad for horses. In fact, precisely as a rash, restive horse is said to feel his oats, so Turkey felt his coat. It made him insolent. He was a man whom prosperity harmed.

Though, concerning the self-indulgent habits of Turkey, I had my own private surmises, yet, touching Nippers, I was well persuaded that, whatever might be his faults in other respects, he was, at least, a temperate young man. But, indeed, Nature herself seemed to have been his vintner, and, at his birth, charged him so thoroughly with an irritable, brandy-like disposition, that all subsequent potations were needless. When I consider how, amid the stillness of my chambers, Nippers would sometimes impatiently rise from his seat, and stooping over his table, spread his arms wide apart, seize the whole desk, and move it, and jerk it, with a grim, grinding motion on the floor, as if the table were a perverse voluntary agent, intent on thwarting and vexing him, I plainly perceive that, for Nippers, brandy-and-water were altogether superfluous.

It was fortunate for me that, owing to its peculiar cause—indigestion—the irritability and consequent nervousness of Nippers were mainly observable in the morning, while in the afternoon he was comparatively mild. So that, Turkey's paroxysms only coming on about twelve o-clock, I never had to do with their eccentricities at one time. Their fits relieved each other, like guards. When Nippers's was on, Turkey's was off; and vice versa. This was a good natural arrangement, under the circumstances.

Ginger Nut, the third on my list, was a lad, some twelve years old. His father was a car-man, ambitious of seeing his son on the bench instead of a cart, before he died. So he sent him to my office, as student at law, errand-boy, cleaner, and sweeper, at the rate of one dollar a week. He had a little desk to himself, but he did not use it much. Upon inspection, the drawer exhibited a great array of the shells of various sorts of nuts. Indeed, to this quick-witted youth, the whole noble science of the law was contained in a nutshell. Not the least among the employments of Ginger Nut, as well as one which he discharged with the most alacrity, was his duty as cake and apple purveyor for Turkey and Nippers. Copying law papers being proverbially a dry, husky sort of business, my two scriveners were fain to moisten their mouths very often with Spitzenbergs, to be had at the numerous stalls nigh the Custom House and Post Office. Also, they sent Ginger Nut very frequently for that peculiar cake—small, flat, round, and very spicy—after which he had been named by them. Of a cold morning, when business was but dull, Turkey would gobble up scores of these cakes, as if they were mere wafers—indeed, they sell them at the rate of six or eight for a penny —the scrape of his pen blending with the crunching of the crisp particles in his mouth. Of all the fiery afternoon blunders and flurried rashnesses of Turkey, was his once moistening a ginger-cake between his lips, and clapping it on to a mortgage, for a seal. I came within an ace of dismissing him then. But he mollified me by making an Oriental bow, and saying—

"With submission, sir, it was generous of me to find you in stationery on my own account."

Now my original business—that of a conveyancer and title hunter, and drawer-up of recondite documents of all sorts—was considerably increased by receiving the Master's office. There was now great work for scriveners. Not only must I push the clerks already with me, but I must have additional help.

In answer to my advertisement, a motionless young man one morning stood upon my office threshold, the door being open, for it was summer. I can see that figure now—pallidly neat, pitiably respectable, incurably forlorn! It was Bartleby.

After a few words touching his qualifications, I engaged him, glad to have among my corps of copyists a man of so singularly sedate an aspect, which I thought might operate beneficially upon the flighty temper of Turkey and the fiery one of Nippers.

I should have stated before that ground glass folding-doors divided my premises into two parts, one of which was occupied by my scriveners, the other by myself. According to my humor, I threw open these doors, or closed them. I resolved to assign Bartleby a corner by the folding-doors, but on my side of them, so as to have this quiet man within easy call, in case any trifling thing was to be done. I placed his desk close up to a small side window in that part of the room, a window which originally had afforded a lateral view of certain grimy backyards and bricks, but which owing to subsequent erections commanded at present no view at all, though it gave some light. Within three feet of the panes was a wall, and the light came down from far above, between two lofty buildings, as from a very small opening in a dome. Still further to a satisfactory arrangement, I procured a high green folding screen, which might entirely isolate Bartleby from my sight, though not remove him from my voice. And thus, in a manner, privacy and society were conjoined.

At first, Bartleby did an extraordinary quantity of writing. As if long famishing for something to copy, he seemed to gorge himself on my documents. There was no pause for digestion. He ran a day and night line, copying by sun-light and by candle-light. I should have been quite delighted with his application, had he been cheerfully industrious. But he wrote on silently, palely, mechanically.

It is, of course, an indispensable part of a scrivener's business to verify the accuracy of his copy, word by word. Where there are two or more scriveners in an office, they assist each other in this examination, one reading from the copy, the other holding the original. It is a very dull, wearisome, and lethargic affair. I can readily imagine that, to some sanguine temperaments, it would be altogether intolerable. For example, I cannot credit that the mettlesome poet, Byron, would have contentedly sat down with Bartleby to examine a law document of, say, five hundred pages, closely written in a crimpy hand.

Now and then, in the haste of business, it had been my habit to assist in comparing some brief document myself, calling Turkey or Nippers for this purpose. One object I had, in placing Bartleby so handy to me behind the screen, was to avail myself of his services on such trivial occasions. It was on the third day, I think, of his being with me, and before any necessity had arisen for having his own writing examined, that, being much hurried to complete a small affair I had in hand, I abruptly called to Bartleby. In my haste and natural expectancy of instant compliance, I sat with my head bent over the original on my desk, and my right hand sideways, and somewhat nervously extended with the copy, so that, immediately upon emerging from his retreat, Bartleby might snatch it and proceed to business without the least delay.

In this very attitude did I sit when I called to him, rapidly stating what it was I wanted him to do—namely, to examine a small paper with me. Imagine my surprise, nay, my consternation, when, without moving from his privacy, Bartleby, in a singularly mild, firm voice, replied, "I would prefer not to."

I sat awhile in perfect silence rallying my stunned faculties. Immediately it occurred to me that my ears had deceived me, or Bartleby had entirely misunderstood my meaning. I repeated my request in the clearest tone I could assume; but in quite as clear a one came the previous reply, "I would prefer not to."

"Prefer not to," echoed I, rising in high excitement, and crossing the room with a stride. "What do you mean? Are you moon-struck? I want you to help me compare this sheet here—take it," and I thrust it towards him.

"I would prefer not to," said he.

I looked at him steadfastly. His face was leanly composed; his gray eye dimly calm. Not a wrinkle of agitation rippled him. Had there been the least uneasiness, anger, impatience or impertinence in his manner; in other words, had there been anything ordinarily human about him, doubtless I should have violently dismissed him from the premises. But as it was, I should have as soon thought of turning my pale plaster-of-Paris bust of Cicero out of doors. I stood gazing at him awhile, as he went on with his own writing, and then reseated myself at my desk. This is very strange, thought I. What had one best do? But my business hurried me. I concluded to forget the matter for the present, reserving it for my future leisure. So, calling Nippers from the other room, the paper was speedily examined.

A few days after this, Bartleby concluded four lengthy documents, being quadruplicates of a week's testimony taken before me in my High Court of Chancery. It became necessary to examine them. It was an important suit, and great accuracy was imperative. Having all things arranged, I called Turkey, Nippers, and Ginger Nut from the next room, meaning to place the four copies in the hands of my four clerks, while I should read from the original. Accordingly, Turkey, Nippers, and Ginger Nut had taken their seats in a row, each with his document in his hand, when I called to Bartleby to join this interesting group.

"Bartleby! quick, I am waiting."

I heard a slow scrape of his chair legs on the uncarpeted floor, and soon he appeared standing at the entrance of his hermitage.

"What is wanted?" said he, mildly.

"The copies, the copies," said I, hurriedly. "We are going to examine them. There"—and I held toward him the fourth quadruplicate.

"I would prefer not to," he said, and gently disappeared behind the screen.

For a few moments I was turned into a pillar of salt, standing at the head of my seated column of clerks. Recovering myself, I advanced toward the screen, and demanded the reason for such extraordinary conduct.

"*Why* do you refuse?"

"I would prefer not to."

With any other man I should have flown outright into a dreadful passion, scorned all further words, and thrust him ignominiously from my presence. But there was something about Bartleby that not only strangely disarmed me, but, in a wonderful manner, touched and disconcerted me. I began to reason with him.

"These are your own copies we are about to examine. It is labor saving to you, because one examination will answer for your four papers. It is common usage. Every copyist is bound to help examine his copy. Is it not so? Will you not speak? Answer!"

"I prefer not to," he replied in a flute-like tone. It seemed to me that, while I had been addressing him, he carefully revolved every statement that I made; fully comprehended the meaning; could not gainsay the irresistible conclusion; but, at the same time, some paramount consideration prevailed with him to reply as he did.

"You are decided, then, not to comply with my request—a request made according to common usage and common sense?"

He briefly gave me to understand that on that point my judgment was sound. Yes: his decision was irreversible.

It is not seldom the case that, when a man is browbeaten in some unprecedented and violently unreasonable way, he begins to stagger in his own plainest faith. He begins, as it were, vaguely to surmise that, wonderful as it may be, all the justice and all the reason is on the other side. Accordingly, if any disinterested persons are present, he turns to them for some reinforcement for his own faltering mind.

"Turkey," said I, "what do you think of this? Am I not right?"

"With submission, sir," said Turkey, in his blandest tone, "I think that you are."

"Nippers," said I, "what do *you* think of it?"

"I think I should kick him out of the office."

(The reader of nice perceptions will here perceive that, it being morning, Turkey's answer is couched in polite and tranquil terms, but Nippers replies in ill-tempered ones. Or, to repeat a previous sentence, Nippers's ugly mood was on duty, and Turkey's off.)

"Ginger Nut," said I, willing to enlist the smallest suffrage in my behalf, "what do *you* think of it?"

"I think, sir, he's a little *luny*," replied Ginger Nut, with a grin.

"You hear what they say," said I, turning towards the screen. "Come forth and do your duty."

But he vouchsafed no reply. I pondered a moment in sore perplexity. But once more business hurried me. I determined again to postpone the consideration of this dilemma to my future leisure. With a little trouble we made out to examine the papers without Bartleby, though at every page or two Turkey deferentially dropped his opinion, that this proceeding was quite out of the common; while Nippers, twitching in his chair with a dyspeptic nervousness, ground out, between his set teeth, occassional hissing maledictions against the stubborn oaf behind the screen. And for his (Nippers's) part, this was the first and the last time he would do another man's business without pay.

Meanwhile Bartleby sat in his hermitage, oblivious to everything but his own peculiar business there.

Some days passed, the scrivener being employed upon another lengthy work. His late remarkable conduct led me to regard his ways narrowly. I observed that he never went to dinner; indeed, that he never went anywhere. As yet I had never, of my personal knowledge, known him to be outside of my office. He was a perpetual sentry in the corner. At about eleven o'clock though, in the morning, I noticed that Ginger Nut would advance toward the opening in Bartleby's screen, as if silently beckoned thither by a gesture invisible to me where I sat. The boy would then leave the office, jingling a few pence, and reappear with a handful of ginger-nuts, which he delivered in the hermitage, receiving two of the cakes for his trouble.

He lives, then, on ginger-nuts, thought I; never eats a dinner, properly speaking; he must be a vegetarian, then; but no; he never eats even vegetables, he eats nothing but ginger-nuts. My mind then ran on in reveries concerning the probable effects upon the human constitution of living entirely on ginger-nuts. Ginger-nuts are so called, because they contain ginger as one of their peculiar constituents, and the final flavoring one. Now, what was ginger? A hot, spicy thing. Was Bartleby hot and spicy? Not at all. Ginger, then, had no effect upon Bartleby. Probably he preferred it should have none.

Nothing so aggravates an earnest person as a passive resistance. If the individual so resisted be of a not inhumane temper, and the resisting one perfectly harmless in his passivity, then, in the better moods of the former, he will endeavor charitably to construe to his imagination what proves impossible to be solved by his judgment. Even so, for the most part, I regarded Bartleby and his ways. Poor fellow! thought I, he means no mischief; it is plain he intends no insolence; his aspect sufficiently evinces that his eccentricities are involuntary. He is useful to me. I can get along with him. If I turn him away, the chances are he will fall in with some less indulgent employer, and then he will be rudely treated, and perhaps driven forth miserably to starve. Yes. Here I can cheaply purchase a delicious self-approval. To befriend Bartleby; to humor him in his strange willfulness, will cost me little or nothing, while I lay up in my soul what will eventually prove a sweet morsel for my conscience. But this mood was not invariable with me. The passiveness of Bartleby sometimes irritated me. I felt strangely goaded on to encounter him in new opposition—to elicit some angry spark from him answerable to my own. But, indeed, I might as well have essayed to strike fire with my knuckles against a bit of Windsor soap. But one afternoon the evil impulse in me mastered me, and the following little scene ensued:

"Bartleby," said I, "when those papers are all copied, I will compare them with you."

"I would prefer not to."

"How? Surely you do not mean to persist in that mulish vagary?" No answer.

I threw open the folding-doors near by, and, turning upon Turkey and Nippers, exclaimed: "Bartleby a second time says he won't examine his papers. What do you think of it, Turkey?"

It was afternoon, be it remembered. Turkey sat glowing like a brass boiler, his bald head steaming, his hands reeling among his blotted papers.

"Think of it?" roared Turkey. "I think I'll just step behind his screen, and black his eyes for him!"

So saying, Turkey rose to his feet and threw his arms into a pugilistic position. He was hurrying away to make good his promise, when I detained him, alarmed at the effect of incautiously rousing Turkey's combativeness after dinner.

"Sit down, Turkey," said I, "and hear what Nippers has to say. What do you think of it, Nippers? Would I not be justified in immediately dismissing Bartleby?"

"Excuse me, that is for you to decide, sir. I think his conduct quite unusual, and, indeed, unjust, as regards Turkey and myself. But it may only be a passing whim."

"Ah," exclaimed I, "you have strangely changed your mind, then —you speak very gently of him now."

"All beer," cried Turkey; "gentleness is effects of beer—Nippers and I dined together to-day. You see how gentle *I* am, sir. Shall I go and black his eyes?"

"You refer to Bartleby, I suppose. No, not to-day, Turkey," I replied. "Pray, put up your fists."

I closed the doors, and again advanced toward Bartleby. I felt additional incentives tempting me to my fate. I burned to be rebelled against again. I remembered that Bartleby never left the office.

"Bartleby," said I, "Ginger Nut is away; just step around to the postoffice, won't you? (it was but a three minutes' walk) and see if there is anything for me."

"I would prefer not to."

"You *will* not?"

"I *prefer* not."

I staggered to my desk and sat there in a deep study. My blind inveteracy returned. Was there any other thing in which I could procure myself to be ignominiously repulsed by this lean, penniless wight?—my hired clerk? What added thing is there, perfectly reasonable, that he will be sure to refuse to do?

"Bartleby!"

No answer.

"Bartleby," in a louder tone.

No answer.

"Bartleby," I roared.

Like a very ghost, agreeably to the laws of magical invocation, at the third summons, he appeared at the entrance of his hermitage.

"Go to the next room, and tell Nippers to come to me."

"I prefer not to," he respectfully and slowly said, and mildly disappeared.

"Very good, Bartleby," said I, in a quiet sort of serenely severe self-possessed tone, intimating the unalterable purpose of some terrible retribution very close at hand. At the moment I half intended something of the kind. But upon the whole, as it was drawing towards my dinner hour, I thought it best to put on my hat and walk home for the day, suffering much from perplexity and distress of mind.

Shall I acknowledge it? The conclusion of this whole business was that it soon became a fixed fact of my chambers, that a pale young scrivener, by the name of Bartleby, had a desk there; that he copied for me at the usual rate of four cents a folio (one hundred words); but he was permanently exempt from examining the work done by him, the duty being transferred to Turkey and Nippers, out of compliment, doubtless, to their superior acuteness; moreover, said Bartleby was never, on any account, to be dispatched on the most trivial errand of any sort; and that, even if entreated to take upon him such a matter, it was generally understood that he would "prefer not to"— in other words, that he would refuse point-blank.

As days passed on, I became considerably reconciled to Bartleby. His steadiness, his freedom from all dissipation, his incessant industry (except when he chose to throw himself into a standing reverie behind his screen), his great stillness, his unalterableness of demeanor under all circumstances, made him a valuable acquisition. One prime thing was this—he was always there—first in the morning, continually through the day, and the last at night. I had a singular confidence in his honesty. I felt my most precious papers perfectly safe in his hands. Sometimes, to be sure, I could not, for the very soul of me, avoid falling into sudden spasmodic passions with him. For it was exceeding difficult to bear in mind all the time those strange peculiarities, privileges, and unheard of exemptions, forming the tacit stipulations on Bartleby's part under which he remained in my office. Now and then, in the eagerness of dispatching pressing business, I would inadvertently summon Bartleby, in a short, rapid tone, to put his finger, say, on the incipient tie of a bit of red tape with which I was about compressing some papers. Of course, from behind the screen the usual answer, "I prefer not to," was sure to come; and then how could a human creature, with the common infirmities of our nature, refrain from bitterly exclaiming upon such perverseness—such unreasonableness? However, every added repulse of this sort which I received only tended to lessen the probability of my repeating the inadvertence.

Here it must be said that, according to the custom of most legal gentlemen occupying chambers in densely populated law buildings, there were several keys to my door. One was kept by a woman residing in the attic, which person weekly scrubbed and daily swept and dusted my apartments. Another was kept by Turkey for convenience' sake. The third I sometimes carried in my own pocket. The fourth I knew not who had.

Now, one Sunday morning I happened to go to Trinity Church, to hear a celebrated preacher, and finding myself rather early on the ground I thought I would walk round to my chambers for a while. Luckily I had my key with me; but upon applying it to the lock, I found it resisted by something inserted from the inside. Quite surprised, I called out; when to my consternation a key was turned from within; and thrusting his lean visage at me, and holding the door ajar, the apparition of Bartleby appeared, in his shirt-sleeves, and otherwise in a strangely tattered deshabille, saying quietly that he was sorry, but he was deeply engaged just then, and—preferred not admitting me at present. In a brief word or two, he moreover added, that perhaps I had better walk round the block two or three times, and by that time he would probably have concluded his affairs.

Now, the utterly unsurmised appearance of Bartleby, tenanting my law-chambers of a Sunday morning, with his cadaverously gentlemanly *nonchalance,* yet withal firm and self-possessed, had such a strange effect upon me, that incontinently I slunk away from my own door, and did as desired. But not without sundry twinges of impotent rebellion against the mild effrontery of this unaccountable scrivener. Indeed, it was his wonderful mildness chiefly which not only disarmed me, but unmanned me, as it were. For I consider that one, for the time, is a sort of unmanned when he tranquilly permits his hired clerk to dictate to him, and order him away from his own premises. Furthermore, I was full of uneasiness as to what Bartleby could possibly be doing in my office in his shirt-sleeves, and in an otherwise dismantled condition, of a Sunday morning. Was anything amiss going on? Nay, that was out of the question. It was not to be thought of for a moment that Bartleby was an immoral person. But what could he be doing there?—copying? Nay again, whatever might be his eccentricities, Bartleby was an eminently decorous person. He would be the last man to sit down to his desk in any state approaching to nudity. Besides, it was Sunday; and there was something about Bartleby that forbade the supposition that he would by any secular occupation violate the proprieties of the day.

Nevertheless, my mind was not pacified; and full of a restless curiosity, at last I returned to the door. Without hindrance I inserted my key, opened it, and entered. Bartleby was not to be seen. I looked round anxiously, peeped behind his screen; but it was very plain that he was gone. Upon more closely examining the place, I surmised that for an indefinite period Bartleby must have ate, dressed, and slept in my office, and that too without plate, mirror, or bed. The cushioned seat of a rickety old sofa in one corner bore the faint impress of a lean, reclining form. Rolled away under his desk, I found a blanket; under the empty grate, a blacking box and brush; on a chair, a tin basin, with soap and a ragged towel; in a newspaper a few crumbs of ginger-nuts and a morsel of cheese. Yes, thought I, it is evident enough that Bartleby has been making his home here, keeping Bachelor's Hall all by himself. Immediately then the thought came sweeping across me, what miserable friendlessness and loneliness are here revealed! His poverty is great; but his solitude, how horrible! Think of it. Of a Sunday, Wall Street is deserted as Petra; and every night of every day it is an emptiness. This building, too, which of week-days hums with industry and life, at nightfall echoes with sheer vacancy, and all through Sunday is forlorn. And here Bartleby makes his home; sole spectator of a solitude which he has seen all populous—a sort of innocent and transformed Marius brooding among the ruins of Carthage!

For the first time in my life a feeling of overpowering stinging melancholy seized me. Before, I had never experienced aught but a not unpleasing sadness. The bond of a common humanity now drew me irresistibly to gloom. A fraternal melancholy! For both I and Bartleby were sons of Adam. I remembered the bright silks and sparkling faces I had seen that day, in gala trim, swan-like sailing down the Mississippi of Broadway; and I contrasted them with the pallid copyist, and thought to myself, Ah, happiness courts the light, so we deem the world is gay; but misery hides aloof, so we deem that misery there is none. These sad fancyings—chimeras, doubtless, of a sick and silly brain—led on to other and more special thoughts, concerning the eccentricities of Bartleby. Presentiments of strange discoveries hovered round me. The scrivener's pale form appeared to me laid out, among uncaring strangers, in its shivering winding-sheet.

Suddenly I was attracted by Bartleby's closed desk, the key in open sight left in the lock.

I mean no mischief, seek the gratification of no heartless curiosity, thought I; besides, the desk is mine, and its contents, too, so I will make bold to look within. Everything was methodically arranged, the papers smoothly placed. The pigeon-holes were deep, and removing the files of documents, I groped into their recesses. Presently I felt something there, and dragged it out. It was an old bandanna handkerchief, heavy and knotted. I opened it, and saw it was a savings bank.

I now recalled all the quiet mysteries which I had noted in the man. I remembered that he never spoke but to answer; that, though at intervals he had considerable time to himself, yet I had never seen him reading—no, not even a newspaper; that for long periods he would stand looking out, at his pale window behind the screen, upon the dead brick wall; I was quite sure he never visited any refectory or eating-house; while his pale face clearly indicated that he never drank beer like Turkey, or tea and coffee even, like other men; that he never went anywhere in particular that I could learn; never went out for a walk, unless, indeed, that was the case at present; that he had declined telling who he was, or whence he came, or whether he had any relatives in the world; that though so thin and pale, he never complained of ill-health. And more than all, I remembered a certain unconscious air of pallid—how shall I call it?—of pallid haughtiness, say, or rather an austere reserve about him, which had positively awed me into my tame compliance with his eccentricities, when I had feared to ask him to do the slightest incidental thing for me, even though I might know, from his long-continued motionlessness, that behind his screen he must be standing in one of those dead-wall reveries of his.

Revolving all these things, and coupling them with the recently discovered fact that he made my office his constant abiding place and home, and not forgetful of his morbid moodiness; revolving all these things, a prudential feeling began to steal over me. My first emotions had been those of pure melancholy and sincerest pity; but just in proportion as the forlornness of Bartleby grew and grew to my imagination, did that same melancholy merge into fear, that pity into repulsion. So true it is, and so terrible, too, that up to a certain point the thought or sight of misery enlists our best affections; but, in certain special cases, beyond that point it does not. They err who would assert that invariably this is owing to the inherent selfishness of the human heart. It rather proceeds from a certain hopelessness of remedying excessive and organic ill. To a sensitive being, pity is not seldom pain. And when at last it is perceived that such pity cannot lead to effectual succor, common sense bids the soul be rid of it. What I saw that morning persuaded me that the scrivener was the victim of innate and incurable disorder. I might give alms to his body; but his body did not pain him; it was his soul that suffered, and his soul I could not reach.

I did not accomplish the purpose of going to Trinity Church that morning. Somehow, the things I had seen disqualified me for the time from church-going. I walked homeward, thinking what I would do with Bartleby. Finally, I resolved upon this—I would put certain calm questions to him the next morning, touching his history, etc., and if he declined to answer them openly and unreservedly (and I supposed he would prefer not), then to give him a twenty dollar bill over and above whatever I might owe him, and tell him his services were no longer required; but that if in any other way I could assist him, I would be happy to do so, especially if he desired to return to his native place, wherever that might be. I would willingly help to defray the expenses. Moreover, if, after reaching home, he found himself at any time in want of aid, a letter from him would be sure of a reply.

The next morning came.

"Bartleby," said I, gently calling to him behind his screen.

No reply.

"Bartleby," said I, in a still gentler tone, "come here; I am not going to ask you to do anything you would prefer not to do—I simply wish to speak to you."

Upon this he noiselessly slid into view.

"Will you tell me, Bartleby, where you were born?"

"I would prefer not to."

"Will you tell me *anything* about yourself?"

"I would prefer not to."

"But what reasonable objection can you have to speak to me? I feel friendly towards you."

He did not look at me while I spoke, but kept his glance fixed upon my bust of Cicero, which, as I then sat, was directly behind me, some six inches above my head.

"What is your answer, Bartleby?" said I, after waiting a considerable time for a reply, during which his countenance remained immovable, only there was the faintest conceivable tremor of the white attenuated mouth.

"At present I prefer to give no answer," he said, and retired into his hermitage.

It was rather weak in me, I confess, but his manner, on this occasion, nettled me. Not only did there seem to lurk in it a certain calm disdain, but his perverseness seemed ungrateful, considering the undeniable good usage and indulgence he had received from me.

Again I sat ruminating what I should do. Mortified as I was at his behavior, and resolved as I had been to dismiss him when I entered my office, nevertheless I strangely felt something superstitious knocking at my heart, and forbidding me to carry out my purpose, and denouncing me for a villain if I dared to breathe one bitter word against this forlornest of mankind. At last, familiarly drawing my chair behind his screen, I sat down and said: "Bartleby, never mind, then, about revealing your history; but let me entreat you, as a friend, to comply as far as may be with the usages of this office. Say now, you will help to examine papers to-morrow or next day: in short, say now, that in a day or two you will begin to be a little reasonable:—say so, Bartleby."

"At present I would prefer not to be a little reasonable," was his mildly cadaverous reply.

Just then the folding-doors opened, and Nippers approached. He seemed suffering from an unusually bad night's rest, induced by severer indigestion than common. He overheard those final words of Bartleby.

"*Prefer not,* eh?" gritted Nippers—"I'd *prefer* him, if I were you, sir," addressing me—"I'd *prefer* him; I'd give him preferences, the stubborn mule! What is it, sir, pray, that he *prefers* not to do now?"

Bartleby moved not a limb.

"Mr. Nippers," said I, "I'd prefer that you would withdraw for the present."

Somehow, of late, I had got into the way of involuntarily using this word "prefer" upon all sorts of not exactly suitable occasions. And I trembled to think that my contact with the scrivener had already and seriously affected me in a mental way. And what further and deeper aberration might it not yet produce? This apprehension had not been without efficacy in determining me to summary measures.

As Nippers, looking very sour and sulky, was departing, Turkey blandly and deferentially approached.

"With submission, sir," said he, "yesterday I was thinking about Bartleby here, and I think that if he would but prefer to take a quart of good ale every day, it would do much towards mending him, and enabling him to assist in examining his papers."

"So you have got the word, too," said I, slightly excited.

"With submission, what word, sir?" asked Turkey, respectfully crowding himself into the contracted space behind the screen, and by so doing, making me jostle the scrivener. "What word, sir?"

"I would prefer to be left alone here," said Bartleby, as if offended at being mobbed in his privacy.

"That's the word, Turkey," said I, *"that's* it."

"Oh, *prefer?* oh yes—queer word. I never use it myself. But, sir, as I was saying, if he would but prefer—"

"Turkey," interrupted I, "you will please withdraw."

"Oh certainly, sir, if you prefer that I should."

As he opened the folding-door to retire, Nippers at his desk caught a glimpse of me, and asked whether I would prefer to have a certain paper copied on blue paper or white. He did not in the least roguishly accent the word "prefer." It was plain that it involuntarily rolled from his tongue. I thought to myself, surely I must get rid of a demented man, who already has in some degree turned the tongues, if not the heads, of myself and clerks. But I thought it prudent not to break the dismission at once.

The next day I noticed that Bartleby did nothing but stand at his window in his dead-wall reverie. Upon asking him why he did not write, he said that he had decided upon doing no more writing.

"Why, how now? what next?" exclaimed I, "do no more writing?"

"No more."

"And what is the reason?"

"Do you not see the reason for yourself?" he indifferently replied.

I looked steadfastly at him, and perceived that his eyes looked dull and glazed. Instantly it occurred to me, that his unexampled diligence in copying by his dim window for the first few weeks of his stay with me might have temporarily impaired his vision.

I was touched. I said something in condolence with him. I hinted that of course he did wisely in abstaining from writing for a while, and urged him to embrace that opportunity of taking wholesome exercise in the open air. This, however, he did not do. A few days after this, my other clerks being absent, and being in a great hurry to dispatch certain letters by the mail, I thought that, having nothing else earthly to do, Bartleby would surely be less inflexible than usual, and carry these letters to the postoffice. But he blankly declined. So, much to my inconvenience, I went myself.

Still added days went by. Whether Bartleby's eyes improved or not, I could not say. To all appearance, I thought they did. But when I asked him if they did, he vouchsafed no answer. At all events, he would do no copying. At last, in reply to my urgings, he informed me that he had permanently given up copying.

"What!" exclaimed I; "suppose your eyes should get entirely well—better than ever before—would you not copy then?"

"I have given up copying," he answered, and slid aside.

He remained as ever, a fixture in my chamber. Nay—if that were possible—he became still more of a fixture than before. What was to be done? He would do nothing in the office; why should he stay there? In plain fact, he had now become a millstone to me, not only useless as a necklace, but afflictive to bear. Yet I was sorry for him.

I speak less than truth when I say that, on his own account, he occasioned me uneasiness. If he would but have named a single relative or friend, I would instantly have written, and urged their taking the poor fellow away to some convenient retreat. But he seemed alone, absolutely alone in the universe. A bit of wreck in the mid-Atlantic. At length, necessities connected with my business tyrannized over all other considerations. Decently as I could, I told Bartleby that in six days' time he must unconditionally leave the office. I warned him to take measures, in the interval, for procuring some other abode. I offered to assist him in this endeavor, if he himself would but take the first step towards a removal. "And when you finally quit me, Bartleby," added I, "I shall see that you go not away entirely unprovided. Six days from this hour, remember."

At the expiration of that period, I peeped behind the screen, and lo! Bartleby was there.

I buttoned up my coat, balanced myself, advanced slowly towards him, touched his shoulder, and said, "The time has come; you must quit this place; I am sorry for you; here is money; but you must go."

"I would prefer not," he replied, with his back still towards me.

"You *must*."

He remained silent.

Now I had an unbounded confidence in this man's common honesty. He had frequently restored to me sixpences and shillings carelessly dropped upon the floor, for I am apt to be very reckless in such shirtbutton affairs. The proceeding, then, which followed will not be deemed extraordinary.

"Bartleby," said I, "I owe you twelve dollars on account; here are thirty-two; the odd twenty are yours—Will you take it?" and I handed the bills towards him.

But he made no motion.

"I will leave them here, then," putting them under a weight on the table. Then taking my hat and cane and going to the door, I tranquilly turned and added, "After you have removed your things from these offices, Bartleby, you will of course lock the door—since every one is now gone for the day but you—and if you please, slip your key underneath the mat, so that I may have it in the morning.

I shall not see you again; so good-by to you. If, hereafter, in your new place of abode, I can be of any service to you, do not fail to advise me by letter. Good-by, Bartleby, and fare you well."

But he answered not a word; like the last column of some ruined temple, he remained standing mute and solitary in the middle of the otherwise deserted room.

As I walked home in a pensive mood, my vanity got the better of my pity. I could not but highly plume myself on my masterly management in getting rid of Bartleby. Masterly I call it, and such it must appear to any dispassionate thinker. The beauty of my procedure seemed to consist in its perfect quietness. There was no vulgar bullying, no bravado of any sort, no choleric hectoring, and striding to and fro across the apartment, jerking out vehement commands for Bartleby to bundle himself off with his beggarly traps. Nothing of the kind. Without loudly bidding Bartleby depart—as an inferior genius might have done—I *assumed* the ground that depart he must; and upon that assumption built all I had to say. The more I thought over my procedure, the more I was charmed with it. Nevertheless, next morning, upon awakening, I had my doubts—I had somehow slept off the fumes of vanity. One of the coolest and wisest hours a man has is just after he awakes in the morning. My procedure seemed as sagacious as ever—but only in theory. How it would prove in practice—there was the rub. It was truly a beautiful thought to have assumed Bartleby's departure; but, after all, that assumption was simply my own, and none of Bartleby's. The great point was, not whether I had assumed that he would quit me, but whether he would prefer so to do. He was more a man of preferences than assumptions.

After breakfast, I walked down town, arguing the probabilities *pro* and *con*. One moment I thought it would prove a miserable failure, and Bartleby would be found all alive at my office as usual; the next moment is seemed certain that I should find his chair empty. And so I kept veering about. At the corner of Broadway and Canal Street, I saw quite an excited group of people standing in earnest conversation.

"I'll take odds he doesn't," said a voice as I passed.

"Doesn't go?—done!" said I, "put up your money."

I was instinctively putting my hand in my pocket to produce my own, when I remembered that this was an election day. The words I had overheard bore no reference to Bartleby, but to the success or non-success of some candidate for the mayoralty. In my intent frame of mind, I had, as it were, imagined that all Broadway shared in my excitement, and were debating the same question with me. I passed on, very thankful that the uproar of the street screened my momentary absentmindedness.

As I had intended, I was earlier than usual at my office door. I stood listening for a moment. All was still. He must be gone. I tried the knob. The door was locked. Yes, my procedure had worked to a charm; he indeed must be vanished. Yet a certain melancholy mixed with this: I was almost sorry for my brilliant success. I was fumbling under the door mat for the key, which Bartleby was to have left there for me, when accidentally my knee knocked against a panel, producing a summoning sound, and in response a voice came to me from within—"Not yet; I am occupied."

It was Bartleby.

I was thunderstruck. For an instant I stood like the man who, pipe in mouth, was killed one cloudless afternoon long ago in Virginia, by summer lightning; at his own warm open window he was killed, and remained leaning out there upon the dreamy afternoon, till some one touched him, when he fell.

"Not gone!" I murmured at last. But again obeying that wondrous ascendancy which the inscrutable scrivener had over me, and from which ascendancy, for all my chafing, I could not completely escape, I slowly went down stairs and out into the street, and while walking round the block, considered what I should next do in this unheard-of perplexity. Turn the man out by an actual thrusting I could not; to drive him away by calling him hard names would not do; calling in the police was an unpleasant idea; and yet, permit him to enjoy his cadaverous triumph over me—this, too, I could not think of. What was to be done? or, if nothing could be done, was there anything further that I could *assume* in the matter? Yes, as before I had prospectively assumed that Bartleby would depart, so now I might retrospectively assume that departed he was. In the legitimate carrying out of this assumption, I might enter my office in a great hurry, and pretending not to see Bartleby at all, walk straight against him as if he were air. Such a proceeding would in a singular degree have the appearance of a home-thrust. It was hardly possible that Bartleby could withstand such an application of the doctrine of assumptions. But upon second thoughts the success of the plan seemed rather dubious. I resolved to argue the matter over with him again.

"Bartleby," said I, entering the office, with a quietly severe expression, "I am seriously displeased. I am pained, Bartleby. I had thought better of you. I had imagined you of such a gentlemanly organization that in any delicate dilemma a slight hint would suffice—in short, an assumption. But it appears I am deceived. Why," I added, unaffectedly starting, "you have not even touched that money yet," pointing to it, just where I had left it the evening previous.

He answered nothing.

"Will you, or will you not, quit me?" I now demanded in a sudden passion, advancing close to him.

"I would prefer *not* to quit you," he replied, gently emphasizing the *not*.

"What earthly right have you to stay here? Do you pay any rent? Do you pay my taxes? Or is this property yours?"

He answered nothing.

"Are you ready to go on and write now? Are your eyes recovered? Could you copy a small paper for me this morning? or help examine a few lines? or step round to the postoffice? In a word, will you do anything at all, to give a coloring to your refusal to depart the premises?"

He silently retired into his hermitage.

I was now in such a state of nervous resentment that I thought it but prudent to check myself at present from further demonstrations. Bartleby and I were alone. I remembered the tragedy of the unfortunate Adams and the still more unfortunate Colt in the solitary office of the latter; and how poor Colt, being dreadfully incensed by Adams, and imprudently permitting himself to get wildly excited, was at unawares hurried into his fatal act—an act which certainly no man could possibly deplore more than the actor himself. Often it had occurred to me in my ponderings upon the subject that had altercation taken place in the public street, or at a private residence, it would not have terminated as it did. It was the cricumstance of being alone in a solitary office, up stairs, of a building entirely unhallowed by humanizing domestic associations—an uncarpeted office, doubtless, of a dusty, haggard sort of appearance—this it must have been, which greatly helped to enhance the irritable desperation of the hapless Colt.

But when this old Adam of resentment rose in me and tempted me concerning Bartleby, I grappled him and threw him. How? Why, simply by recalling the divine injunction: "A new commandment give I unto you, that ye love one another." Yes, this it was that saved me. Aside from higher considerations, charity often operates as a vastly wise and prudent principle—a great safeguard to its possessor. Men have committed murder for jealousy's sake, and anger's sake, and hatred's sake, and selfishness' sake, and spiritual pride's sake; but no man that ever I heard of ever committed a diabolical murder for sweet charity's sake. Mere self-interest, then, if no better motive can be enlisted, should, especially with high-tempered men, prompt all beings to charity and philanthropy. At any rate, upon the occasion in question, I strove to drown my exasperated feelings towards the scrivener by benevolently construing his conduct. Poor fellow, poor fellow! thought I, he don't mean anything; and besides, he has seen hard times, and ought to be indulged.

I endeavored, also, immediately to occupy myself, and at the same time to comfort my despondency. I tried to fancy, that in the course of the morning, at such time as might prove agreeable to him, Bartleby, of his own free accord, would emerge from his hermitage and take up some decided line of march in the direction of the door. But no. Half-past twelve o'clock came; Turkey began to glow in the face, overturn his inkstand, and become generally obstreperous; Nippers abated down into quietude and courtesy; Ginger Nut munched his noon apple; and Bartleby remained standing at his window in one of his profoundest dead-wall reveries. Will it be credited? Ought I to acknowledge it? That afternoon I left the office without saying one further word to him.

Some days now passed, during which, at leisure intervals I looked a little into *Edwards on the Will,* and *Priestley on Necessity.* Under the circumstances, those books induced a salutary feeling. Gradually I slid into the persuasion that these troubles of mine, touching the scrivener, had been all predestinated from eternity, and Bartleby was billeted upon me for some mysterious purpose of an all-wise Providence, which it was not for a mere mortal like me to fathom. Yes, Bartleby, stay there behind your screen, thought I; I shall persecute you no more; you are harmless and noiseless as any of these old chairs; in short, I never feel so private as when I know you are here. At last I see it, I feel it; I penetrate to the predestinated purpose of my life. I am content. Others may have loftier parts to enact; but my mission in this world, Bartleby, is to furnish you with office room for such period as you may see fit to remain.

I believe that this wise and blessed frame of mind would have continued with me, had it not been for the unsolicited and uncharitable remarks obtruded upon me by my professional friends who visited the rooms. But thus it often is, that the constant friction of illiberal minds wears out at last the best resolves of the more generous. Though to be sure, when I reflected upon it, it was not strange that people entering my office should be struck by the peculiar aspect of the unaccountable Bartleby, and so be tempted to throw out some sinister observations concerning him. Sometimes an attorney, having business with me, and calling at my office, and finding no one but the scrivener there, would undertake to obtain some sort of precise information from him touching my whereabouts; but without heeding his idle talk, Bartleby would remain standing immovable in the middle of the room. So after contemplating him in that position for a time, the attorney would depart, no wiser than he came.

Also, when a reference was going on, and the room full of lawyers and witnesses, and business driving fast, some deeply occupied legal gentleman present, seeing Bartleby wholly unemployed, would request him to run round to his (the legal gentleman's) office and fetch some papers for him. Thereupon, Bartleby would tranquilly decline, and yet remain idle as before. Then the lawyer would give a great stare, and turn to me. And what could I say? At last I was made aware that all through the circle of my professional acquaintance, a whisper of wonder was running round, having reference to the strange creature I kept at my office. This worried me very much. And as the idea came upon me of his possibly turning out a long-lived man, and keep occupying my chambers, and denying my authority, and perplexing my visitors, and scandalizing my professional reputation, and casting a general gloom over the premises; keeping soul and body together to the last upon his savings (for doubtless he spent but half a dime a day), and in the end perhaps outlive me, and claim possession of my office by right of his perpetual occupancy: as all these dark anticipations crowded upon me more and more, and my friends continually intruded their relentless remarks upon the apparition in my room, a great change was wrought in me. I resolved to gather all my faculties together, and forever rid me of this intolerable incubus.

Ere revolving any complicated project, however, adapted to this end, I first simply suggested to Bartleby the propriety of his permanent departure. In a calm and serious tone, I commended the idea to his careful and mature consideration. But, having taken three days to meditate upon it, he apprised me that his original determination remained the same; in short, that he still preferred to abide with me.

What shall I do? I now said to myself, buttoning up my coat to the last button. What shall I do? what ought I to do? what does conscience say I *should* do with this man, or, rather, ghost. Rid myself of him, I must; go, he shall. But how? You will not thrust him, the poor, pale, passive mortal—you will not thrust such a helpless creature out of your door? you will not dishonor yourself by such cruelty? No, I will not, I cannot do that. Rather would I let him live and die here, and then mason up his remains in the wall. What, then, will you do? For all your coaxing, he will not budge. Bribes he leaves under your own paper-weight on your table; in short, it is quite plain that he prefers to cling to you.

Then something severe, something unusual must be done. What! surely you will not have him collared by a constable, and commit his innocent pallor to the common jail? And upon what ground could you procure such a thing to be done?—a vagrant, is he? What! he a vagrant, a wanderer, who refuses to budge? It is because he will *not* be a vagrant, then, that you seek to count his *as* a vagrant. That is too absurd. No visible means of support: there I have him. Wrong again: for indubitably he *does* support himself, and that is the only unanswerable proof that any man can show of his possessing the means so to do. No more, then. Since he will not quit me, I must quit him. I will change my offices; I will move elsewhere, and give him fair notice that if I find him on my new premises I will then proceed against him as a common trespasser.

Acting accordingly, next day I thus addressed him: "I find these chambers too far from the City Hall; the air is unwholesome. In a word, I propose to remove my offices next week, and shall no longer require your services. I tell you this now, in order that you may seek another place."

He made no reply, and nothing more was said.

On the appointed day I engaged carts and men, proceeded to my chambers, and, having but little furniture, everything was removed in a few hours. Throughout, the scrivener remained standing behind the screen, which I directed to be removed the last thing. It was withdrawn, and, being folded up like a huge folio, left him the motionless occupant of a naked room. I stood in the entry watching him a moment, while something from within me upbraided me.

I re-entered, with my hand in my pocket—and—and my heart in my mouth.

"Good-by, Bartleby; I am going—good-by, and God some way bless you; and take that," slipping something in his hand. But it dropped upon the floor, and then—strange to say—I tore myself from him whom I had so longed to be rid of.

Established in my new quarters, for a day or two I kept the door locked, and started at every footfall in the passages. When I returned to my rooms, after any little absence, I would pause at the threshold for an instant, and attentively listen, ere applying my key. But these fears were needless. Bartleby never came nigh me.

I thought all was going well, when a perturbed-looking stranger visited me, inquiring whether I was the person who had recently occupied rooms at No.——Wall Street.

Full of forebodings, I replied that I was.

"Then, sir," said the stranger, who proved a lawyer, "you are responsible for the man you left there. He refuses to do any copying; he refuses to do anything; he says he prefers not to; and he refuses to quit the premises."

"I am very sorry, sir," said I, with assumed tranquillity, but an inward tremor, "but, really, the man you allude to is nothing to me —he is no relation or apprentice of mine, that you should hold me responsible for him."

"In mercy's name, who is he?"

"I certainly cannot inform you. I know nothing about him. Formerly I employed him as a copyist; but he has done nothing for me now for some time past."

"I shall settle him, then—good morning, sir."

Several days passed, and I heard nothing more; and, though I often felt a charitable prompting to call at the place and see poor Bartleby, yet a certain squeamishness, of I know not what, withheld me.

All is over with him, by this time, thought I, at last, when, through another week, no further intelligence reached me. But, coming to my room the day after, I found several persons waiting at my door in a high state of nervous excitement.

"That's the man—here he comes," cried the foremost one, whom I recognized as the lawyer who had previously called upon me alone.

"You must take him away, sir, at once," cried a portly person among them, advancing upon me, and whom I knew to be the landlord of No.—— Wall Street. "These gentlemen, my tenants, cannot stand it any longer; Mr. B——," pointing to the lawyer, "has turned him out of his room, and he now persists in haunting the building generally, sitting upon the banisters of the stairs by day, and sleeping in the entry by night. Everybody is concerned; clients are leaving the offices; some fears are entertained of a mob; something you must do, and that without delay."

Aghast at this torrent, I fell back before it, and would fain have locked myself in my new quarters. In vain I persisted that Bartleby was nothing to me—no more than to anyone else. In vain—I was the last person known to have anything to do with him, and they held me to the terrible account. Fearful, then, of being exposed in the papers (as one person present obscurely threatened), I considered the matter, and, at length, said, that if the lawyer would give me a confidential interview with the scrivener, in his (the lawyer's) own room, I would, that afternoon, strive my best to rid them of the nuisance they complained of.

Going up stairs to my old haunt, there was Bartleby silently sitting upon the banister at the landing.

"What are you doing here, Bartleby?" said I.

"Sitting upon the banister," he mildly replied.

I motioned him into the lawyer's room, who then left us.

"Bartleby," said I, "are you aware that you are the cause of great tribulation to me, by persisting in occupying the entry after being dismissed from the office?"

No answer.

"Now one of two things must take place. Either you must do something, or something must be done to you. Now what sort of business would you like to engage in? Would you like to re-engage in copying for some one?"

"No; I would prefer not to make any change."

"Would you like a clerkship in a dry-goods store?"

"There is too much confinement about that. No, I would not like a clerkship; but I am not particular."

"Too much confinement," I cried, "why, you keep yourself confined all the time!"

"I would prefer not to take a clerkship," he rejoined, as if to settle that little item at once.

"How would a bar-tender's business suit you? There is no trying of the eyesight in that."

"I would not like it at all; though, as I said before, I am not particular."

His unwonted wordiness inspirited me. I returned to the charge.

"Well, then, would you like to travel through the country collecting bills for the merchants? That would improve your health."

"No, I would prefer to be doing something else."

"How, then, would going as a companion to Europe, to entertain some young gentleman with your conversation—how would that suit you?"

"Not at all. It does not strike me that there is anything definite about that. I like to be stationary. But I am not particular."

"Stationary you shall be, then," I cried, now losing all patience, and, for the first time in all my exasperating connection with him, fairly flying into a passion. "If you do not go away from these premises before night, I shall feel bound—indeed, I *am* bound—to—to—to quit the premises myself!" I rather absurdly concluded, knowing not with what possible threat to try to frighten his immobility into compliance. Despairing of all further efforts, I was precipitately leaving him, when a final thought occurred to me—one which had not been wholly unindulged before.

"Bartleby," said I, in the kindest tone I could assume under such exciting circumstances, "will you go home with me now—not to my office, but my dwelling—and remain there till we can conclude upon some convenient arrangement for you at our leisure? Come, let us start now, right away."

"No, at present I would prefer not to make any change at all."

I answered nothing; but, effectually dodging every one by the suddenness and rapidity of my flight, rushed from the building, ran up Wall Street towards Broadway, and, jumping into the first omnibus, was soon removed from pursuit. As soon as tranquillity returned, I distinctly perceived that I had now done all that I possibly could, both in respect to the demands of the landlord and his tenants, and with regard to my own desire and sense of duty, to benefit Bartleby, and shield him from rude persecution. I now strove to be entirely carefree and quiescent; and my conscience justified me in attempt; though, indeed, it was not so successful as I could have wished. So fearful was I of being again hunted out by the incensed landlord and his exasperated tenants, that, surrendering my business to Nippers for a few days, I drove about the upper part of the town and through the suburbs, in my rockaway, crossed over to Jersey City and Hoboken, and paid fugitive visits to Manhattanville and Astoria. In fact, I almost lived in my rockaway for the time.

When again I entered my office, lo, a note from the landlord lay upon the desk. I opened it with trembling hands. It informed me that the writer had sent to the police, and had Bartleby removed to the Tombs as a vagrant. Moreover, since I knew more about him than any one else, he wished me to appear at that place, and make a suitable statement of the facts. These tidings had a conflicting effect upon me. At first I was indignant, but, at last, almost approved. The landlord's energetic, summary disposition had led him to adopt a procedure which I do not think I would have decided upon myself; and yet, as a last resort, under such peculiar circumstances, it seemed the only plan.

As I afterwards learned, the poor scrivener, when told that he must be conducted to the Tombs, offered not the slightest obstacle, but, in his pale, unmoving way, silently acquiesced.

Some of the compassionate and curious bystanders joined the party; and headed by one of the constables arm-in-arm with Bartleby, the silent procession filed its way through all the noise, and heat, and joy of the roaring thoroughfares at noon.

The same day I received the note, I went to the Tombs, or, to speak more properly, the Halls of Justice. Seeking the right officer, I stated the purpose of my call, and was informed that the individual I described was, indeed, within. I then assured the functionary that Bartleby was a perfectly honest man, and greatly to be compassionated, however unaccountably eccentric. I narrated all I knew, and closed by suggesting the idea of letting him remain in as indulgent confinement as possible, till something less harsh might be done—though, indeed, I hardly knew what. At all events, if nothing else could be decided upon, the almshouse must receive him. I then begged to have an interview.

Being under no disgraceful charge, and quite serene and harmless in all his ways, they had permitted him freely to wander about the prison, and, especially, in the inclosed grass-platted yards thereof. And so I found him there, standing all alone in the quietest of the yards, his face towards a high wall, while all around, from the narrow slits of the jail windows, I thought I saw peering out upon him the eyes of murderers and thieves.

"Bartleby!"

"I know you," he said, without looking round, "and I want nothing to say to you."

"It was not I that brought you here, Bartleby," said I, keenly pained at his implied suspicion. "And to you, this should not be so vile a place. Nothing reproachful attaches to you by being here. And see, it is not so sad a place as one might think. Look, there is the sky, and here is the grass."

"I know where I am," he replied, but would say nothing more, and so I left him.

As I entered the corridor again, a broad meat-like man, in an apron, accosted me, and, jerking his thumb over his shoulder, said, "Is that your friend?"

"Yes."

"Does he want to starve? If he does, let him live on the prison fare, that's all."

"Who are you?" asked I, not knowing what to make of such an unofficially speaking person in such a place.

"I am the grub-man. Such gentlemen as have friends here hire me to provide them with something good to eat."

"Is this so?" said I, turning to the turnkey.

He said it was.

"Well, then," said I, slipping some silver into the grub-man's hands (for so they called him), "I want you to give particular attention to my friend there; let him have the best dinner you can get. And you must be as polite to him as possible."

"Introduce me, will you?" said the grub-man, looking at me with an expression which seemed to say he was all impatience for an opportunity to give a specimen of his breeding.

Thinking it would prove of benefit to the scrivener, I acquiesced, and, asking the grub-man his name, went up with him to Bartleby.

"Bartleby, this is a friend; you will find him very useful to you."

"Your sarvant, sir, your sarvant," said the grub-man, making a low salutation behind his apron. "Hope you find it pleasant here, sir; nice grounds—cool apartments—hope you'll stay with us some time—try to make it agreeable. What will you have for dinner to-day?"

"I prefer not to dine to-day," said Bartleby, turning away. "It would disagree with me; I am unused to dinners." So saying, he slowly moved to the other side of the inclosure, and took up a position fronting the dead-wall.

"How's this?" said the grub-man, addressing me with a stare of astonishment. "He's odd, ain't he?"

"I think he is a little deranged," said I, sadly.

"Deranged? deranged is it? Well, now, upon my word, I thought that friend of yourn was a gentleman forger; they are always pale and genteel-like, them forgers. I can't help pity 'em—can't help it, sir. Did you know Monroe Edwards?" he added, touchingly, and paused, then, laying his hand piteously on my shoulder, sighed, "He died of consumption at Sing-Sing. So you weren't acquainted with Monroe?"

"No, I was never socially acquainted with any forgers. But I cannot stop longer. Look to my friend yonder. You will not lose by it. I will see you again."

Some few days after this, I again obtained admission to the Tombs, and went through the corridors in quest of Bartleby, but without finding him.

"I saw him coming from his cell not long ago," said a turnkey, "may be he's gone to loiter in the yards."

So I went in that direction.

"Are you looking for the silent man?" said another turnkey, passing me. "Yonder he lies—sleeping in the yard there. 'Tis not twenty minutes since I saw him lie down."

The yard was entirely quiet. It was not accessible to the common prisoners. The surrounding walls, of amazing thickness, kept off all sounds behind them. The Egyptian character of the masonry weighed upon me with its gloom. But a soft imprisoned turf grew under foot. The heart of the eternal pyramids, it seemed, wherein, by some strange magic, through the clefts, grass seed, dropped by birds, had sprung.

Strangely huddled at the base of the wall, his knees drawn up, and lying on his side, his head touching the cold stones, I saw the wasted Bartleby. But nothing stirred. I paused; then went close up to him; stooped over, and saw that his dim eyes were open; otherwise he seemed profoundly sleeping. Something prompted me to touch him. I felt his hand, when a tingling shiver ran up my arm and down my spine to my feet.

The round face of the grub-man peered upon me now. "His dinner is ready. Won't he dine today, either? Or does he live without dining?"

"Lives without dining," said I, and closed the eyes.

"Eh!—He's asleep, ain't he?"

"With kings and counselors," murmured I.

There would seem little need for proceeding further in this history. Imagination will readily supply the meager recital of poor Bartleby's interment. But, ere parting with the reader, let me say that if this little narrative has sufficiently interested him to awaken curiosity as to who Bartleby was, and what manner of life he led prior to the present narrator's making his acquaintance, I can only reply that in such curiosity I fully share, but am wholly unable to gratify it. Yet here I hardly know whether I should divulge one little item of rumor, which came to my ear a few months after the scrivener's decease. Upon what basis it rested, I could never ascertain, and hence how true it is I cannot tell. But, inasmuch as this vague report has not been without a certain suggestive interest to me, however sad, it may prove the same with some others; and so I will briefly mention it. The report was this: that Bartleby had been a subordinate clerk in the Dead Letter Office at Washington, from which he had been suddenly removed by a change in the administration. When I think over this rumor, hardly can I express the emotions which seize me. Dead letters! does it not sound like dead men? Conceive a man by nature and misfortune prone to a pallid hopelessness, can any business seem more fitted to heighten it than that of continually handling these dead letters, and assorting them for the flames? For by the cart-load they are annually burned. Sometimes from out the folded paper the pale clerk takes a ring—the finger it was meant for, perhaps, moulders in the grave; a bank-note sent in swiftest charity—he whom it would relieve nor eats nor hungers any more; pardon for those who died despairing; hope for those who died unhoping; good tidings for those who died stifled by unrelieved calamities. On errands of life, these letters speed to death.

Ah, Bartleby! Ah, humanity!

Using the Action Line to Identify Structural Peculiarities

Writing an unusually detailed action summary probably is essential for getting objective control over "Bartleby." As he writes, the reader should identify and make notes about unusual characteristics revealed by the story's structure. However, he should persist in listing actions until his summary is entirely finished before he studies each special clue. The first peculiarity is that despite the unusually long exposition, there are almost no expository actions on the part of the protagonist to record in the action summary. There are instead a great many actions of the other law clerks and the narrator essential to an understanding of the habits and nature of the narrator. A second major structural peculiarity is that the action could be written as numerous little action lines, each complete in itself. In every episode from the inciting action to the climax, the narrator and Bartleby seem to act out the same provocation, the same response, the same crisis, and the same resolution. However, in each apparent repetition, the reader can uncover something vital and new, usually about the natures of both the lawyer and Bartleby and certainly about the development of the conflict. A third major peculiarity is the reoccurrence of deliberations by the narrator at the end of every episode. Since deeds, speeches, and changes of character that stem from deliberation are the highest revelation of character, these passages will have to be studied with exceptional attention because in these deliberations the narrator makes, modifies, rejects, and usually does not act on decisions at all! While he is completing his action line, the reader should mark the points at which deliberations occur and separately record the content of each deliberation. Later, the reader should determine how many of the narrator's desired but rejected actions are performed later by others without the narrator's objection on Bartleby's behalf.

Once the action line is completed, it is imperative that the reader determine who is the protagonist. Who is the grammatical subject of most sentences? Who is the content subject of most paragraphs? Through whose mind is most of the watching or judging done? Who is the person present when all major actions are performed, particularly at the beginning and end of the story? Who is, or should be, affected most by the resolution? As the evidence accumulates, the reader may be very much surprised to discover that he is proving that the narrator, not Bartleby, is the major character. However, he may balk at believing that the narrator properly fits the last test. Rather than set his judgment so early in his study of the story, the reader will do well to decide, instead, to gather material for exhaustive character analyses of both the narrator and Bartleby.

Reliability of the Narrator

Since the narrator seems to be the protagonist, the reader needs especially to examine what point of view means in "Bartleby." The narrator tells the story in retrospect. That means that he should be able to recognize and interpret the importance of actions, conversations, and thoughts that he might not have considered significant had he recorded them as they occurred. It means, also, that he as a human being has some purpose for telling the story of Bartleby. That purpose may assure that he is reasonably objective or it may guarantee that his narrative cannot be trusted. Early in the exposition the narrator asserts his reasons; but does the story bear him out? About whom does he talk most—himself or Bartleby? (Can his self-centeredness be defended because of the obvious truth that as a first-person narrator he cannot know what Bartleby is thinking?) If on so important a matter as why he wrote the story at all, there is a discrepancy—obvious to the reader but not to the narrator—between the narrator's intention and his performance, can he be trusted in any of his opinions? The answer to such a question should never be based on a single piece of evidence. Therefore, one of the major steps of study is for the reader to examine and evaluate every assertion that the narrator makes about himself. The greatest surprise for almost any reader probably will be his final detailed awareness that this lawyer knows as little of his real motives as Skvortsoff did of his. If he perceives himself so poorly, even in retrospect, how well does he remember Bartleby? Nevertheless, does his training or his nature suggest that he will be accurate in his recording of events even if his interpretations are not reliable?

An estimate of the accuracy of this narrator is so critical to a reading of "Bartleby" that the reader must go far beyond a simple identification of the narrator's ostensible purposes, his training as a lawyer, and his natural meticulous accuracy in matters of fact. His accuracy depends also on the degree to which all of his other traits color his perception, and most of them are established in the long exposition in which the narrator deliberately talks, not of Bartleby, but of himself. What may startle most a reader who has responded to the predicament and personality of Bartleby is the insistence with which the narrator illustrates that his habits and attitudes have not changed as a result of his contact with Bartleby. This insistence may seem unimportant unless the reader recognizes that the narrator's telling the story of Bartleby at all is a repetition of the conflict between himself and Bartleby—but, this time, a conflict totally under his control. In fact, the narrator's failure to recognize his own complete selfish wilfulness may be the reader's most important key to the nature of the narrator's inner conflict.

Close Questioning to Infer the Role of Minor Characters In Defining Major Characters

So subtle a story as "Bartleby," moreover, cannot be understood fully in the light of only major traits of the protagonist. Therefore, the reader should pursue particularly the technique of questioning details closely and writing down in order whatever minute insights he gains. Especially in "Bartleby" the reader should be alert to every detail of the human relationships of this narrator. What sort of law does he practice? Why? What are his relations with persons with money and power, and how does he feel about those people? How does he handle the very few setbacks to his anticipations, particularly the abolition of the office of Master in Chancery? Just how violent is what he calls his "outburst"? What is his attitude toward both Turkey and Nippers? What is there in his way of speaking about them that indicates that when he thinks of them he compares them to himself, much to his own self-satisfaction? What is his way of correcting his employees? Why does he not fire them? What does this show of his habit? What does it show of his nature? How does he habitually justify his allowing them their own ways when they oppose him?

A single incident which the narrator treats in some detail demands close attention because it provides the pattern of action with which the reader must contrast the episodes that constitute the narrator's conflict with Bartleby. The narrator in introducing Turkey explains that after noon Turkey is prone to make blots on the documents he copies as well as to behave noisily and impatiently. He explains: "Now, valuing his morning services as I did, and resolved not to lose them ... and being a man of peace, unwilling by my admonitions to call for unseemly retorts from him, I took upon me ... to hint to him, very kindly, that, perhaps, now that he was growing old, it might be well to abridge his labors...." The careful reader will notice that the narrator's argument is as devious as his sentence. He wants to keep Turkey's useful services and he does not want any more afternoon ink blots and noise. Yet, he hints instead that it is concern with Turkey's age that prompts him to give him all afternoons off. That argument failing, the narrator at least intimates that the blots are a concern. "With submission, Sir," says Turkey, "... a blot or two of a warm afternoon is not to be severely urged against gray hairs.... With submission, Sir, we are both getting old." In effect, Turkey refuses not to appear in the afternoons, and he offers back "with submission" the narrator's own excuse of age. Faced by Turkey's refusal, the narrator records: "The appeal to my fellow-feeling was hardly to be resisted. At all events, I saw that go he would not so I made up my mind to let him stay, resolving ... nevertheless, to see to it that, during the afternoon he had to do with my less important papers." Given some human quality by which he could profess himself warmed, the narrator dismisses Turkey's refusal to go and, furthermore, persuades himself that letting Turkey stay is his own decision. Not having gotten what he intended but having persuaded himself of a change in his wishes, he simply avoids the circumstances that could cause him to have to speak to Turkey about the matter again. This whole habit of action is what the reader must contrast later with the inciting action, the protagonist's response, and the narrator's consequent new deliberation. Repeated episode after episode, that new pattern is Melville's major device for revealing character in a depth that increases as the intensity of the conflict increases.

 The reader may need to examine other incidents in the exposition with almost this much care. Certainly he should continue to raise questions through the remainder of the exposition. What about Nippers' appearance appeals to the narrator, and what about Turkey's offends him? What is the characteristic subject of his humor, illustrated here in his remark about Turkey and the new coat? How does he feel about even so small a deviation by one of his employees from what he expected? What are his major grounds for believing himself superior to each of the persons in his employ? Why does he choose to hire Bartleby? What have his reasons to do with either Bartleby's qualifications or Bartleby's probable idea of what the job entails? Did he expect from Bartleby or from any of his clerks simply that they do their jobs? The reader should have no difficulty now in naming the narrator's major habitual traits. He also should make, then, a statement of what he believes the narrator's basic nature to be. The next significant necessity is that the reader discover precisely what Bartleby is like and how he differs in nature, in habit, and in emotions from Turkey and Nippers. Then the reader must consider why those differences cause the narrator and Bartleby to be in conflict.

Inferring Objective Evidence of Character from Biased Narration

How does this almost silent, stationary character so completely win the sympathy of most readers yet so absolutely antagonize the narrator? Perhaps he is most singularly attractive because he does only what he prefers to, even though that preference makes him completely unsuited for the realities of the business world of Wall Street. Because he is shown almost always as negative—preferring *not* to do something—it is easy to overlook the facts of his positive nature. Clearly, then, the reader should examine each of his responses for both what he prefers and what he does not prefer. The reader should keep simultaneously an especially close record of precisely how the narrator's actions deny Bartleby's needs as implied in his preferences. To study Bartleby's preferences in chronological order, the reader should recall first what he learns only at the end of the story: "that Bartleby had been a subordinate clerk at the Dead Letter Office in Washington." Turned out of that job by a change in administration, Bartleby apparently prefers to become a scrivener. The narrator has indulged in a long consideration of what it would mean to work in a dead letter office. The reader must speculate himself about what working in such an office must mean to a man like Bartleby. If he keeps his objectivity instead of joining the narrator in his habitual sentimentalizing about humanity, the perceptive reader may see an irony that the narrator does not perceive even by the time that he completes the narrative. The narrator suggests: "Conceive a man by nature and misfortune prone to a pallid hopelessness; can any business seem more fitted to heighten it than that of continually handling these dead letters, and assorting them for the flames?" The reader sees the irony, of course, that it is Bartleby's conflict with the narrator, not his work in the Dead Letter Office, that brings him finally to hopelessness and death.

What is the difference between his work at the Dead Letter Office and his work on Wall Street? Why would he prefer copying legal papers to destroying dead letters? Hired as a law copyist, how effectively does Bartleby work? What about his performance annoys the narrator? The narrator suggests that he would not expect a "mettlesome poet" like Byron to examine manuscripts and admits that it is "a very dull, worrisome and lethargic affair," which he himself is willing to conduct. What does Bartleby's preferring not to examine his work suggest about the difference between his basic nature and what his appearance leads the narrator to expect? Does the narrator consider that his clerk might in any way be a creative person like a Byron whose erratic behavior could be justified? The reader will do well to speculate constantly about how Bartleby has come to seem so mechanical and unemotional while there still remains in him a will that permits him passively to resist even the power of his employer to which conventions of business expect him to bow.

The reader surely must be aware that Bartleby is indeed wrong from the point of view of business not to be willing to interrupt his work even at the whim of the man who hires him—and wrong not to read copy with the other clerks—and wrong not to explain his reasons for declining. Does the narrator's hiring Bartleby no more for his skill as a copyist than for his convenience to the narrator or his supposed sobering influence on Turkey and Nippers justify Bartleby's violation of the conventional subservient position of an employee to an employer? The more a reader speculates in this way the more frustrated he will become both with the narrator and with Bartleby because neither acts as he should within a business relationship.

If a new employee is insolent, as Bartleby surely is, the expectation in the business world is that he will be fired. Why isn't Bartleby? Turkey and Nippers are not fired both because they perform satisfactorily in quantity and quality for low wages and because overlooking their insubordination permits the narrator not only to feel magnanimous and superior but also to justify his paying them so poorly. The simplest answer is that Bartleby is not fired because it is not the habit of the narrator to fire anyone. However, Bartleby violates the employee's pattern by showing no human feeling that the narrator can use as an excuse to ignore the gap between his real grounds for not acting and his supposed grounds. Why then does the narrator not fire Bartleby simply to remove the irritation? To fire Bartleby, to remove Bartleby from his offices by force, to do anything directly for Bartleby in prison would be to commit himself to action rather than to talk. He cannot act at all about Bartleby if he is to say simultaneously on the one hand that business is business, that though he is a very humane man benignly tolerant of the human failings of his employees he cannot allow his personal feelings in any way to influence his business judgment, and on the other hand that he runs his business by working with his friends.

Now the reader can see that Bartleby must be studied not only for what he prefers and what he prefers not to but also for what in the basic nature of the narrator is exposed directly by each of Bartleby's negative preferences. That pattern is clear in the episode that involves the inciting action, particularly when it is contrasted with the pattern of the narrator's report of his asking Turkey not to come to the office after noon.

Inciting Action: Motive

Just before the inciting action begins, Bartleby is described as doing "an extraordinary quantity of writing ... copying by sun-light and by candle-light." The reader may infer from Bartleby's diligence that Bartleby prefers writing copy that will preserve ideas that he would have had to destroy if they had come to the Dead Letter Office. The narrator, acting according to habit, "abruptly called to Bartleby" while without looking up he held out the copy that he wanted checked "so that immediately upon emerging from his retreat Bartleby might snatch it and proceed to business without delay." The narrator describes his "surprise, nay ... consternation" when Bartleby replies for the first time, "I would prefer not to." Here the reader sees underlined emphatically the narrator's most consistent habitual attitude: his expectation of instant compliance with his least request. Because we see Bartleby only through the eyes of the narrator, it is much more difficult to know what Bartleby's motives are. However, there can be no doubt that he prefers to continue his copying and, by inference, prefers not to give up his own determination of what he will do, even to an employer whom he surely must recognize has the right to order, not to ask, the particular work of an employee. So surprised is the narrator by Bartleby's refusal that he presumes the incident could not have happened, repeats his request, and receives the same answer. If Bartleby has not considered before he speaks what his refusal could cost him, the narrator's repetition of the question surely makes Bartleby's alternatives absolutely clear in any ordinary business circumstances. As a human being, he has a right to act on his preferences. As an employee, he is expected to defer to an employer. That unexpected second "I would prefer not" underlines the basic nature of Bartleby. He acts not by habit but by deliberation and awaits tranquilly whatever consequences attach to his preferences. Bartleby's unexpectedly exercising his right as a human being to preferences even in an office conflicts directly with another of the narrator's most basic assumptions—that wages buy the instant submission of his employees. The conflict is under way when the narrator rises "in high excitement," strides across the room, and thrusts the sheet toward Bartleby saying, "I want you to help me compare this sheet here—take it." Bartleby's third rejection of an order from the narrator in his power role as employer is as incredible to the narrator as the affrontery of Trippetta was to the king in "Hop-Frog." However, the deepest offense is to the narrator's image of himself—an image that the narrator cannot admit to himself is in error. What makes the third response of Bartleby most frustrating to the narrator is that Bartleby offers no justification whatever for his refusal and demonstrates no human weakness that permits the narrator to excuse his failure to comply. With Turkey, the narrator did not persist in action that might cost him services which he finds useful because he could rationalize that he himself decided whatever Turkey actually chose to do. When he says that he would have been able to have "violently dismissed him from the premises" had he detected in Bartleby "anything ordinarily human about him," what he means is that he could excuse Bartleby, just as he did Turkey, had he found it. Bartleby denies him that refuge of believing that it is he, the narrator, who chooses among alternatives.

Now the impossible is demanded by Bartleby: either the narrator must act morally according to what he says about charity and love or he must act expediently as business demands. His nature will not let him become involved with any human being either way; yet, a face-saving avoidance of action is not present. Therefore, he is driven to provoke over and over the same conduct from Bartleby, seeking always a weakness in Bartleby that will vindicate him as charitable and right, hence superior. Each of the episodes of the story after the inciting action depends, first, on this necessity of the narrator to provoke Bartleby rather than commit himself to any real relationship and, second, on the constancy with which Bartleby persists in doing what he prefers.

Deliberation: Key to the Narrator's Character

Real deliberation is new to the narrator because he has so seldom failed to have his wishes satisfied immediately. The more frustrated he becomes, the more he thinks; and the more he thinks, the more he reveals the depths of himself. The narrator stands gazing at Bartleby, then reseats himself thinking, "What had one best do?" That his pose of objectivity is indeed a pose is clear even in the way he phrases his thoughts. He removes the question from any personal concern by asking what the impersonal "one" should do in general. Instead of the simple, expedient, appropriate business action of firing Bartleby on the spot, he asks what "best to do," a question with moral overtones. Next, "Because my business hurried me," he decides only to "reserve the matter for my future leisure." This step is complicated. On the one hand, his business permits him little leisure; on the other hand, since quite as much as Bartleby he does only what he prefers in his business, he always has leisure if he wishes it.

In summary, there are three vital exceptions to the narrator's habitual pattern that mark the difference between how he acts and thinks in the episode involving the inciting action and how he dealt habitually with Turkey. (1) The narrator actually responds to Bartleby with overt anger; (2) he finds no human frailty in Bartleby that he can use to justify his inaction; and (3) he actually thinks of a violent act to solve the problem: "I should have violently dismissed him from the premises."

The pattern that the reader must check throughout the rest of the story should now be clearly seen:

> 1. Because the narrator has been able to make no satisfactory rationalization of Bartleby's failure to submit to him, the narrator will deliberately choose, as he himself says, "to encounter him in new opposition."
> 2. He will ask Bartleby to do something which he knows Bartleby will prefer not to do.

3. The narrator will argue the reasonableness of his request and the unreasonableness of Bartleby's preference.

4. Bartleby will agree that he is unreasonable but will persist in his preference.

5. The narrator will decide that business decrees that he handle the problem at his leisure.

6. While attempting to pay no attention to Bartleby, the narrator will observe him very closely for a period of time.

7. The narrator will argue that he is being kind and indulgent until he almost persuades himself he has reason to forgive Bartleby.

8. The urge to provoke Bartleby again overcomes his rationalizations.

Each time that the pattern is repeated, the reader must watch carefully for potential insights into the characters of the two men. When a few days after the inciting action the narrator decides to examine Bartleby's four copies of a document, he demands, "Bartleby! quick, I am waiting." Bartleby prefers to scrape his chair back slowly and to inquire mildly, "What is wanted?" Again Bartleby is preferring not to respond to the demand that he comply immediately to the wishes of the narrator. However, he adds the additional aggravation of suggesting that it is reasonable for a human being to know what is demanded before he decides whether he will comply, even with the request of an employer who can fire him for asking. The reader must realize now that it is this sort of abrasive action, or nonaction, on the part of Bartleby that provokes the characteristic deliberation on the part of the narrator. What may not be so apparent is that Bartleby as a human being silently asks of the narrator some personal recognition of his own human needs—a response that has no official place in the conventions of business. It is precisely that very sort of response that the narrator prides himself on making out of the generosity of his heart. Ironically, he never makes it because he so constantly thinks only of his own interests that he can interpret deviation from his expectation only as attack. Consequently, according to his habit, he busily manufactures a conventionally pious rationalization for not facing his selfish refusal to become involved.

Emotional Needs: Key to the Conflict

Much evidence in this story suggests that what Bartleby needs is some human relationship. To a sensitive man like Bartleby, however, the narrator's responses after deliberation are what is most "fitted to heighten his pallid hopelessness." For example, in the deliberation following his discovery that apparently Bartleby lives on ginger nuts, the narrator admits that "nothing so aggravates an earnest person as passive resistance." However, he remembers only a moment later that "He is useful to me...." Therefore, he decides to befriend Bartleby; "to humor him in his strange wilfulness," since friendship and tolerance "will cost me little or nothing," and will pay off in Bartleby's continued usefulness. How the narrator slowly takes away Bartleby's last hope is clearly identified in the irony of that decision. Having decided to be Bartleby's friend because it will cost him nothing, the narrator, at his first opportunity, deliberately provokes Bartleby to a negative response. The irony of claiming friendship yet acting antagonistically is not lost on Bartleby. "Surely you do not mean to persist in that mulish vagary?" the narrator asks, then records, "No answer." What the reader must surely see is that Bartleby knows the potential cost of acting by his preferences—particularly the cost of making a man like the narrator live up to his pious words. At any confrontation in the story, the narrator need not continue in his pattern if he is ready to accept the cost of decision. All he need do is say either as a businessman, "Then if you prefer not, you are fired," or as a friend, "If you prefer not, you needn't." Bartleby is prepared for either. The narrator's answer shows that he is determined to be related to Bartleby only on his private, selfish terms that demand of Bartleby compliance in all things.

If the reader has followed the suggestion that he keep a careful chronological record of the contents of the narrator's deliberations, those notes should reveal in sequence the increasing elaborateness with which the narrator must philosophize about love and charity to prevent himself from taking action of increasing violence against

Bartleby. Each deliberation can easily be checked against the action summary to see how the narrator's successive demands on Bartleby leave less and less room in which Bartleby can comply. The reader needs to analyze particularly carefully the scene in which the narrator, having found him in the office on Sunday, determines after an exceptionally long deliberation not only that Bartleby must go but also with what tests he will justify his dismissal.

The narrator says to him the next morning: "I am not going to ask you to do anything you would prefer not to do—I simply wish to speak to you." As it becomes increasingly clear to Bartleby that the narrator is saying one thing and doing another, Bartleby "kept his glance fixed on the bust of Cicero"; showed "only the faintest tremor of the white, attenuated mouth"; and answered, "At present I prefer to give no answer." Melville offers the reader a very subtle symbolic clue to the tremor of Bartleby's mouth in Bartleby's focusing his attention on the bust of Cicero rather than on the narrator. The ablest of the defense lawyers of Rome, Cicero, chose exile rather than influence bought by helping to destroy the power of the Roman Senate. Brought back from exile, Cicero sided with Octavian against Marc Antony who had participated in that destruction. When Antony, Octavian, and Lepidus formed the second triumvirate, Octavian gave Antony permission to kill his friend Cicero. Antony's troops nailed Cicero's head and right hand to the platform where he had often spoken against Antony. Since the tremor of Bartleby's mouth is the only action of his which isn't in Bartleby's control, one must assume that Bartleby sees the bust of Cicero as a symbol both of the narrator's moral blindness and of the hopelessness of his own position. The reader recognizes readily how little like Cicero is this narrator who views himself as "one of those unambitious lawyers who never address a jury," who "seldom lose my temper; much more seldom indulge in dangerous indignation at wrongs and outrages...," and who conceive of friendship as something that "would cost me little or nothing." There is also an ironic parallel between the fate of Octavian's friend and of Bartleby as the friend of the narrator. Bartleby's responses throughout the rest of the story are a result of his acceptance in this scene of the irony of his relationship to the narrator.

Analysis of Action to Show Crisis

To complete his study of Bartleby's character, the reader will do best to analyze very precisely every response that Bartleby makes from this point on. Why must he reject the narrator's request that he be "a little reasonable"? Why does he "prefer to be left alone here" when everyone crowds into his office? Perhaps most important, why does he reply "indifferently" when pressed for a reason for doing no more writing, "Do you not see the reason for yourself?" This line undoubtedly poses a major problem, for it can be argued very persuasively that Bartleby is at least partially blind, particularly if his way of moving in prison and his simple statement, "I know where I am," are examined closely. However, regardless of whether or not Bartleby is blind, he still makes no appeal to the narrator either for understanding or help; and he refuses to explain now or later whether the narrator is correct in thinking that he is blind or that his eyes have been damaged. The reader can never know from the facts whether or not Bartleby is blind because the viewpoint throughout the story is the narrator's, and he is so consistently concerned only with himself that he never bothers to find out. However, "a man by nature and misfortune prone to a pallid hopelessness" could well be indifferent even to the loss of his sight had he lost something far more valuable. If the reason for his not writing is the loss of his hope rather than his eyesight, that reason he also leaves to be supplied by the narrator.

What should at least begin to be clear is that each man demands of the other the one thing that each is unable to give. What is even more remarkable is that the two men are acting from identical motives: their preferences. However, there is a tremendous difference in their awareness of the cost of so acting and an even greater difference in their capacity to accept and pay that cost. Perhaps the response of the narrator to Bartleby's preference for staying in the office is most revealing of that greatest difference.

Bartleby stays when he either cannot or will not write and when he will not demonstrate his usefulness in any other way. Yet, quite clearly, Bartleby can leave the office; for he does, despite his preference, when the new renter puts him out. Nor does he force his reentrance to that office once the new renter's decision is made. His roaming the building rather than leaving it is still a matter of preference, not an emotional or physical inability to do so. Nor is Bartleby unaware of reality when he answers the narrator's agitated "What are you doing here?" with his reasonable, factual "Sitting upon the banister."

On the other hand, the narrator permits Bartleby to stay because he prefers to let him rather than face the alternatives. The narrator has always before been able to buy compliance with his preferences. Therefore, he has never had to examine his actions to see if they accord with his words. Faced by Bartleby's directly contradictory promises and unable to buy him off, the narrator flees frantically from him to new quarters. Yet, he feels somehow that he tears himself from Bartleby rather than wishing to be free—an emotion that is almost strong enough to commit him to involvement as a human being. His flight having proved unsuccessful but his decision to remain uninvolved encouraged by his separation from Bartleby, the narrator is forced by his society to confront Bartleby in the scene where Bartleby sits on the banister.

Here, perhaps more clearly than at any other point in the story, the reader may be able to determine what Bartleby represents to the narrator. For the first time, the narrator says the exact truth: "... you are the cause of great tribulation to me by persisting in occupying the entry after being dismissed from the office." Bartleby makes no answer and the narrator continues, "Either you must do something or something must be done to you." Without question, this statement identifies a crisis for the narrator, but he again evades the issue between himself and Bartleby by naming a series of totally unsuitable jobs, each of which Bartleby cannot and will not prefer. Each suggestion is met by extensive, very reasonable reinforcements of Bartleby's preference. The narrator cannot tolerate Bartleby's removing by reasonableness his last grounds for feeling superior. Therefore, the narrator, "fairly flying into a passion," cries: "Stationary you shall be," and almost commits himself to direct action in relation to Bartleby. However, on the spur of the moment the narrator thinks of one last offer with which he may force Bartleby to turn "his immobility into compliance." He offers to take Bartleby home. Because the one thing that the narrator has consistently refused to do is to involve himself, Bartleby recognizes that the offer of his home is not on the narrator's part generosity, but a last possible offer to bring him to the narrator's terms. When Bartleby rejects him this last time, the narrator flees again and returns only after Bartleby has been committed to the Tombs. Bartleby accepts the cost of living as he prefers—even the necessity of colliding so abrasively and so constantly with the narrator and of being taken to the Tombs because he will not conform, either, to society in general. In prison Bartleby must recognize completely what he first glimpsed when he gazed at the bust of Cicero: the narrator refuses to know himself enough either to accept the cost of friendship with Bartleby or to pay the price of rejecting him honestly. It is the narrator's final leaving of decision about Bartleby to others—his refusal to accept human responsibility—that makes Bartleby say without turning, "I know you, and I want nothing to say to you." And it is at least a vague apprehension of what his failure to act means that makes the narrator think before he calls on Bartleby that "all around, from the narrow slits of the jail, I thought I saw peering out upon him the eyes of murderers and thieves." However, the narrator keeps the defense of reason to the end. He explains truthfully and factually what is true of his direct action but not of his omission of concern: "it was not I who brought you here, Bartleby." He persuades himself, furthermore, that it is he who has the right to be offended that Bartleby should think so unreasonably that he had some part in Bartleby's being escorted by police to prison. He even goes on to reason for Bartleby that being in prison is not so bad for someone who prefers to be stationary and spends so much time in dead-wall reveries. He is right, in all reason.

When a man like Bartleby "prefers," he leaves another person only the alternative of total commitment either to him or against him. Positive involvement is finally what all human beings desire of others and is the heart of the humanistic ethic to which the narrator gives lip service when he exclaims at the end of his narrative, "Ah, Bartleby! Ah, humanity!" However, the narrator's prime conviction is "that the easiest way of life is the best." What is human of himself he incarcerates with Bartleby by his failure to act. The expedient businessman who remains can resolve the conflict climaxed by Bartleby's death by writing this detached, rational biography. He can even recognize that the lack of a complete life history represents "an irreparable loss to literature." However, he sees no personal loss or any loss to humanity in the loss of the actual man. Without Bartleby the narrator is "an eminently safe man," as objective and rational as the Wall Street where he works "in the cool tranquility of a snug retreat...."

QUESTIONS FOR DISCUSSION AND WRITING

1. What are the major traits of the two main characters?
2. How do minor characters help to define the major characters?
3. How do Bartleby's actions after the scene where he gazes at the bust of Cicero show that Bartleby has accepted the irony of his relationship to the narrator?
4. What is the irony of the narrator's not being able to go on to church after seeing Bartleby?
5. What are the steps in the narrator's pattern of deliberation when he returns from traveling around New York and finds Bartleby in jail?
6. What are the actions, particularly of the narrator, that immediately precede and follow Bartleby's crisis in the prison?
7. In the scene where the narrator offers to find Bartleby any number of public contact jobs, what is the difference between the narrator's asserted motives and his real motives?
8. What does the narrator intend to establish about himself in the

exposition before he introduces Bartleby? Does he succeed in his intention?

9. How is the exposition of the story the resolution of the narrator's conflict?

10. What is the difference between the point of view in "The Beggar" and in "Bartleby"?

11. In "Bartleby" what identical emotion of the protagonist and the antagonist produce the inciting action and the protagonist's response? Do Hop-Frog and the king have identical emotions in conflict? Do Skvortsoff and Lushkoff?

The Hollow of the Three Hills

NATHANIEL HAWTHORNE

In those strange old times, when fantastic dreams and madmen's reveries were realised among the actual circumstances of life, two persons met together at an appointed hour and place. One was a lady, graceful in form and fair of feature, though pale and troubled, and smitten with an untimely blight in what should have been the fullest bloom of her years; the other was an ancient and meanly-dressed woman, of ill-favoured aspect, and so withered, shrunken, and decrepit, that even the space since she began to decay must have exceeded the ordinary term of human existence. In the spot where they encountered no mortal could observe them. Three little hills stood by each other, and down in the midst of them sunk a hollow basin, almost mathematically circular, two or three hundred feet in breadth, and of such depth that a stately cedar might but just be visible above the sides. Dwarf pines were numerous upon the hills, and partly fringed the outer verge of the intermediate hollow; within which there was nothing but the brown grass of October, and here and there a tree-trunk, that had fallen long ago, and lay mouldering with no green successor from its roots. One of these masses of decaying wood, formerly a majestic oak, rested close beside a pool of green and sluggish water at the bottom of the basin. Such scenes as this (so grey tradition tells) were once the resort of a power of evil and his plighted subjects; and here, at midnight or on the dim verge of evening, they were said to stand round the mantling pool, disturbing its putrid waters in the performance of an impious baptismal rite. The chill beauty of an autumnal sunset was now gilding the three hill-tops, whence a paler tint stole down their sides into the hollow.

"Here is our pleasant meeting come to pass," said the aged crone, "according as thou hast desired. Say quickly what thou wouldest have of me, for there is but a short hour that we may tarry here."

As the old, withered woman spoke, a smile glimmered on her countenance, like lamplight on the wall of a sepulchre. The lady trembled, and cast her eyes upward to the verge of the basin, as if meditating to return with her purpose unaccomplished. But it was not so ordained.

"I am a stranger in this land, as you know," said she, at length. "Whence I come it matters not; but I have left those behind me with whom my fate was intimately bound, and from whom I am cut off for ever. There is a weight in my bosom that I cannot away with, and I have come hither to inquire of their welfare."

"And who is there by this green pool that can bring thee news from the ends of the earth?" cried the old woman, peering into the lady's face. "Not from my lips mayest thou hear these tidings; yet, be thou bold, and the daylight shall not pass away from yonder hill-top before thy wish be granted."

"I will do your bidding though I die," replied the lady, desperately.

The old woman seated herself on the trunk of the fallen tree, threw aside the hood that shrouded her grey locks, and beckoned her companion to draw near.

"Kneel down," she said, "and lay your forehead on my knees."

She hesitated a moment, but the anxiety that had long been kindling burned fiercely up within her. As she knelt down, the border of her garment was dipped into the pool; she laid her forehead on the old woman's knees, and the latter drew a cloak about the lady's face, so that she was in darkness. Then she heard the muttered words of prayer, in the midst of which she started, and would have arisen.

"Let me flee—let me flee and hide myself, that they may not look upon me!" she cried. But, with returning recollection, she hushed herself, and was still as death.

For it seemed as if other voices—familiar in infancy, and unforgotten through many wanderings, and in all the vicissitudes of her heart and fortune—were mingling with the accents of the prayer. At first the words were faint and indistinct, not rendered so by distance, but rather resembling the dim pages of a book which we strive to read by an imperfect and gradually brightening light. In such a manner, as the prayer proceeded, did those voices strengthen upon the ear; till at length the petition ended, and the conversation of an aged man, and of a woman broken and decayed like himself, became distinctly audible to the lady as she knelt. But those strangers appeared not to stand in the hollow depth between the three hills. Their voices were encompassed and re-echoed by the walls of a chamber, the windows of which were rattling in the breeze; the regular vibration of a clock, the crackling of a fire, and the tinkling of the embers as they fell among the ashes, rendered the scene almost as vivid as if painted to the eye. By a melancholy hearth sat these two old people, the man calmly despondent, the woman querulous and tearful, and their words were all of sorrow. They spoke of a daughter, a wanderer they knew not where, bearing dishonour along with her, and leaving shame and affliction to bring their grey heads to the grave. They alluded also to other and more recent woe, but in the midst of their talk their voices seemed to melt into the sound of the wind sweeping mournfully among the autumn leaves; and when the lady lifted her eyes, there was she kneeling in the hollow between three hills.

"A weary and lonesome time yonder old couple have of it," remarked the old woman, smiling in the lady's face.

"And did you also hear them?" exclaimed she, a sense of intolerable humiliation triumphing over her agony and fear.

"Yea; and we have yet more to hear," replied the old woman. "Wherefore cover thy face quickly."

Again the withered hag poured forth the monotonous words of a prayer that was not meant to be acceptable in heaven; and soon in the pauses of her breath strange murmurings began to thicken, gradually increasing, so as to drown and overpower the charm by which they grew. Shrieks pierced through the obscurity of sound, and were succeeded by the singing of sweet female voices, which in their turn gave way to a wild roar of laughter, broken suddenly by groanings and sobs, forming altogether a ghastly confusion of terror and mourning and mirth. Chains were rattling, fierce and stern voices uttered threats, and the scourge resounded at their command. All these noises deepened and became substantial to the listener's ear, till she could distinguish every soft and dreamy accent of the love songs, that died causelessly into funeral hymns. She shuddered at the unprovoked wrath which blazed up like the spontaneous kindling of flame, and she grew faint at the fearful merriment raging miserably around her. In the midst of this wild scene, where unbound passions jostled each other in a drunken career, there was one solemn voice of a man, and a manly and melodious voice it might once have been. He went to and fro continually, and his feet sounded upon the floor. In each member of that frenzied company, whose own burning thoughts had become their exclusive world, he sought an auditor for the story of his individual wrong, and interpreted their laughter and tears as his reward of scorn or pity. He spoke of woman's perfidy, of a wife who had broken her holiest vows, of a home and heart made desolate. Even as he went on, the shout, the laugh, the shriek, the sob, rose up in unison, till they changed into the hollow, fitful, and uneven sound of the wind, as it fought among the pine-trees on those three lonely hills. The lady looked up, and there was the withered woman smiling in her face.

"Couldst thou have thought there were such merry times in a madhouse?" inquired the latter.

"True, true," said the lady to herself, "there is mirth within its walls, but misery, misery without."

"Wouldst thou hear more?" demanded the old woman.

"There is one other voice I would fain listen to again," replied the lady, faintly.

"Then lay down thy head speedily upon my knees, that thou mayst get thee hence before the hour be past."

The golden skirts of day were yet lingering upon the hills, but deep shades obscured the hollow and the pool, as if sombre night were rising thence to overspread the world. Again that evil woman began to weave her spell. Long did it proceed unanswered, till the knolling of a bell stole in among the intervals of her words, like a clang that had travelled far over valley and rising ground, and was just ready to die in the air. The lady shook upon her companion's knees as she heard that boding sound. Stronger it grew and sadder, and deepened into the tone of a death-bell knolling dolefully from some ivy-mantled tower, and bearing tidings of mortality and woe to the cottage, to the hall, and to the solitary wayfarer, that all might weep for the doom appointed in turn to them. Then came a measured tread, passing slowly, slowly on, as of mourners with a coffin, their garments trailing on the ground, so that the ear could measure the length of their melancholy array. Before them went the priest reading the burial service, while the leaves of his book were rustling in the breeze. And though no voice but his was heard to speak aloud, still there were revilings and anathemas whispered, but distinct, from women and from men, breathed against the daughter who had wrung the aged hearts of her parents, the wife who had betrayed the trusting fondness of her husband, the mother who had sinned against natural affection and left her child to die. The sweeping sound of the funeral train faded away like a thin vapour, and the wind, that just before had seemed to shake the coffin-pall, moaned sadly round the verge of the hollow between three hills. But when the old woman stirred the kneeling lady she lifted not her head.

"Here has been a sweet hour's sport," said the withered crone, chuckling to herself.

Atmosphere

Its Relation to Effect, Recognition, and Theme

The term **atmosphere** denotes the general emotional conditions within which characters must act and readers must understand them. In "The Hollow of the Three Hills," the major character quite clearly is overcome by guilt, fear, and foreboding—attitudes with which the author colors the descriptions so that natural objects seem somehow to have a supernatural power capable of imposing this sense of guilt. Since a sensitive reader suspends his disbelief, he responds to the atmosphere much as the characters do. Consequently, this emotional element is added to his intellectual understanding of the conflict of the characters so that together they induce the effect. This dual emotional and intellectual **effect** makes possible the reader's **recognition:** his conscious awareness of his personal relationship to existence as it is experienced by the characters in this particular story. (Sometimes a first-person retrospective narrator experiences the recognition first and shares it with the reader.) When the reader generalizes his recognition, he arrives at the story's **theme.**

Clearly, atmosphere is a simpler term than effect, since one may identify the atmosphere of the story, yet fail to appreciate its total effect. Sometimes such a failure is the author's because he lacks the art to involve the emotions and the mind (hence the awareness) of the reader. Sometimes, however, the reader himself either cannot or will not become involved enough in a very well-written story to experience its effect. If either the reader or the writer fails, it will be almost impossible for the reader to identify the central theme because he gains no personal recognition from the effect.

The Contribution of the Setting

Awareness of the details of the setting is crucial to understanding any story. Since the **setting** establishes not only the historical and the specific time of the action but also the general geographic location and the precise scene where the action occurs, the setting is vital to the conflict. Besides providing a background that draws partly on the reader's own experience and information, the setting serves the simple, practical purpose of getting the characters together at the right instant. (Imagine what would happen to "The Hollow of the Three Hills" if the crone and the lady arrived at the pool on different days.) Also, especially by description of place, the emotional color of the atmosphere is established in the exposition. The more symbolic the story, the more important atmosphere will be, and consequently the more description of the setting will be used to produce the atmosphere. Regardless of the emphasis of the story, however, the reader who wishes eventually to identify themes in literature will do well to examine closely the setting of every story, not merely those in which atmosphere is emphasized.

The setting of the "The Hollow of the Three Hills" involves **historical time** and **specific time**. Specifically, it is the hour of sunset in October. The historical time is, clearly, completely outside real human experience. The omniscient narrator says that the story takes place "In those strange old times when fantastic dreams and madmen's reveries were realized among the actual circumstances of life. . . ." No reader now believes that such a period of history existed, but he does know that there have been periods when such beliefs were truly held. Nevertheless, he must willingly believe those characters are real or at least possible or he will miss the effect.

The Contribution of Realistic Detail

Though the time may be only generally established historically, both the specific time in any story and the specific place depend on realistic details. In "The Hollow of the Three Hills," many of the specific details of place and person reinforce the atmosphere of the ancient time and are involved directly in the creation of the atmosphere of the story. As an author frequently does if the atmosphere is a major factor in the effect, Hawthorne here begins the description of the place with the major details of the landscape: "Three little hills stood by each other." Then he leads the reader's eye from the top of the hills to the "hollow basin" in their midst, traces its edge as "mathematically circular," and names its diameter as two or three hundred feet and its depth such "that a stately cedar might but just be visible above the sides." Because the descriptive detail is so realistically precise, the supernatural elements also are made far more believable. The more Hawthorne moves from the general to the specific, the more he reinforces not only the distance in time but also its strangeness. That reinforcement comes precisely from the connotation of key nouns and adjectives—words chosen for their emotional color. The pines upon the hills and fringing the middle level of the hollow are dwarfed; the grass of the rest of the hollow is of the brown, dead color of October; and no trees grow, though moldering tree trunks lie about.

This specific spot where the action of the story is set contains a "formerly ... majestic oak," here described as "one of these masses of decaying wood," and "a pool of green and sluggish water" described also as "mantling"—covered with green, wrinkling scum—and "putrid." In such a setting typified by natural decay, in a spot where "no mortal could observe them in those strange old times," it is appropriate that the protagonist should meet a "meanly-dressed woman, of ill-favored aspect" so ancient "that even the space since she began to decay must have exceeded the ordinary term of human existence." Clearly the setting, both as time and place, general and specific, is a major factor in establishing the atmosphere of evil and foreboding.

The Contribution of Repetition as a Key to Symbol

Whenever an author takes such great care to describe in such minute detail the physical objects in the setting and to repeat those characteristics (for example, the decay of the trees) as characteristics of the persons, the reader may be sure that the story is symbolic. Therefore, he can interpret the story in part by methodically collecting examples of these repetitions. Usually the key to what he should collect comes early in the first paragraph. Hawthorne suggests the four major elements of "The Hollow of the Three Hills" in the very first sentence: "what is strange, what is old, fantastic dreams and madmen's reveries." The reader can see that the hollow in the hills with its basin, the traditions (themselves old) that this was the resort of a power of evil (the putrid pool) and his plighted subjects (the old crone) all are old and all are strange. Before he has read three sentences, the reader also must be aware that he must deal not only with age, but also with destruction, decay, and, especially, death. The lady is "blighted," the old woman is "withered, shrunken, and decrepit" and has begun to decay; the fallen tree trunks are "mouldering," and the pool is "putrid." Examples of the other elements are equally easy to collect.

This appearance of decay reflected in the crone should alert the reader to look for evidence of decay in the protagonist. Clearly, the decay of the young woman is not so much external as internal. If the reader collects his evidence carefully enough he will discover that each episode explores a more serious failure of the woman to meet her moral responsibilities. That each failure causes her progressively more pain as she accepts her guilt can also be verified. As she sees clearly the cost of her actions, particularly the cost to others, she is more and more overcome until she herself dies after the funeral of her child is enacted before her. The setting mirrors the young woman's moral decline.

The Contribution of Character

In the atmosphere of many stories, setting is the most important single factor. However, traits of the characters often contribute much to it. In "The Hollow of the Three Hills," for instance, the atmosphere of death and evil is perhaps more intensified by the old crone than even by the setting. Seen first as "withered, shrunken, and decrepit," her smile glimmers "like lamplight on the wall of a sepulchre." Her grey hair is "shrouded" by a hood, and she mutters—not murmurs—prayers "not meant to be acceptable in heaven." The atmosphere is intensified further when the narrator introduces the lady in "what should have been the fullest bloom of her years" as instead "pale and troubled and smitten with an untimely blight." Without question her attitudes and emotions, displayed completely by actions that are not habitual, depict some form of fear that permeates the atmosphere.

The Contribution of the Conflict

Although the setting and the characters establish the atmosphere, the nature and development of the conflict contribute greatly to it also. Since the reader's interest increases as the conflict approaches the climax, that contribution of action to the atmosphere should be expected. When the withered crone and the troubled lady meet at the mantling pool by the mouldering oak, the reader feels immediately that their actions must lead to disaster. When, in contrast to his own feeling of pity, the old withered woman smiles at their "pleasant meeting," the reader's mind adds his intellectual knowledge of what comes from compacts with the devil to his emotional involvement.

Effect

The Contribution of Atmosphere

Almost at the instant that the reader's intellectual awareness of the significance of an action joins his emotional response, the reader is involved in the effect of the story rather than simply in its atmosphere. From another way of looking at it, the atmosphere heightens the reader's awareness by involving his emotions so that when he begins to intuit the meaning of an action he understands the story as a complex whole instead of reacting only emotionally to elements of it. The atmosphere, then, is the emotional climate to which a reader responds and within which the characters understand each other and themselves. His response is both intellectual and emotional —not only to the emotional atmosphere but also to the factual level of characters, their conflict, and resolution. Most especially this effect produces the reader's recognition of his personal share of whatever aspect of the human condition concerns the author in that particular story.

The Contribution of Intellect

In "The Hollow of the Three Hills," the atmosphere of dread established by the setting and the introduction of the characters prepares the reader emotionally to align his sympathies with the lady against the crone. Simultaneously, the reader supplies from his own knowledge awareness of what comes from compacts with evil powers. Therefore, he is prepared both emotionally and intellectually for the smiling crone to set the conflict in action by saying that if the lady is bold her wish will be granted. He is fully aware, also, how the lady's desperate response—"I will do your bidding though I die"—commits her irreversibly to the conflict and foreshadows her death. The reader who wishes to experience completely the effect that the author intends must recreate in his own mind, as exactly as he can, what the author intended when he created his story. In this story, he must imagine precisely with what emotions the lady hears the voices in each vision, and he must also imagine with what evil joy the old woman watches that suffering. If he reads carefully, the reader will be intellectually aware by the end of the story both of how intensely the lady has been tormented by her every wrong action and of how each wrong seemed to come inevitably once that first error was made. Therefore, the reader should experience some emotional anguish because of his empathy for the woman's inability either to erase or to avoid her actions; and he should feel, also, some shock at her death despite his preparation for it by her response to the inciting action and in the whole atmosphere of the story. He should feel, also, a particularly strong revulsion for the withered woman's final chuckle at the "sweet hour's sport." Unless the reader examines carefully that revulsion, however, he may miss the final effect of the story.

Recognition: The Result of the Effect

With shock and dismay the reader may see that while he felt for the lady in her plight, he has maintained his superiority to her errors and has unconsciously felt that what she got, she deserved. The final result, then, is the reader's appalled recognition that he, like the crone, has enjoyed the woman's suffering and her death. If he enjoys his moral superiority, he must enjoy equally her death as the final horror of her life. With that recognition must come the reader's intellectual acceptance that he shares the evil of the crone.

Theme

The reader's recognition that he is evil as well as good permits him to perceive the story's theme: the sinner who recognizes his guilt but can do nothing but suffer the consciousness of it is superior to any human being (or crone) who judges that failure but finds himself without fault. Clearly, the atmosphere has helped the reader to feel the plight of a human being; the effect has enabled him to recognize his personal reaction to this aspect of the human condition; and his recognition of his own fallibility points the way to the theme of the story.

To be sure that he moves correctly from effect to theme, hence understands "The Hollow of the Three Hills" thoroughly, the reader still needs to study the details of the action in the dream-like recollections of the young woman. That these are complete scenes should prepare the reader for cumulative repetition somewhat like that in "Bartleby," with each episode and each of its parts progressively more serious. The reader will have to infer what action of the lady produces in each vision the particular effect on the lives of others. Studying details of both her reaction and that of the crone is essential to experiencing the effect of the story and hence to recognizing the story's theme.

A Mark of Hawthorne's Style: Ambiguity

Another recurrence in "The Hollow of the Three Hills" worth close study illustrates a famous Hawthorne trademark. He deliberately makes it equally possible that nature or that the supernatural causes certain events. For example, when day is dying in such a hollow in a real autumn, there often is a wind. In Hawthorne's fictitious hollow, where the lady also is dying as she examines the actions of her life and their consequences, each "fantastic dream" ends with the lady's raising her head to see nothing but the empty hollow and to hear the wind among the leaves. Also, just before the final scene, the sun touches only the hilltop as the light dies out of the hollow and from the pool. The poor light makes distinguishing shadow from reality difficult. Finally, when "The sweeping sound of the funeral train faded away like a thin vapor," the narrator explains that "the wind that just before had seemed to shake the coffin-pall, moaned sadly round the verge of the hollow between three hills." The reader has a choice: to believe that these things somehow "were realized among the actual circumstances of life" or to explain scientifically that some natural phenomenon (the wind) is interpreted by the young lady's sensitive and suggestive mind in her dreams and reveries. The ambiguity lets the story have the same effect on the reader who makes either choice. Hawthorne's deliberate use of ambiguity to avoid alienating a reader marks his skill in guaranteeing an effect that permits each reader's recognition and his subsequent possible assent to the story's universal theme.

The Universality of Themes

Universal themes are statements of facts of human experience in and of the universe and of human nature rather than prescriptions for living. For example, there is a great deal of difference between the moral of "The Unicorn in the Garden"—"Don't count your boobies until they are hatched" (practical advice for wives planning to institutionalize husbands whose abberations annoy the wives)—and its theme. Thurber's comment on mankind in the story touches numbers of universal themes: the need of human beings to share discoveries, the difficulty of communicating about things that matter (even the difficulty of finding someone with whom to attempt communication), the selfish preoccupations that blind men to the needs and values of others, and many more. Every man can testify that these statements are true in his knowledge and his experience. That —and not the skill or invention of the author—is what makes themes universal.

To say that many universal themes are present in every work of literature is not to suggest that a particular story has several central themes, any one of which equally well describes the major statement of the story about man's nature and the universe. Every facet of a well-written short story—even the glimpses of other universal truth —contributes to a single theme for that particular story. The central theme of "The Unicorn in the Garden" comprehends the whole story: the natures of the characters, the development and resolution of their conflict, and the quality of their insight into their motives. "The Unicorn in the Garden" says: a person who judges himself superior to another and attempts to use that supposed superiority against his inferior will always be defeated. The story does not preach that one should not feel or act that way. It only points out what happens universally if one does. A universal theme leaves a reader free to disregard it, but at his own risk.

By now the reader no doubt has realized that the theme of "The Unicorn in the Garden" is similar in many respects to the theme of "The Hollow of the Three Hills." That a tragic story and a comic one both make much the same statements about the danger of judging other persons testifies to the universality of the themes. That each story makes a different observation about particular consequences of such judgment marks the uniqueness of each story's individual universal comment.

Verifying the Theme as the Author's Personal View

A reader almost always may safely assume that the narrator's view of the human condition is also the author's view if, as Hawthorne does in "The Hollow of the Three Hills," an author chooses to use an omniscient narrator. However, the reader should beware of stating that a story's theme is the author's until he can show that theme recurring fairly consistently in other of the author's works. Hawthorne is ideal for study to verify an author's concern with a particular theme because, in "The Hollow of the Three Hills," Hawthorne treats even more directly than in most stories the theme of nearly every short story and novel that he ever wrote.

QUESTIONS FOR DISCUSSION AND WRITING

1. What is the setting of "The Hollow of the Three Hills"?
2. What is the relation between symbol and atmosphere?
3. What does realistic detail contribute to the atmosphere?
4. What does repetition contribute to the atmosphere?

5. What is the contribution of character to the atmosphere?
6. What does atmosphere contribute to the effect? what does the conflict?
7. What is the contribution of intellect to the effect?
8. Why are both the emotional and the intellectual effects necessary for the reader's recognition?
9. Why is the recognition necessary to the reader's statement of the theme?
10. What does Hawthorne's ambiguity contribute to the story?
11. What is the theme?
12. Is the theme of "The Hollow of the Three Hills" universal?
13. What is the setting of "Hop-Frog"?
14. Why is the setting so important to the atmosphere of "Hop-Frog"?
15. In "Hop-Frog" what is the emotional effect? the intellectual effect? the reader's recognition?
16. What universal relation between rationality, moral deliberation, and indulgence or control of emotions does the recognition permit the reader to see in "Hop-Frog"?
17. How is that theme in "Hop-Frog" similar to and different from the theme of "The Hollow of the Three Hills"? In other words, how do the two stories show about each other that universal themes stating facts about the nature of man apply in stories where they are not the central theme?
18. In what way are the crone, Hop-Frog, and the reader involved with the theme of "The Hollow of the Three Hills"?
19. In terms of the stories' themes, how similar are the defeats of Mrs. Quabarl in "The Schartz-Metterklume Method" and the wife in "The Unicorn in the Garden"?

The Secret Sharer

JOSEPH CONRAD

I

On my right hand there were lines of fishing-stakes resembling a mysterious system of half-submerged bamboo fences, incomprehensible in its division of the domain of tropical fishes, and crazy of aspect as if abandoned for ever by some nomad tribe of fishermen now gone to the other end of the ocean; for there was no sign of human habitation as far as the eye could reach. To the left a group of barren islets, suggesting ruins of stone walls, towers, and blockhouses, had its foundation set in a blue sea that itself looked solid, so still and stable did it lie below my feet; even the track of light from the westering sun shone smoothly, without that animated glitter which tells of an imperceptible ripple. And when I turned my head to take a parting glance at the tug which had just left us anchored outside the bar, I saw the straight line of the flat shore joined to the stable sea, edge to edge, with a perfect and unmarked closeness, in one levelled floor half brown, half blue under the enormous dome of the sky. Corresponding in their insignificance to the islets of the sea, two small clumps of trees, one on each side of the only fault in the impeccable joint, marked the mouth of the river Meinam we had just left on the first preparatory stage of our homeward journey; and, far back on the inland level, a larger and loftier mass, the grove surrounding the great Paknam pagoda, was the only thing on which the eye could rest from the vain task of exploring the monotonous sweep of the horizon. Here and there gleams as of a few scattered pieces of silver marked the windings of the great river; and on the nearest of them, just within the bar, the tug steaming right into the land became lost to my sight, hull and funnel and masts, as though the impassive earth had swallowed her up without an effort, without a tremor. My eye followed the light cloud of her smoke, now here, now there, above the plain, according to the devious curves of the stream, but always fainter and farther away, till I lost it at last behind the mitre-shaped hill of the great pagoda. And then I was left alone with my ship, anchored at the head of the Gulf of Siam.

She floated at the starting-point of a long journey, very still in an immense stillness, the shadows of her spars flung far to the eastward by the setting sun. At that moment I was alone on her decks. There was not a sound in her—and around us nothing moved, nothing lived, not a canoe on the water, not a bird in the air, not a cloud in the sky. In this breathless pause at the threshold of a long passage we seemed to be measuring our fitness for a long and arduous enterprise, the appointed task of both our existences to be carried out, far from all human eyes, with only sky and sea for spectators and for judges.

There must have been some glare in the air to interfere with one's sight, because it was only just before the sun left us that my roaming eyes made out beyond the highest ridge of the principal islet of the group something which did away with the solemnity of perfect solitude. The tide of darkness flowed on swiftly; and with tropical suddenness a swarm of stars came out above the shadowy earth, while I lingered yet, my hand resting lightly on my ship's rail as if on the shoulder of a trusted friend. But, with all that multitude of celestial bodies staring down at once, the comfort of quiet communion with her was gone for good. And there were also disturbing sounds by this time—voices, footsteps forward; the steward flitted along the main-deck, a busily ministering spirit; a hand-bell tinkled urgently under the poop-deck....

I found my two officers waiting for me near the supper table, in the lighted cuddy. We sat down at once, and as I helped the chief mate, I said:

"Are you aware that there is a ship anchored inside the islands? I saw her mastheads above the ridge as the sun went down."

He raised sharply his simple face, overcharged by a terrible growth of whisker, and emitted his usual ejaculations: "Bless my soul, sir! You don't say so!"

My second mate was a round-cheeked, silent young man, grave beyond his years, I thought; but as our eyes happened to meet I detected a slight quiver on his lips. I looked down at once. It was not my part to encourage sneering on board my ship. It must be said, too, that I knew very little of my officers. In consequence of certain events of no particular significance, except to myself, I had been appointed to the command only a fortnight before. Neither did I know much of the hands forward. All these people had been together for eighteen months or so, and my position was that of the only stranger on board. I mention this because it has some bearing on what is to follow. But what I felt most was my being a stranger to the ship; and if all the truth must be told, I was somewhat of a stranger to myself. The youngest man on board (barring the second mate), and untried as yet by a position of the fullest responsibility, I was willing to take the adequacy of the others for granted. They had simply to be equal to their tasks; but I wondered how far I should turn out faithful to that ideal conception of one's own personality every man sets up for himself secretly.

Meantime the chief mate, with an almost visible effect of collaboration on the part of his round eyes and frightful whiskers, was trying to evolve a theory of the anchored ship. His dominant trait was to take all things into earnest consideration. He was of a painstaking turn of mind. As he used to say, he "liked to account to himself" for practically everything that came in his way, down to a miserable scorpion he had found in his cabin a week before. The why and the wherefore of that scorpion—how it got on board and came to select his room rather than the pantry (which was a dark place and more what a scorpion would be partial to), and how on earth it managed to drown itself in the inkwell of his writing desk— had exercised him infinitely. The ship within the islands was much more easily accounted for; and just as we were about to rise from table he made his pronouncement. She was, he doubted not, a ship from home lately arrived. Probably she drew too much water to cross the bar except at the top of spring tides. Therefore she went into that natural harbour to wait for a few days in preference to remaining in an open roadstead.

"That's so," confirmed the second mate, suddenly, in his slightly hoarse voice. "She draws over twenty feet. She's the Liverpool ship *Sephora* with a cargo of coal. Hundred and twenty-three days from Cardiff."

We looked at him with surprise.

"The tugboat skipper told me when he came on board for your letters, sir," explained the young man. "He expects to take her up the river the day after tomorrow."

After thus overwhelming us with the extent of his information he slipped out of the cabin. The mate observed regretfully that he "could not account for that young fellow's whims." What prevented him telling us all about it at once, he wanted to know.

I detained him as he was making a move. For the last two days the crew had had plenty of hard work, and the night before they had very little sleep. I felt painfully that I—a stranger—was doing something unusual when I directed him to let all hands turn in without setting an anchor-watch. I proposed to keep on deck myself till one o-clock or thereabouts. I would get the second mate to relieve me at that hour.

"He will turn out the cook and the steward at four," I concluded, "and then give you a call. Of course at the slightest sign of any sort of wind we'll have the hands up and make a start at once."

He concealed his astonishment. "Very well, sir." Outside the cuddy he put his head in the second mate's door to inform him of my unheard-of caprice to take a five hours' anchor-watch on myself. I heard the other raise his voice incredulously—"What? The Captain himself?" Then a few more murmurs, a door closed, then another. A few moments later I went on deck.

My strangeness, which had made me sleepless, had prompted that unconventional arrangement, as if I had expected in those solitary hours of the night to get on terms with the ship of which I knew nothing, manned by men of whom I knew very little more. Fast alongside a wharf, littered like any ship in port with a tangle of unrelated things, invaded by unrelated shore people, I had hardly seen her yet properly. Now, as she lay cleared for sea, the stretch of her main-deck seemed to me very fine under the stars. Very-fine, very roomy for her size, and very inviting. I descended the poop and paced the waist, my mind picturing to myself the coming passage through the Malay Archipelago, down the Indian Ocean, and up the Atlantic. All its phases were familiar enough to me, every characteristic, all the alternatives which were likely to face me on the high seas—everything! ... except the novel responsibility of command. But I took heart from the reasonable thought that the ship was like other ships, the men like other men, and that the sea was not likely to keep any special surprises for my discomfiture.

Arrived at that comforting conclusion, I bethought myself of a cigar and went below to get it. All was still down there. Everybody at the after end of the ship was sleeping profoundly. I came out again on the quarter-deck, agreeably at ease in my sleeping-suit on that warm breathless night, barefooted, a glowing cigar in my teeth, and, going forward, I was met by the profound silence of the fore end of the ship. Only as I passed the door of the forecastle I heard a deep, quiet, trustful sigh of some sleeper inside. And suddenly I rejoiced in the great security of the sea as compared with the unrest of the land, in my choice of that untempted life presenting no disquieting problems, invested with an elementary moral beauty by the absolute straightforwardness of its appeal and by the singleness of its purpose.

The riding-light in the fore-rigging burned with a clear, untroubled, as if symbolic, flame, confident and bright in the mysterious shades of the night. Passing on my way aft along the other side of the ship, I observed that the rope side-ladder, put over, no doubt, for the master of the tug when he came to fetch away our letters, had not been hauled in as it should have been. I became annoyed at this, for exactitude in small matters is the very soul of discipline. Then

I reflected that I had myself peremptorily dismissed my officers from duty, and by my own act had prevented the anchor-watch being formally set and things properly attended to. I asked myself whether it was wise ever to interfere with the established routine of duties even from the kindest of motives. My action might have made me appear eccentric. Goodness only knew how that absurdly whiskered mate would "account" for my conduct, and what the whole ship thought of that informality of their new captain. I was vexed with myself.

Not from compunction certainly, but, as it were mechanically, I proceeded to get the ladder in myself. Now a side-ladder of that sort is a light affair and comes in easily, yet my vigorous tug, which should have brought it flying on board, merely recoiled upon my body in a totally unexpected jerk. What the devil! . . . I was so astounded by the immovableness of that ladder that I remained stock-still, trying to account for it to myself like that imbecile mate of mine. In the end, of course, I put my head over the rail.

The side of the ship made an opaque belt of shadow on the darkling glassy shimmer of the sea. But I saw at once something elongated and pale floating very close to the ladder. Before I could form a guess a faint flash of phosphorescent light, which seemed to issue suddenly from the naked body of a man, flickered in the sleeping water with the elusive, silent play of summer lightning in a night sky. With a gasp I saw revealed to my stare a pair of feet, the long legs, a broad livid back immersed right up to the neck in a greenish cadaverous glow. One hand, awash, clutched the bottom rung of the ladder. He was complete but for the head. A headless corpse! The cigar dropped out of my gaping mouth with a tiny plop and a short hiss quite audible in the absolute stillness of all things under heaven. At that I suppose he raised up his face, a dimly pale oval in the shadow of the ship's side. But even then I could only barely make out down there the shape of his black-haired head. However, it was enough for the horrid, frost-bound sensation which had gripped me about the chest to pass off. The moment of vain exclamations was past, too. I only climbed on the spare spar and leaned over the rail as far as I could, to bring my eyes nearer to that mystery floating alongside.

As he hung by the ladder, like a resting swimmer, the sea-lightning played about his limbs at every stir; and he appeared in it ghastly, silvery, fish-like. He remained as mute as a fish too. He made no motion to get out of the water, either. It was inconceivable that he should not attempt to come on board, and strangely troubling to suspect that perhaps he did not want to. And my first words were prompted by just that troubled incertitude.

"What's the matter?" I asked in my ordinary tone, speaking down to the face upturned exactly under mine.

"Cramp," it answered, no louder. Then slightly anxious, "I say, no need to call any one."

"I was not going to," I said.

"Are you alone on deck?"

"Yes."

I had somehow the impression that he was on the point of letting go the ladder to swim away beyond my ken—mysterious as he came. But, for the moment, this being appearing as if he had risen from the bottom of the sea (it was certainly the nearest land to the ship) wanted only to know the time. I told him. And he, down there, tentatively:

"I suppose your captain's turned in?"

"I am sure he isn't," I said.

He seemed to struggle with himself, for I heard something like the low, bitter murmur of doubt. "What's the good?" His next words came out with a hesitating effort.

"Look here, my man. Could you call him out quietly?"

I thought the time had come to declare myself.

"*I* am the captain."

I heard a "By Jove!" whispered at the level of the water. The phosphorescence flashed in the swirl of the water all about his limbs, his other hand seized the ladder.

"My name's Leggatt."

The voice was calm and resolute. A good voice. The self-possession of that man had somehow induced a corresponding state in myself. It was very quietly that I remarked:

"You must be a good swimmer."

"Yes. I've been in the water practically since nine o'clock. The question for me now is whether I am to let go this ladder and go on swimming till I sink from exhaustion, or—to come on board here."

I felt this was no mere formula of desperate speech, but a real alternative in the view of a strong soul. I should have gathered from this that he was young; indeed, it is only the young who are ever confronted by such clear issues. But at the time it was pure intuition on my part. A mysterious communication was established already between us two—in the face of that silent, darkened tropical sea. I was young, too; young enough to make no comment. The man in the water began suddenly to climb up the ladder, and I hastened away from the rail to fetch some clothes.

Before entering the cabin I stood still, listening in the lobby at the foot of the stairs. A faint snore came through the closed door of the chief mate's room. The second mate's door was on the hook, but the darkness in there was absolutely soundless. He, too, was young and could sleep like a stone. Remained the steward, but he was not likely to wake up before he was called. I got a sleeping-suit out of my room and, coming back on deck, saw the naked man from the sea sitting on the mainhatch, glimmering white in the darkness, his elbows on his knees and his head in his hands. In a moment he had concealed his damp body in a sleeping-suit of the same grey-stripe pattern as the one I was wearing and followed me like my double on the poop. Together we moved right aft, barefooted, silent.

"What is it?" I asked in a deadened voice, taking the lighted lamp out of the binnacle, and raising it to his face.

"An ugly business."

He had rather regular features; a good mouth; light eyes under somewhat heavy, dark eyebrows; a smooth, square forehead; no growth on his cheeks; a small, brown moustache, and a well-shaped, round chin. His expression was concentrated, meditative, under the inspecting light of the lamp I held up to his face; such as a man thinking hard in solitude might wear. My sleeping-suit was just right for his size. A well-knit young fellow of twenty-five at most. He caught his lower lip with the edge of white, even teeth.

"Yes," I said, replacing the lamp in the binnacle. The warm, heavy tropical night closed upon his head again.

"There's a ship over there," he murmured.

"Yes, I know. The *Sephora*. Did you know of us?"

"Hadn't the slightest idea. I am the mate of her—" He paused and corrected himself. "I should say I *was*."

"Aha! Something wrong?"

"Yes. Very wrong indeed. I've killed a man."

"What do you mean? Just now?"

"No, on the passage. Weeks ago. Thirty-nine south. When I say a man—"

"Fit of temper," I suggested, confidently.

The shadowy, dark head, like mine, seemed to nod imperceptibly above the ghostly grey of my sleeping-suit. It was, in the night, as though I had been faced by my own reflection in the depths of a sombre and immense mirror.

"A pretty thing to have to own up to for a Conway boy," murmured my double, distinctly.

"You're a Conway boy?"

"I am," he said, as if startled. Then, slowly... "Perhaps you too—"

It was so; but being a couple of years older I had left before he joined. After a quick interchange of dates a silence fell; and I thought suddenly of my absurd mate with his terrific whiskers and the "Bless my soul—you don't say so" type of intellect. My double gave me an inkling of his thoughts by saying: "My father's a parson in Norfolk. Do you see me before a judge and jury on that charge? For myself I can't see the necessity. There are fellows that an angel from heaven—And I am not that. He was one of those creatures that are just simmering all the time with a silly sort of wickedness. Miserable devils that have no business to live at all. He wouldn't do his duty and wouldn't let anybody else do theirs. But what's the good of talking! You know well enough the sort of ill-conditioned snarling cur—"

He appealed to me as if our experiences had been as identical as our clothes. And I knew well enough the pestiferous danger of such a character where there are no means of legal repression. And I knew well enough also that my double there was no homicidal ruffian. I did not think of asking him for details, and he told me the story roughly in brusque, disconnected sentences. I needed no more. I saw it all going on as though I were myself inside that other sleeping-suit.

"It happened while we were setting a reefed foresail, at dusk. Reefed foresail! You understand the sort of weather. The only sail we had left to keep the ship running; so you may guess what it had been like for days. Anxious sort of job, that. He gave me some of his cursed insolence at the sheet. I tell you I was overdone with this terrific weather that seemed to have no end to it. Terrific, I tell you—and a deep ship. I believe the fellow himself was half crazed with funk. It was not time for gentlemanly reproof, so I turned round and felled him like an ox. He up and at me. We closed just as an awful sea made for the ship. All hands saw it coming and took to the rigging, but I had him by the throat, and went on shaking him like a rat, the men above us yelling, 'Look out! look out!' Then a crash as if the sky had fallen on my head. They say that for over ten minutes hardly anything was to be seen of the ship—just the three masts and a bit of the forecastle head and of the poop all awash driving along in a smother of foam. It was a miracle that they found us, jammed together behind the forebits. It's clear that I meant business, because I was holding him by the throat still when they picked us up. He was black in the face. It was too much for them. It seems they rushed us aft together, gripped as we were, screaming 'Murder!' like a lot of lunatics, and broke into the cuddy. And the ship running for her life, touch and go all the time, any minute her last in a sea fit to turn your hair grey only a-looking at it. I understand that the skipper, too, started raving like the rest of them. The man had been deprived of sleep for more than a week, and to have this sprung on him at the height of a furious gale nearly drove him out of his mind. I wonder they didn't fling me overboard after getting the carcass of their precious shipmate out of my fingers. They had rather a job to separate us, I've been told. A sufficiently fierce story to make an old judge and a respectable jury sit up a bit. The first thing I heard when I came to myself was the maddening howling of that endless gale, and on that the voice of the old man. He was hanging onto my bunk, staring into my face out of his sou'wester.

" 'Mr. Leggatt, you have killed a man. You can act no longer as chief mate of this ship.' "

His care to subdue his voice made it sound monotonous. He rested a hand on the end of the skylight to steady himself with, and all that time did not stir a limb, so far as I could see. "Nice little tale for a quiet tea-party," he concluded in the same tone.

One of my hands, too, rested on the end of the skylight; neither did I stir a limb, so far as I knew. We stood less than a foot from each other. It occurred to me that if old "Bless my soul—you don't say so" were to put his head up the companion and catch sight of us, he would think he was seeing double, or imagine himself come upon a scene of weird witchcraft; the strange captain having a quiet confabulation by the wheel with his own grey ghost. I became very much concerned to prevent anything of the sort. I heard the other's soothing undertone.

"My father's a parson in Norfolk," it said. Evidently he had forgotten he had told me this important fact before. Truly a nice little tale.

"You had better slip down into my stateroom now," I said, moving off stealthily. My double followed my movements; our bare feet made no sound; I let him in, closed the door with care, and, after giving a call to the second mate, returned on deck for my relief.

"Not much sign of any wind yet," I remarked when he approached.

"No, sir. Not much," he assented, sleepily, in his hoarse voice, with just enough deference, no more, and barely suppressing a yawn.

"Well, that's all you have to look out for. You have got your orders."

"Yes, sir."

I paced a turn or two on the poop and saw him take up his position face forward with his elbow in the rat-lines of the mizzen-rigging before I went below. The mate's faint snoring was still going on peacefully. The cuddy lamp was burning over the table on which stood a vase with flowers, a polite attention from the ship's provision merchant—the last flowers we should see for the next three months at the very least. Two bunches of bananas hung from the beam symmetrically, one on each side of the rudder-casing. Everything was as before in the ship—except that two of her captain's sleeping-suits were simultaneously in use, one motionless in the cuddy, the other keeping very still in the captain's stateroom.

It must be explained here that my cabin had the form of the capital letter L, the door being within the angle and opening into the short part of the letter. A couch was to the left, the bed-place to the right; my writing-desk and the chronometers' table faced the door. But any one opening it, unless he stepped right inside, had no view of what I call the long (or vertical) part of the letter. It contained some lockers surmounted by a bookcase; and a few clothes, a thick jacket or two, caps, oilskin coat, and such like, hung on hooks. There was at the bottom of that part a door opening into my bath-room, which could be entered also directly from the saloon. But that way was never used.

The mysterious arrival had discovered the advantage of this particular shape. Entering my room, lighted strongly by a big bulkhead lamp swung on gimbals above my writing-desk, I did not see him anywhere till he stepped out quietly from behind the coats hung in the recessed part.

"I heard somebody moving about, and went in there at once," he whispered.

I, too, spoke under my breath.

"Nobody is likely to come in here without knocking and getting permission."

He nodded. His face was thin and the sunburn faded, as though he had been ill. And no wonder. He had been, I heard presently, kept under arrest in his cabin for nearly seven weeks. But there was nothing sickly in his eyes or in his expression. He was not a bit like me really; yet, as we stood leaning over my bed-place, whispering side by side, with our dark heads together and our backs to the door, anybody bold enough to open it stealthily would have been treated to the uncanny sight of a double captain busy talking in whispers with his other self.

"But all this doesn't tell me how you came to hang on to our side-ladder," I inquired, in the hardly audible murmurs we used, after he had told me something more of the proceedings on board the *Sephora* once the bad weather was over.

"When we sighted Java Head I had had time to think all those matters out several times over. I had six weeks of doing nothing else, and with only an hour or so every evening for a tramp on the quarterdeck."

He whispered, his arms folded on the side of my bed-place, staring through the open port. And I could imagine perfectly the manner of this thinking out—a stubborn if not a steadfast operation; something of which I should have been perfectly incapable.

"I reckoned it would be dark before we closed with the land," he continued, so low that I had to strain my hearing, near as we were to each other, shoulder touching shoulder almost. "So I asked to speak to the old man. He always seemed very sick when he came to see me —as if he could not look me in the face. You know, that foresail saved the ship. She was too deep to have run long under bare poles. And it was I that managed to set it for him. Anyway, he came. When I had him in my cabin—he stood by the door looking at me as if I had the halter round my neck already—I asked him right away to leave my cabin door unlocked at night while the ship was going through Sunda Straits. There would be the Java coast within two or three miles, off Angier Point. I wanted nothing more. I've had a prize for swimming my second year in the Conway."

"I can believe it," I breathed out.

"God only knows why they locked me in every night. To see some of their faces you'd have thought they were afraid I'd go about at night strangling people. Am I a murdering brute? Do I look it? By Jove! If I had been he wouldn't have trusted himself like that into my room. You'll say I might have chucked him aside and bolted out, there and then—it was dark already. Well, no. And for the same reason I wouldn't think of trying to smash the door. There would have been a rush to stop me at the noise, and I did not mean to get into a confounded scrimmage. Somebody else might have got killed—for I would not have broken out only to get chucked back, and I did not want any more of that work. He refused, looking more sick than ever. He was afraid of the men, and also of that old second mate of his who had been sailing with him for years—a grey-headed old humbug; and his steward, too, had been with him devil knows how long—seventeen years or more—a dogmatic sort of loafer who hated me like poison, just because I was the chief mate. No chief mate ever made more than one voyage in the *Sephora,* you know. Those two old chaps ran the ship. Devil only knows what the skipper wasn't afraid of (all his nerve went to pieces altogether in that hellish spell of bad weather we had)—of what the law would do to him—of his wife, perhaps. Oh, yes! she's on board. Though I don't think she would have meddled. She would have been only too glad to have me out of the ship in any way. The 'brand of Cain' business, don't you see. That's all right. I was ready enough to go off wandering on the face of the earth—and that was price enough to pay for an Abel of that sort. Anyhow, he wouldn't listen to me. 'This thing must take its course. I represent the law here.' He was shaking like a leaf. 'So you won't?' 'No!' 'Then I hope you will be able to sleep on that,' I said, and turned my back on him. 'I wonder that *you* can,' cries he, and locks the door.

"Well, after that, I couldn't. Not very well. That was three weeks ago. We have had a slow passage through the Java Sea; drifted about Carimata for ten days. When we anchored here they thought, I suppose, it was all right. The nearest land (and that's five miles) is the ship's destination; the consul would soon set about catching me; and there would have been no object in bolting to these islets there. I don't suppose there's a drop of water on them. I don't know how it was, but tonight that steward, after bringing me my supper, went out to let me eat it, and left the door unlocked. And I ate it—all there was, too. After I had finished I strolled out on the quarter-deck. I don't know that I meant to do anything. A breath of fresh air was all I wanted, I believe. Then a sudden temptation came over me. I kicked off my slippers and was in the water before I had made up my mind fairly. Somebody heard the splash and they raised an awful hullabaloo. 'He's gone! Lower the boats! He's committed suicide! No, he's swimming.' Certainly I was swimming. It's not so easy for a swimmer like me to commit suicide by drowning. I landed on the nearest islet before the boat left the ship's side. I heard them pulling about in the dark, hailing, and so on, but after a bit they gave up. Everything quieted down and the anchorage became as still as death. I sat down on a stone and began to think. I felt certain they would start searching for me at daylight. There was no place to hide on those stony things—and if there had been, what would have been the good? But now I was clear of that ship, I was not going back. So after a while I took off all my clothes, tied them up in a bundle with a stone inside, and dropped them in the deep water on the outer side of that islet. That was suicide enough for me. Let them think what they liked, but I didn't mean to drown myself. I meant to swim till I sank—but that's not the same thing. I struck out for another of these little islands, and it was from that one that I first saw your riding-light. Something to swim for. I went on easily, and on the way I came upon a flat rock a foot or two above water. In the daytime, I dare say, you might make it out with glass from your poop. I scrambled up on it and rested myself for a bit. Then I made another start. That last spell must have been over a mile."

His whisper was getting fainter and fainter, and all the time he stared straight out through the porthole, in which there was not even a star to be seen. I had not interrupted him. There was something that made comment impossible in his narrative, or perhaps in himself; a sort of feeling, a quality, which I can't find a name for. And when he ceased, all I found was a futile whisper: "So you swam for our light?"

"Yes—straight for it. It was something to swim for. I couldn't see any stars low down because the coast was in the way, and I couldn't see the land, either. The water was like glass. One might have been swimming in a confounded thousand-feet deep cistern with no place for scrambling out anywhere; but what I didn't like was the notion of swimming round and round like a crazed bullock before I gave out; and as I didn't mean to go back... No. Do you see me being hauled back, stark naked, off one of these little islands by the scruff of the neck and fighting like a wild beast? Somebody would have got killed for certain, and I did not want any of that. So I went on. Then your ladder—"

"Why didn't you hail the ship?" I asked, a little louder.

He touched my shoulder lightly. Lazy footsteps came right over our heads and stopped. The second mate had crossed from the other side of the poop and might have been hanging over the rail, for all we knew.

"He couldn't hear us talking—could he?" My double breathed into my very ear, anxiously.

His anxiety was an answer, a sufficient answer, to the question I had put to him. An answer containing all the difficulty of that situation. I closed the porthole quietly, to make sure. A louder word might have been overheard.

"Who's that?" he whispered then.

"My second mate. But I don't know much more of the fellow than you do."

And I told him a little about myself. I had been appointed to take charge while I least expected anything of the sort, not quite a fortnight ago. I didn't know either the ship or the people. Hadn't had the time in port to look about me or size anybody up. And as to the crew, all they knew was that I was appointed to take the ship home. For the rest, I was almost as much of a stranger on board as himself, I said. And at the moment I felt it most acutely. I felt that it would take very little to make me a suspect person in the eyes of the ship's company.

He had turned about meantime; and we, the two strangers in the ship, faced each other in identical attitudes.

"Your ladder—" he murmured, after a silence. "Who'd have thought of finding a ladder hanging over at night in a ship anchored out here! I felt just then a very unpleasant faintness. After the life

I've been leading for nine weeks, anybody would have got out of condition. I wasn't capable of swimming round as far as your rudder-chains. And, lo and behold! there was a ladder to get hold of. After I gripped it I said to myself, 'What's the good?' When I saw a man's head looking over I thought I would swim away presently and leave him shouting—in whatever language it was. I didn't mind being looked at. I—I liked it. And then you speaking to me so quietly—as if you had expected me—made me hold on a little longer. It had been a confounded lonely time—I don't mean while swimming. I was glad to talk a little to somebody that didn't belong to the *Sephora*. As to asking for the captain, that was a mere impulse. It could have been no use, with all the ship knowing about me and the other people pretty certain to be round here in the morning. I don't know—I wanted to be seen, to talk with somebody, before I went on. I don't know what I would have said. . . . 'Fine night, isn't it?' or something of the sort."

"Do you think they will be round here presently?" I asked with some incredulity.

"Quite likely," he said, faintly.

He looked extremely haggard all of a sudden. His head rolled on his shoulders.

"H'm. We shall see then. Meantime get into that bed," I whispered. "Want help? There."

It was a rather high bed-place with a set of drawers underneath. This amazing swimmer really needed the lift I gave him by seizing his leg. He tumbled in, rolled over on his back, and flung one arm across his eyes. And then, with his face nearly hidden, he must have looked exactly as I used to look in that bed. I gazed upon my other self for a while before drawing across carefully the two green serge curtains which ran on a brass rod. I thought for a moment of pinning them together for greater safety, but I sat down on the couch, and once there I felt unwilling to rise and hunt for a pin. I would do it in a moment. I was extremely tired, in a peculiarly intimate way, by the strain of stealthiness, by the effort of whispering and the general secrecy of this excitement. It was three o'clock by now and I had been on my feet since nine, but I was not sleepy; I could not have gone to sleep. I sat there, fagged out, looking at the curtains, trying to clear my mind of the confused sensation of being in two places at once, and greatly bothered by an exasperating knocking in my head. It was a relief to discover suddenly that it was not in my head at all, but on the outside of the door. Before I could collect myself, the words "Come in" were out of my mouth, and the steward entered with a tray, bringing in my morning coffee. I had slept, after all, and I was so frightened that I shouted, "This way! I am here, steward," as though he had been miles away. He put down the tray on the table next the couch and only then said, very quietly, "I can see you are here, sir." I felt him give me a keen look, but I dared not meet his eyes just then. He must have wondered why I had drawn the curtains of my bed before going to sleep on the couch. He went out, hooking the door open as usual.

I heard the crew washing decks above me. I knew I would have been told at once if there had been any wind. Calm, I thought, and I was doubly vexed. Indeed, I felt dual more than ever. The steward reappeared suddenly in the doorway. I jumped up from the couch so quickly that he gave a start.

"What do you want here?"

"Close your port, sir—they are washing decks."

"It is closed," I said, reddening.

"Very well, sir." But he did not move from the doorway and returned my stare in an extraordinary, equivocal manner for a time. Then his eyes wavered, all his expression changed, and in a voice unusually gentle, almost coaxingly:

"May I come in to take the empty cup away, sir?"

"Of course!" I turned my back on him while he popped in and out. Then I unhooked and closed the door and even pushed the bolt. This sort of thing could not go on very long. The cabin was as hot as an oven, too. I took a peep at my double, and discovered that he had not moved, his arm was still over his eyes; but his chest heaved; his hair was wet; his chin glistened with perspiration. I reached over him and opened the port.

"I must show myself on deck," I reflected.

Of course, theoretically, I could do what I liked, with no one to say nay to me within the whole circle of the horizon; but to lock my cabin door and take the key away I did not dare. Directly I put my head out of the companion I saw the group of my two officers, the second mate barefooted, the chief mate in long india-rubber boots, near the break of the poop, and the steward half-way down the poop-ladder talking to them eagerly. He happened to catch sight of me and dived, the second ran down on the main-deck shouting some order or other, and the chief mate came to meet me, touching his cap.

There was a sort of curiosity in his eye that I did not like. I don't know whether the steward had told them that I was "queer" only, or downright drunk, but I know the man meant to have a good look at me. I watched him coming with a smile which, as he got into point-blank range, took effect and froze his very whiskers. I did not give him time to open his lips.

"Square the yards by lifts and braces before the hands go to breakfast."

It was the first particular order I had given on board that ship; and I stayed on deck to see it executed, too. I had felt the need of asserting myself without loss of time. That sneering young cub got taken down a peg or two on that occasion, and I also seized the opportunity of having a good look at the face of every foremast man as they filed past me to go to the after braces. At breakfast time, eating nothing myself, I presided with such frigid dignity that the two mates were only too glad to escape from the cabin as soon as decency permitted; and all the time the dual working of my mind distracted me almost to the point of insanity. I was constantly watching myself, my secret self, as dependent on my actions as my own personality, sleeping in that bed, behind that door which faced me as I sat at the head of the table. It was very much like being mad, only it was worse because one was aware of it.

I had to shake him for a solid minute, but when at last he opened his eyes it was in the full possession of his senses, with an inquiring look.

"All's well so far," I whispered. "Now you must vanish into the bath-room."

He did so, as noiseless as a ghost, and then I rang for the steward, and facing him boldly, directed him to tidy up my stateroom while I was having my bath—"and be quick about it." As my tone admitted of no excuses, he said, "Yes, sir," and ran off to fetch his dust-pan and brushes. I took a bath and did most of my dressing, splashing, and whistling softly for the steward's edification, while the secret sharer of my life stood drawn up bolt upright in that little space, his face looking very sunken in daylight, his eyelids lowered under the stern, dark line of his eyebrows drawn together by a slight frown.

When I left him there to go back to my room the steward was finishing dusting. I sent for the mate and engaged him in some insignificant conversation. It was, as it were, trifling with the terrific character of his whiskers; but my object was to give him an opportunity for a good look at my cabin. And then I could at last shut, with a clear conscience, the door of my stateroom and get my double back into the recessed part. There was nothing else for it. He had to sit still on a small folding stool, half smothered by the heavy coats hanging there. We listened to the steward going into the bath-room out of the saloon, filling the water-bottles there, scrubbing the bath, setting things to rights, whisk, bang, clatter—out again into the saloon—turn the key—click. Such was my scheme for keeping my second self invisible. Nothing better could be contrived under the circumstances. And there we sat; I at my writing-desk ready to appear busy with some papers, he behind me out of sight of the door. It would not have been prudent to talk in daytime; and I could not have stood the excitement of that queer sense of whispering to myself. Now and then, glancing over my shoulder, I saw him far back there, sitting rigidly on the low stool, his bare feet close together, his arms folded, his head hanging on his breast—and perfectly still. Anybody would have taken him for me.

I was fascinated by it myself. Every moment I had to glance over my shoulder. I was looking at him when a voice outside the door said:

"Beg pardon, sir."

"Well!" ... I kept my eyes on him, and so when the voice outside the door announced, "There's a ship's boat coming our way, sir," I saw him give a start—the first movement he had made for hours. But he did not raise his bowed head.

"All right. Get the ladder over."

I hesitated. Should I whisper something to him? But what? His immobility seemed to have been never disturbed. What could I tell him he did not know already? ... Finally I went on deck.

II

The skipper of the *Sephora* had a thin red whisker all round his face, and the sort of complexion that goes with hair of that colour; also the particular, rather smeary shade of blue in the eyes. He was not exactly a showy figure; his shoulders were high, his stature but middling—one leg slightly more bandy than the other. He shook hands, looking vaguely around. A spiritless tenacity was his main characteristic, I judged. I behaved with a politeness which seemed to disconcert him. Perhaps he was shy. He mumbled to me as if he were ashamed of what he was saying; gave his name (it was something like Archbold—but at this distance of years I hardly am sure), his ship's name, and a few other particulars of that sort, in the manner of a criminal making a reluctant and doleful confession. He had had terrible weather on the passage out—terrible—terrible—wife aboard, too.

By this time we were seated in the cabin and the steward brought in a tray with a bottle and glasses. "Thanks! No." Never took liquor. Would have some water, though. He drank two tumblerfuls. Terrible thirsty work. Ever since daylight had been exploring the islands round his ship.

"What was that for—fun?" I asked, with an appearance of polite interest.

"No!" He sighed. "Painful duty."

As he persisted in his mumbling and I wanted my double to hear every word, I hit upon the notion of informing him that I regretted to say I was hard of hearing.

"Such a young man, too!" he nodded, keeping his smeary blue, unintelligent eyes fastened upon me. "What was the cause of it—some disease?" he inquired, without the least sympathy and as if he thought that, if so, I'd got no more than I deserved.

"Yes; disease," I admitted in a cheerful tone which seemed to shock him. But my point was gained, because he had to raise his voice to give me his tale. It is not worth while to record that version. It was just over two months since all this had happened, and he had thought so much about it that he seemed completely muddled as to its bearings, but still immensely impressed.

"What would you think of such a thing happening on board your own ship? I've had the *Sephora* for these fifteen years. I am a well-known shipmaster."

He was densely distressed—and perhaps I should have sympathized with him if I had been able to detach my mental vision from the unsuspected sharer of my cabin as though he were my second self. There he was on the other side of the bulkhead, four or five feet from us, no more, as we sat in the saloon. I looked politely at Captain Archbold (if that was his name), but it was the other I saw, in a grey sleeping-suit, seated on a low stool, his bare feet close together, his arms folded, and every word said between us falling into the ears of his dark head bowed on his chest.

"I have been at sea now, man and boy, for seven-and-thirty years, and I've never heard of such a thing happening in an English ship. And that it should be my ship. Wife on board, too."

I was hardly listening to him.

"Don't you think," I said, "that the heavy sea which, you told me, came aboard just then might have killed the man? I have seen the sheer weight of a sea kill a man very neatly, by simply breaking his neck."

"Good God!" he uttered, impressively, fixing his smeary blue eyes on me. "The sea! No man killed by the sea ever looked like that." He seemed positively scandalized at my suggestion. And as I gazed at him, certainly not prepared for anything original on his part, he advanced his head close to mine and thrust his tongue out at me so suddenly that I couldn't help starting back.

After scoring over my calmness in this graphic way he nodded wisely. If I had seen the sight, he assured me, I would never forget it as long as I lived. The weather was too bad to give the corpse a proper sea burial. So next day at dawn they took it up on the poop, covering its face with a bit of bunting; he read a short prayer, and then, just as it was, in its oilskins and long boots, they launched it amongst those mountainous seas that seemed ready every moment to swallow up the ship herself and the terrified lives on board of her.

"That reefed foresail saved you," I threw in.

"Under God—it did," he exclaimed fervently. "It was by a special mercy, I firmly believe, that it stood some of those hurricane squalls."

"It was the setting of that sail which—" I began.

"God's own hand in it," he interrupted me. "Nothing less could have done it. I don't mind telling you that I hardly dared to give the order. It seemed impossible that we could touch anything without losing it, and then our last hope would have been gone."

The terror of that gale was on him yet. I let him go on for a bit, then said, casually—as if returning to a minor subject:

"You were very anxious to give up your mate to the shore people, I believe?"

He was. To the law. His obscure tenacity on that point had in it something incomprehensible and a little awful; something, as it were, mystical, quite apart from his anxiety that he should not be suspected of "countenancing any doings of that sort." Seven-and-thirty virtuous years at sea, of which over twenty of immaculate command, and the last fifteen in the *Sephora,* seemed to have laid him under some pitiless obligation.

"And you know," he went on, groping shamefacedly amongst his feelings, "I did not engage that young fellow. His people had some interest with my owners. I was in a way forced to take him on. He looked very smart, very gentlemanly, and all that. But do you know —I never liked him, somehow. I am a plain man. You see, he wasn't exactly the sort for the chief mate of a ship like the *Sephora.*"

I had become so connected in thoughts and impressions with the secret sharer of my cabin that I felt as if I, personally, were being given to understand that I, too, was not the sort that would have done for the chief mate of a ship like the *Sephora*. I had no doubt of it in my mind.

"Not at all the style of man. You understand," he insisted, superfluously, looking at me.

I smiled urbanely. He seemed at a loss for a while.

"I suppose I must report a suicide."

"Beg pardon?"

"Sui-cide! That's what I'll have to write to my owners directly I get in."

"Unless you manage to recover him before tomorrow," I assented, dispassionately.... "I mean, alive."

He mumbled something which I really did not catch, and I turned my ear to him in a puzzled manner. He fairly bawled:

"The land—I say, the mainland is at least seven miles off my anchorage."

"About that."

My lack of excitement, of curiosity, of surprise, of any sort of pronounced interest, began to arouse his distrust. But except for the felicitous pretense of deafness I had not tried to pretend anything. I had felt utterly incapable of playing the part of ignorance properly, and therefore was afraid to try. It is also certain that he had brought some ready-made suspicions with him, and that he viewed my politeness as a strange and unnatural phenomenon. And yet how else could I have received him? Not heartily! That was impossible for psychological reasons, which I need not state here. My only object was to keep off his inquiries. Surlily? Yes, but surliness might have provoked a point-blank question. From its novelty to him and from its nature, punctilious courtesy was the manner best calculated to restrain the man. But there was the danger of his breaking through my defense bluntly. I could not, I think, have met him by a direct lie, also for psychological (not moral) reasons. If he had only known how afraid I was of his putting my feeling of identity with the other to the test!

But, strangely enough—(I thought of it only afterwards)—I believe that he was not a little disconcerted by the reverse side of that weird situation, by something in me that reminded him of the man he was seeking—suggested a mysterious similitude to the young fellow he had distrusted and disliked from the first.

However that might have been, the silence was not very prolonged. He took another oblique step.

"I reckon I had no more than a two-mile pull to your ship. Not a bit more."

"And quite enough, too, in this awful heat," I said.

Another pause full of mistrust followed. Necessity, they say, is mother of invention, but fear, too, is not barren of ingenious suggestions. And I was afraid he would ask me point-blank for news of my other self.

"Nice little saloon, isn't it?" I remarked, as if noticing for the first time the way his eyes roamed from one closed door to the other. "And very well fitted out, too. Here, for instance," I continued, reaching over the back of my seat negligently and flinging the door open, "is my bath-room."

He made an eager movement, but hardly gave it a glance. I got up, shut the door of the bath-room, and invited him to have a look round, as if I were very proud of my accommodation. He had to rise and be shown round, but he went through the business without any raptures whatever.

"And now we'll have a look at my stateroom," I declared, in a voice as loud as I dared to make it, crossing the cabin to the starboard side with purposely heavy steps.

He followed me in and gazed around. My intelligent double had vanished. I played my part.

"Very convenient—isn't it?"

"Very nice. Very comf..." He didn't finish and went out brusquely as if to escape from some unrighteous wiles of mine. But it was not to be. I had been too frightened not to feel vengeful; I felt I had him on the run, and I meant to keep him on the run. My polite insistence must have had something menacing in it, because he gave in suddenly. And I did not let him off a single item; mate's room, pantry, storerooms, the very sail-locker which was also under the poop—he had to look into them all. When at last I showed him out on the quarter-deck he drew a long, spiritless sigh, and mumbled dismally that he must really be going back to his ship now. I desired my mate, who had joined us, to see to the captain's boat.

The man of whiskers gave a blast on the whistle which he used to wear hanging round his neck, and yelled, *"Sephora's* away!" My double down there in my cabin must have heard, and certainly could not feel more relieved than I. Four fellows came running out from somewhere forward and went over the side, while my own men, appearing on deck too, lined the rail. I escorted my visitor to the gangway ceremoniously, and nearly overdid it. He was a tenacious beast. On the very ladder he lingered, and in that unique, guiltily conscientious manner of sticking to the point:

"I say . . . you . . . you don't think that—"

I covered his voice loudly:

"Certainly not. . . . I am delighted. Goodbye."

I had an idea of what he meant to say, and just saved myself by the privilege of defective hearing. He was too shaken generally to insist, but my mate, close witness of that parting, looked mystified and his face took on a thoughtful cast. As I did not want to appear as if I wished to avoid all communication with my officers, he had the opportunity to address me.

"Seems a very nice man. His boat's crew told our chaps a very extraordinary story, if what I am told by the steward is true. I suppose you had it from the captain, sir?"

"Yes. I had a story from the captain."

"A very horrible affair—isn't it, sir?"

"It is."

"Beats all these tales we hear about murders in Yankee ships."

"I don't think it beats them. I don't think it resembles them in the least."

"Bless my soul—you don't say so! But of course I've no acquaintance whatever with American ships, not I, so I couldn't go against your knowledge. It's horrible enough for me.... But the queerest part is that those fellows seemed to have some idea the man was hidden aboard here. They had really. Did you ever hear of such a thing?"

"Preposterous—isn't it?"

We were walking to and fro athwart the quarter-deck. No one of the crew forward could be seen (the day was Sunday), and the mate pursued:

"There was some little dispute about it. Our chaps took offense. 'As if we would harbour a thing like that,' they said. 'Wouldn't you like to look for him in our coalhole?' Quite a tiff. But they made it up in the end. I suppose he did drown himself. Don't you, sir?"

"I don't suppose anything."

"You have no doubt in the matter, sir?"

"None whatever."

I left him suddenly. I felt I was producing a bad impression, but with my double down there it was most trying to be on deck. And it was almost as trying to be below. Altogether a nerve-trying situation. But on the whole I felt less torn in two when I was with him. There was no one in the whole ship whom I dared take into my confidence. Since the hands had got to know his story, it would have been impossible to pass him off for any one else, and an accidental discovery was to be dreaded now more than ever....

The steward being engaged in laying the table for dinner, we could talk only with our eyes when I first went down. Later in the afternoon we had a cautious try at whispering. The Sunday quietness of the ship was against us; the elements, the men were against us—everything was against us in our secret partnership; time itself—for this could not go on forever. The very trust in Providence was, I suppose, denied to his guilt. Shall I confess that this thought cast me down very much? And as to the chapter of accidents which counts for so much in the book of success, I could only hope that it was closed. For what favourable accident could be expected?

"Did you hear everything?" were my first words as soon as we took up our position side by side, leaning over my bed-place.

He had. And the proof of it was his earnest whisper, "The man told you he hardly dared to give the order."

I understood the reference to be to that saving foresail.

"Yes. He was afraid of it being lost in the setting."

"I assure you he never gave the order. He may think he did, but he never gave it. He stood there with me on the break of the poop after the maintopsail blew away, and whimpered about our last hope—positively whimpered about it and nothing else—and the night coming on! To hear one's skipper go on like that in such weather was enough to drive any fellow out of his mind. It worked me up into a sort of desperation. I just took it into my own hands and went away from him, boiling, and—But what's the use telling you? *You* know! . . . Do you think that if I had not been pretty fierce with them I should have got the men to do anything? Not I! The bo's'n perhaps? Perhaps! It wasn't a heavy sea—it was a sea gone mad! I suppose the end of the world will be something like that; and a man may have the heart to see it coming once and be done with it—but to have to face it day after day—I don't blame anybody. I was precious little better than the rest. Only—I was an officer of that old coal-wagon, anyhow—"

"I quite understand," I conveyed that sincere assurance into his ear. He was out of breath with whispering; I could hear him pant slightly. It was all very simple. The same strung-up force which had given twenty-four men a chance, at least, for their lives, had, in a sort of recoil, crushed an unworthy mutinous existence.

But I had no leisure to weigh the merits of the matter—footsteps in the saloon, a heavy knock. "There's enough wind to get under way with, sir." Here was the call of a new claim upon my thoughts and even upon my feelings.

"Turn the hands up," I cried through the door. "I'll be on deck directly."

I was going out to make the acquaintance of my ship. Before I left the cabin our eyes met—the eyes of the only two strangers on board. I pointed to the recessed part where the little camp-stool awaited him and laid my fingers on my lips. He made a gesture—somewhat vague —a little mysterious, accompanied by a faint smile, as if of regret.

This is not the place to enlarge upon the sensations of a man who feels for the first time a ship move under his feet to his own independent word. In my case they were not unalloyed. I was not wholly alone with my command; for there was that stranger in my cabin. Or rather, I was not completely and wholly with her. Part of me was absent. That mental feeling of being in two places at once affected me physically as if the mood of secrecy had penetrated my very soul. Before an hour had elapsed since the ship had begun to move, having occasion to ask the mate (he stood by my side) to take a compass bearing of the Pagoda, I caught myself reaching up to his ear in whispers. I say I caught myself, but enough had escaped to startle the man. I can't describe it otherwise than by saying that he shied. A grave, preoccupied manner, as though he were in possession of some perplexing intelligence, did not leave him henceforth. A little later I moved away from the rail to look at the compass with such a stealthy gait that the helmsman noticed it—and I could not help noticing the unusual roundness of his eyes. These are trifling instances, though it's to no commander's advantage to be suspected of ludicrous eccentricities. But I was also more seriously affected. There are to a seaman certain words, gestures, that should in given conditions come as naturally, as instinctively as the winking of a menaced eye. A certain order should spring on to his lips without thinking; a certain sign should get itself made, so to speak, without reflection. But all unconscious alertness had abandoned me. I had to make an effort of will to recall myself back (from the cabin) to the conditions of the moment. I felt that I was appearing an irresolute commander to those people who were watching me more or less critically.

And, besides, there were the scares. On the second day out, for instance, coming off the deck in the afternoon (I had straw slippers on my bare feet) I stopped at the open pantry door and spoke to the steward. He was doing something there with his back to me. At the sound of my voice he nearly jumped out of his skin, as the saying is, and incidentally broke a cup.

"What on earth's the matter with you?" I asked, astonished.

He was extremely confused. "Beg your pardon, sir. I made sure you were in your cabin."

"You see I wasn't."

"No, sir. I could have sworn I had heard you moving in there not a moment ago. It's most extraordinary . . . very sorry, sir."

I passed on with an inward shudder. I was so identified with my secret double that I did not even mention the fact in those scanty, fearful whispers we exchanged. I suppose he had made some slight noise of some kind or other. It would have been miraculous if he hadn't at one time or another. And yet, haggard as he appeared, he looked always perfectly self-controlled, more than calm—almost invulnerable. On my suggestion he remained almost entirely in the bath-room, which, upon the whole, was the safest place. There could be really no shadow of an excuse for any one ever wanting to go in there, once the steward had done with it. It was a very tiny place. Sometimes he reclined on the floor, his legs bent, his head sustained on one elbow. At others I would find him on the camp stool, sitting in his grey sleeping-suit and with his cropped dark hair like a patient, unmoved convict. At night I would smuggle him into my bed-place, and we would whisper together with the regular footfalls of the officer of the watch passing and repassing over our heads. It was an infinitely miserable time. It was lucky that some tins of fine preserves were stowed in a locker in my stateroom; hard bread I could always get hold of; and so he lived on stewed chicken, paté de foie gras, asparagus, cooked oysters, sardines—on all sorts of abominable sham delicacies out of tins. My early morning coffee he always drank; and it was all I dared do for him in that respect.

Every day there was the horrible manoeuvring to go through so that my room and then the bath-room should be done in the usual way. I came to hate the sight of the steward, to abhor the voice of that harmless man. I felt that it was he who would bring on the disaster of discovery. It hung like a sword over our heads.

The fourth day out, I think (we were then working down the east side of the Gulf of Siam, tack for tack, in light winds and smooth water)—the fourth day, I say, of this miserable juggling with the unavoidable, as we sat at our evening meal, that man, whose slightest movement I dreaded, after putting down the dishes ran up on deck busily. This could not be dangerous. Presently he came down again;

and then it appeared that he had remembered a coat of mine which I had thrown over a rail to dry after having been wetted in a shower which had passed over the ship in the afternoon. Sitting stolidly at the head of the table I became terrified at the sight of the garment on his arm. Of course he made for my door. There was no time to lose.

"Steward," I thundered. My nerves were so shaken that I could not govern my voice and conceal my agitation. This was the sort of thing that made my terrifically whiskered mate tap his forehead with his forefinger. I had detected him using that gesture while talking on deck with a confidential air to the carpenter. It was too far to hear a word, but I had no doubt that this pantomine could only refer to the strange new captain.

"Yes, sir," the pale-faced steward turned resignedly to me. It was this maddening course of being shouted at, checked without rhyme or reason, arbitrarily chased out of my cabin, suddenly called into it, sent flying out of his pantry on incomprehensible errands, that accounted for the growing wretchedness of his expression.

"Where are you going with that coat?"

"To your room, sir."

"Is there another shower coming?"

"I'm sure I don't know, sir. Shall I go up again and see, sir?"

"No! never mind."

My object was attained, as of course my other self in there would have heard everything that passed. During this interlude my two officers never raised their eyes off their respective plates; but the lip of that confounded cub, the second mate, quivered visibly.

I expected the steward to hook my coat on and come out at once. He was very slow about it; but I dominated my nervousness sufficiently not to shout after him. Suddenly I became aware (it could be heard plainly enough) that the fellow for some reason or other was opening the door of the bath-room. It was the end. The place was literally not big enough to swing a cat in. My voice died in my throat and I went stony all over. I expected to hear a yell of surprise and terror, and made a movement, but had not the strength to get on my legs. Everything remained still. Had my second self taken the poor wretch by the throat? I don't know what I could have done next moment if I had not seen the steward come out of my room, close the door, and then stand quietly by the sideboard.

"Saved," I thought. "But, no! Lost! Gone! He was gone!"

I laid my knife and fork down and leaned back in my chair. My head swam. After a while, when sufficiently recovered to speak in a steady voice, I instructed my mate to put the ship round at eight o'clock himself.

"I won't come on deck," I went on. "I think I'll turn in, and unless the wind shifts I don't want to be disturbed before midnight. I feel a bit seedy."

"You did look middling bad a little while ago," the chief mate remarked without showing any great concern.

They both went out, and I stared at the steward clearing the table. There was nothing to be read on that wretched man's face. But why did he avoid my eyes, I asked myself. Then I thought I should like to hear the sound of his voice.

"Steward!"

"Sir!" Startled as usual.

"Where did you hang up that coat?"

"In the bath-room, sir." The usual anxious tone. "It's not quite dry yet, sir."

For some time longer I sat in the cuddy. Had my double vanished as he had come? But of his coming there was an explanation, whereas his disappearance would be inexplicable.... I went slowly into my dark room, shut the door, lighted the lamp, and for a time dared not turn round. When at last I did I saw him standing bolt-upright in the narrow recessed part. It would not be true to say I had a shock, but an irresistible doubt of his bodily existence flitted through my mind. Can it be, I asked myself, that he is not visible to other eyes than mine? It was like being haunted. Motionless, with a grave face, he raised his hands slightly at me in a gesture which meant clearly, "Heavens! what a narrow escape!" Narrow indeed. I think I had come creeping quietly as near insanity as any man who has not actually gone over the border. That gesture restrained me, so to speak.

The mate with the terrific whiskers was now putting the ship on the other tack. In the moment of profound silence which follows upon the hands going to their stations I heard on the poop his raised voice: "Hard alee!" and the distant shout of the order repeated on the main-deck. The sails, in that light breeze, made but a faint fluttering noise. It ceased. The ship was coming round slowly; I held my breath in the renewed stillness of expectation; one wouldn't have thought that there was a single living soul on her decks. A sudden brisk shout, "Mainsail haul!" broke the spell, and in the noisy cries and rush overhead of the men running away with the main-brace we two, down in my cabin, came together in our usual position by the bed-place.

He did not wait for my question. "I heard him fumbling here and just managed to squat myself down in the bath," he whispered to me. "The fellow only opened the door and put his arm in to hang the coat up. All the same—"

"I never thought of that," I whispered back, even more appalled than before at the closeness of the shave, and marvelling at that something unyielding in his character which was carrying him through so finely. There was no agitation in his whisper. Whoever was being driven distracted, it was not he. He was sane. And the proof of his sanity was continued when he took up the whispering again.

"It would never do for me to come to life again."

It was something that a ghost might have said. But what he was alluding to was his old captain's reluctant admission of the theory of suicide. It would obviously serve his turn—if I had understood at all the view which seemed to govern the unalterable purpose of his action.

"You must maroon me as soon as ever you can get amongst these islands off the Cambodge shore," he went on.

"Maroon you! We are not living in a boy's adventure tale," I protested. His scornful whispering took me up.

"We aren't indeed! There's nothing of a boy's tale in this. But there's nothing else for it. I want no more. You don't suppose I am afraid of what can be done to me? Prison or gallows or whatever they may please. But you don't see me coming back to explain such things to an old fellow in a wig and twelve respectable tradesmen, do you? What can they know whether I am guilty or not—or of *what* I am guilty, either? That's my affair. What does the Bible say? 'Driven off the face of the earth.' Very well. I am off the face of the earth now. As I came at night so I shall go."

"Impossible!" I murmured. "You can't."

"Can't? . . . Not naked like a soul on the Day of Judgment, I shall freeze on to this sleeping-suit. The Last Day is not yet—and . . . you have understood thoroughly. Didn't you?"

I felt suddenly ashamed of myself. I may say truly that I understood—and my hesitation in letting that man swim away from my ship's side had been a mere sham sentiment, a sort of cowardice.

"It can't be done now till next night," I breathed out. "The ship is on the off-shore tack and the wind may fail us."

"As long as I know that you understand," he whispered. "But of course you do. It's a great satisfaction to have got somebody to understand. You seem to have been there on purpose." And in the same whisper, as if we two whenever we talked had to say things to each other which were not fit for the world to hear, he added, "It's very wonderful."

We remained side by side talking in our secret way—but sometimes silent or just exchanging a whispered word or two at long intervals. And as usual he stared through the port. A breath of wind came now and again into our faces. The ship might have been moored in dock, so gently and on an even keel she slipped through the water, that did not murmur even at our passage, shadowy and silent like a phantom sea.

At midnight I went on deck, and to my mate's great surprise put the ship round on the other tack. His terrible whiskers flitted round me in silent criticism. I certainly should not have done it if it had been only a question of getting out of that sleepy gulf as quickly as possible. I believe he told the second mate, who relieved him, that it was a great want of judgment. The other only yawned. That intolerable cub shuffled about so sleepily and lolled against the rails in such a slack, improper fashion that I came down on him sharply.

"Aren't you properly awake yet?"

"Yes, sir! I am awake."

"Well, then, be good enough to hold yourself as if you were. And keep a look-out. If there's any current we'll be closing with some islands before daylight."

The east side of the gulf's fringed with islands, some solitary, others in groups. On the blue background of the high coast they seem to float on silvery patches of calm water, arid and grey, or dark green and rounded like clumps of evergreen bushes, with the larger ones, a mile or two long, showing the outlines of ridges, ribs of grey rock under the dank mantle of matted leafage. Unknown to trade, to travel, almost to geography, the manner of life they harbour is an unsolved secret. There must be villages—settlements of fishermen at least—on the largest of them, and some communication with the world is probably kept up by native craft. But all that forenoon, as we headed for them, fanned along by the faintest of breezes, I saw no sign of man or canoe in the field of the telescope I kept on pointing at the scattered group.

At noon I gave no orders for a change of course, and the mate's whiskers became much concerned and seemed to be offering themselves unduly to my notice. At last I said:

"I am going to stand right in. Quite in—as far as I can take her."

The stare of extreme surprise imparted an air of ferocity also to his eyes, and he looked truly terrific for a moment.

"We're not doing well in the middle of the gulf," I continued, casually. "I am going to look for the land breezes tonight."

"Bless my soul! Do you mean, sir, in the dark amongst the lot of all them islands and reefs and shoals?"

"Well—if there are any regular land breezes at all on this coast one must get close inshore to find them, mustn't one?"

"Bless my soul!" he exclaimed again under his breath. All that afternoon he wore a dreamy, contemplative appearance which in him was a mark of perplexity. After dinner I went into my stateroom as if I meant to take some rest. There we two bent our dark heads over a half-unrolled chart lying on my bed.

"There," I said. "It's got to be Koh-ring. I've been looking at it ever since sunrise. It has got two hills and a low point. It must be inhabited. And on the coast opposite there is what looks like the mouth of a biggish river—with some town, no doubt, not far up. It's the best chance for you that I can see."

"Anything. Koh-ring let it be."

He looked thoughtfully at the chart as if surveying chances and distances from a lofty height—and following with his eyes his own figure wandering on the blank land of Cochin-China, and then passing off that piece of paper clean out of sight into uncharted regions. And it was as if the ship had two captains to plan her course for her. I had been so worried and restless running up and down that I had not had the patience to dress that day. I had remained in my sleeping-suit, with straw slippers and a soft floppy hat. The closeness of the heat in the gulf had been most oppressive, and the crew were used to see me wandering in that airy attire.

"She will clear the south point as she heads now," I whispered into his ear. "Goodness only knows when, though, but certainly after dark. I'll edge her in to half a mile, as far as I may be able to judge in the dark—"

"Be careful," he murmured, warningly—and I realized suddenly that all my future, the only future for which I was fit, would perhaps go irretrievably to pieces in any mishap to my first command.

I could not stop a moment longer in the room. I motioned him to get out of sight and made my way on the poop. That unplayful cub had the watch. I walked up and down for a while thinking things out, then beckoned him over.

"Send a couple of hands to open the two quarter-deck ports," I said, mildly.

He actually had the impudence, or else so forgot himself in his wonder at such an incomprehensible order, as to repeat:

"Open the quarter-deck ports! What for, sir?"

"The only reason you need concern yourself about is because I tell you to do so. Have them opened wide and fastened properly."

He reddened and went off, but I believe made some jeering remark to the carpenter as to the sensible practice of ventilating a ship's quarter-deck. I know he popped into the mate's cabin to impart the fact to him because the whiskers came on deck, as it were by chance, and stole glances at me from below—for signs of lunacy or drunkenness, I suppose.

A little before supper, feeling more restless than ever, I rejoined, for a moment, my second self. And to find him sitting so quietly was surprising, like something against nature, inhuman.

I developed my plan in a hurried whisper.

"I shall stand in as close as I dare and then put her round. I will presently find means to smuggle you out of here into the sail-locker, which communicates with the lobby. But there is an opening, a sort of square for hauling the sails out, which gives straight on the quarter-deck and which is never closed in fine weather, so as to give air to the sails. When the ship's way is deadened in stays and all the hands are aft at the main-braces you will have a clear road to slip out and get overboard through the open quarter-deck port. I've had them both fastened up. Use a rope's end to lower yourself into the water so as to avoid a splash—you know. It could be heard and cause some beastly complication."

He kept silent for a while, then whispered, "I understand."

"I won't be there to see you go," I began with an effort. "The rest ... I only hope I have understood, too."

"You have. From first to last"—and for the first time there seemed to be a faltering, something strained in his whisper. He caught hold of my arm, but the ringing of the supper bell made me start. He didn't, though; he only released his grip.

After supper I didn't come below again till well past eight o'clock. The faint, steady breeze was loaded with dew; and the wet, darkened sails held all there was of propelling power in it. The night, clear and starry, sparkled darkly, and the opaque, lightless patches shifting slowly against the low stars were the drifting islets. On the port bow there was a big one more distant and shadowily imposing by the great space of sky it eclipsed.

On opening the door I had a back view of my very own self looking at a chart. He had come out of the recess and was standing near the table.

"Quite dark enough," I whispered.

He stepped back and leaned against my bed with a level, quiet glance. I sat on the couch. We had nothing to say to each other. Over our heads the officer of the watch moved here and there. Then I heard him move quickly. I knew what that meant. He was making for the companion; and presently his voice was outside my door.

"We are drawing in pretty fast, sir. Land looks rather close."

"Very well," I answered. "I am coming on deck directly."

I waited till he was gone out of the cuddy, then rose. My double moved too. The time had come to exchange our last whispers, for neither of us was ever to hear each other's natural voice.

"Look here!" I opened a drawer and took out three sovereigns. "Take this anyhow. I've got six and I'd give you the lot, only I must keep a little money to buy some fruit and vegetables for the crew from native boats as we go through Sunda Straits."

He shook his head.

"Take it," I urged him, whispering desperately. "No one can tell what—"

He smiled and slapped meaningly the only pocket of the sleeping-jacket. It was not safe, certainly. But I produced a large old silk handkerchief of mine, and tying the three pieces of gold in a corner, pressed it on him. He was touched, I suppose, because he took it at last and tied it quickly round his waist under the jacket, on his bare skin.

Our eyes met; several seconds elapsed, till, our glances still mingled, I extended my hand and turned the lamp out. Then I passed through the cuddy, leaving the door of my room wide open....

"Steward!"

He was still lingering in the pantry in the greatness of his zeal, giving a rub-up to a plated cruet stand the last thing before going to bed. Being careful not to wake up the mate, whose room was opposite, I spoke in an undertone.

He looked round anxiously. "Sir!"

"Can you get me a little hot water from the galley?"

"I am afraid, sir, the galley fire's been out for some time now."

"Go and see."

He flew up the stairs.

"Now," I whispered, loudly, into the saloon—too loudly, perhaps, but I was afraid I couldn't make a sound. He was by my side in an instant—the double captain slipped past the stairs—through a tiny dark passage . . . a sliding door. We were in the sail-locker, scrambling on our knees over the sails. A sudden thought struck me. I saw myself wandering barefooted, bareheaded, the sun beating on my dark poll. I snatched off my floppy hat and tried hurriedly in the dark to ram it on my other self. He dodged and fended off silently. I wonder what he thought had come to me before he understood and suddenly desisted. Our hands met gropingly, lingered united in a steady, motionless clasp for a second. . . . No word was breathed by either of us when they separated.

I was standing quietly by the pantry door when the steward returned.

"Sorry, sir. Kettle barely warm. Shall I light the spirit-lamp?"

"Never mind."

I came out on deck slowly. It was now a matter of conscience to shave the land as close as possible—for now he must go overboard whenever the ship was put in stays. Must! There could be no going back for him. After a moment I walked over to leeward and my heart flew into my mouth at the nearness of the land on the bow. Under any other circumstances I would not have held on a minute longer. The second mate had followed me anxiously.

I looked on till I felt I could command my voice.

"She will weather," I said then in a quiet tone.

"Are you going to try that, sir?" he stammered out incredulously.

I took no notice of him and raised my tone just enough to be heard by the helmsman.

"Keep her good full."

"Good full, sir."

The wind fanned my cheek, the sails slept, the world was silent. The strain of watching the dark loom of the land grow bigger and denser was too much for me. I had shut my eyes—because the ship must go closer. She must! The stillness was intolerable. Were we standing still?

When I opened my eyes the second view started my heart with a thump. The black southern hill of Koh-ring seemed to hang right over the ship like a towering fragment of the everlasting night. On that enormous mass of blackness there was not a gleam to be seen, not a sound to be heard. It was gliding irresistibly towards us and yet seemed already within reach of the hand. I saw the vague figures of the watch grouped in the waist, gazing in awed silence.

"Are you going on, sir?" inquired an unsteady voice at my elbow.

I ignored it. I had to go on.

"Keep her full. Don't check her way. That won't do now," I said, warningly.

"I can't see the sails very well," the helmsman answered me, in strange, quavering tones.

Was she close enough? Already she was, I won't say in the shadow of the land, but in the very blackness of it, already swallowed up as it were, gone too close to be recalled, gone from me altogether.

"Give the mate a call," I said to the young man who stood at my elbow as still as death. "And turn all hands up."

My tone had a borrowed loudness reverberated from the height of the land. Several voices cried out together: "We are all on deck, sir."

Then stillness again, with the great shadow gliding closer, towering higher, without a light, without a sound. Such a hush had fallen on the ship that she might have been a bark of the dead floating in slowly under the very gate of Erebus.

"My God! Where are we?"

It was the mate moaning at my elbow. He was thunderstruck, and as it were deprived of the moral support of his whiskers. He clapped his hands and absolutely cried out, "Lost!"

"Be quiet," I said, sternly.

He lowered his tone, but I saw the shadowy gesture of his despair.

"What are we doing here?"

"Looking for the land wind."

He made as if to tear his hair, and addressed me recklessly.

"She will never get out. You have done it, sir. I knew it'd end in something like this. She will never weather, and you are too close now to stay. She'll drift ashore before she's round. O my God!"

I caught his arm as he was raising it to batter his poor devoted head, and shook it violently.

"She's ashore already," he wailed, trying to tear himself away.

"Is she? . . . Keep good full there!"

"Good full, sir," cried the helmsman in a frightened, thin, child-like voice.

I hadn't let go the mate's arm and went on shaking it. "Ready about, do you hear? You go forward"—shake—"and stop there"—shake—"and hold your noise"—shake—"and see these head-sheets properly overhauled"—shake, shake—shake.

And all the time I dared not look towards the land lest my heart should fail me. I released my grip at last and he ran forward as if fleeing for dear life.

I wondered what my double there in the sail-locker thought of this commotion. He was able to hear everything—and perhaps he was able to understand why, on my conscience, it had to be thus close—no less. My first order "Hard alee!" re-echoed ominously under the towering shadow of Koh-ring as if I had shouted in a mountain gorge. And then I watched the land intently. In that smooth water and light wind it was impossible to feel the ship coming-to. No! I could not feel her. And my second self was making now ready to slip out and lower himself overboard. Perhaps he was gone already . . . ?

The great black mass brooding over our very mastheads began to pivot away from the ship's side silently. And now I forgot the secret stranger ready to depart, and remembered only that I was a total stranger to the ship. I did not know her. Would she do it? How was she to be handled?

I swung the mainyard and waited helplessly. She was perhaps stopped, and her very fate hung in the balance, with the black mass of Koh-ring like the gate of the everlasting night towering over her taffrail. What would she do now? Had she way on her yet? I stepped to the side swiftly, and on the shadowy water I could see nothing except a faint phosphorescent flash revealing the glassy smoothness of the sleeping surface. It was impossible to tell—and I had not learned yet the feel of my ship. Was she moving? What I needed was something easily seen, a piece of paper, which I could throw overboard and watch. I had nothing on me. To run down for it I didn't dare. There was no time. All at once my strained, yearning stare distinguished a white object floating within a yard of the ship's side. White on the black water. A phosphorescent flash passed under it. What was that thing? ... I recognized my own floppy hat. It must have fallen off his head ... and he didn't bother. Now I had what I wanted—the saving mark for my eyes. But I hardly thought of my other self, now gone from the ship, to be hidden for ever from all friendly faces, to be a fugitive and a vagabond on the earth, with no brand of the curse on his sane forehead to stay a slaying hand ... too proud to explain.

And I watched the hat—the expression of my sudden pity for his mere flesh. It had been meant to save his homeless head from the dangers of the sun. And now—behold—it was saving the ship, by serving me for a mark to help out the ignorance of my strangeness. Ha! It was drifting forward, warning me just in time that the ship had gathered sternway.

"Shift the helm," I said in a low voice to the seaman standing still like a statue.

The man's eyes glistened wildly in the binnacle light as he jumped round to the other side and spun round the wheel.

I walked to the break of the poop. On the overshadowed deck all hands stood by the forebraces waiting for my order. The stars ahead seemed to be gliding from right to left. And all was so still in the world that I heard the quiet remark, "She's round," passed in a tone of intense relief between two seamen.

"Let go and haul."

The foreyards ran round with a great noise, amidst cheery cries.

And now the frightful whiskers made themselves heard giving various orders. Already the ship was drawing ahead. And I was alone with her. Nothing! no one in the world should stand now between us, throwing a shadow on the way of silent knowledge and mute affection, the perfect communion of a seaman with his first command.

Walking to the taffrail, I was in time to make out, on the very edge of a darkness thrown by a towering black mass like the very gateway of Erebus—yes, I was in time to catch an evanescent glimpse of my white hat left behind to mark the spot where the secret sharer of my cabin and of my thoughts, as though he were my second self, had lowered himself into the water to take his punishment; a free man, a proud swimmer striking out for a new destiny.

Theme

The reader should come to recognize some precise comment on the human condition that underlies the conflict of the characters in every story. In "The Secret Sharer," the author invents a narrator-protagonist who involves the reader deliberately in that narrator's own awareness as it develops throughout the story. The recognition necessary for theme is delayed in stories about characters who are themselves blind or whose narrators do not interpret for the reader. In "Hop-Frog," the reader feels emotionally the effect of horror at the burning of the king, and he intellectually appreciates the inevitability of some such act once Hop-Frog's humanity is removed by wine. However, not until the reader experiences this dual effect can he recognize that he has a dwarf in himself who has encouraged Hop-Frog's revenge without concern for its outcome. In "The Hollow of the Three Hills," the reader's recognition again is delayed until he not only shares the suffering of the young lady and feels revulsion at the crone's relishing her pain but also until, intellectually, he thinks of his moral superiority to her. Only after the resolution is he prepared to recognize that his own intellectual pride is condemned by the author's identification of the reader's sense of superiority with the crone's devilish pleasure. In "The Unicorn in the Garden," Thurber states the reader's recognition as a humorous moral: "Don't count your boobies before they are hatched." Again, that awareness comes only after the reader delights emotionally in the complete reversal of the wife's expectations and becomes aware intellectually that the wife has mistakenly believed that she knows her husband thoroughly. Recognition, then, is the reader's awareness of his very specific personal relationship to that single story. When a reader generalizes the recognition of a particular story, he arrives at a universal theme that can be discovered in very diverse literature. Theme, then, is the generalization of a reader's recognition to a level of universal significance.

The Importance of Point of View

Without question, Conrad's subject in "The Secret Sharer" is serious; therefore, he must wish to communicate some understanding of the human condition that he considers worth the reader's effort. For that communication he chooses to illuminate a period of crisis in the life of a young and intelligent man. The introspective and intelligent narrator shares in retrospect every step of his experience with Leggatt and with himself and his ship. Even though many years have elapsed, every detail of his action is still vivid, and his recollection of his emotions and his thoughts is extremely clear. Furthermore, he now can see clearly both the universal truths about the human condition that his experience revealed to him and how that recognition developed as his relationship with Leggatt unfolded.

Since Conrad wants the reader to participate consciously in the narrator's recognition at each moment of the action, he has the narrator elaborately explain both his intellectual and emotional awareness and, almost without exception, provide some physical symbol for whatever idea engrosses him at the time of an action. The reader must not only follow the action but also identify these symbols and recognize their parallel in the internal intellectual world of the narrator. Then the reader can safely interpret them also in terms of his own personal experience.

Clues for Identifying Symbols

Just as in "The Hollow of the Three Hills" and all other symbolic stories, any object or idea or action that is repeated constantly must be thought of as symbolic. Deciding precisely what a symbol stands for is a matter first of looking closely at the literal object for its real qualities and second of determining how each quality is compared to, reflected in, or associated with some attitude or aspect of a character, a problem, or an action. Certain universal symbols will be even more obvious because of their sheer size, their distance from man, or their importance in relation to the situation in which they occur. The sea as the unknown or psychologically as the unconscious, the stars as observers for the power of the universe, nakedness as the unprotected natural man—all these have to be recognized as universal symbols. The third most important signal that symbols are present—besides universality and repetition—is the recurrence of objects or persons in the same sequence or relationship. The most obvious sequence symbol from "The Secret Sharer" is, of course, the close identification of the Captain and Leggatt, each in pajamas. In this particular story, a unique stylistic clue to symbol is Conrad's use of alliteration. Whether consciously or not, Conrad has chosen for almost every major symbol in the story a word that begins with "s": the secret sharer, the stable sea, the ship, the sun, the stars, the sleeping suits, even the initial line of fishing stakes.

The Literal Level of a Complex Story

As always, the reader's first study of a complex story should be of its literal level. When this complexity is apparent in style rather than in action, the reader may be wise to study first the facts of setting and atmosphere and to postpone his preparation of an action line. Such a postponement is indicated here because in the first sentence of "The Secret Sharer" the reader is caught by the philosophical nature of the narrator, hence in the philosophical nature of his story. A man looks down into a tropical sea at fishing-stakes, but he does not see them merely as stakes for securing set fish nets. He thinks of them as "resembling" fences and he sees their lack of system as "mysterious," "incomprehensible," and "crazy of aspect." To the logical mind of this man, even an imaginary fence requires a human builder, so he completes his imagining with a "nomad tribe" which in its wanderings built and then abandoned the fence to go "to the other end of the ocean." Returning at the semicolon to the real world, the narrator looks completely around him and sees "no sign of human habitation as far as the eye could reach." Here is the first specific setting: a tropical sea clear enough to reveal partially what lies beneath its surface. And here is introduced the narrator, a very close observer, obviously with time on his hands—time that he spends interpreting the significance of what lies about him. Specifically, his vocabulary betrays that at this moment he views the world in terms of mystery and incomprehensibility, perhaps because of, rather than despite, his wish to understand and explain. Clearly, this is a complex narrator who is himself going to examine the significance of what he thinks and does and is going to see both his actions and his ideas reflected—even interpreted—in the literal world. The problem for the reader is to recognize Conrad's stylistic devices for moving the story on the levels of action, idea, symbol, and emotion.

Linguistic clues almost always signal this narrator's symbolic interpretation of the natural world. In the first sentence he sees the lines of fishing stakes as "resembling" fences that appear "as if they were abandoned." The small bare islands "suggesting" the remains of a civilization have their foundations in a sea that "looked" like half of a floor. Whenever the narrator says "as if," "as though," "I wondered," "we seemed," or any such words that directly express a comparison, the reader may expect what follows to be an interpretation of the symbolic significance of the object to the narrator.

In this first scene, a major emphasis of the narrator's repetition (hence his identification of symbols) falls on the silence and the stillness and the solitude of the first scene. The ship is anchored. There is no wind. Even the tug's smoke, which marked the only movement, disappears. With these details, the narrator conditions the reader particularly to accept his interpretation of the significance of "this breathless pause at the threshold of a long passage." In fact, the reader should realize here that the journey itself is the key symbol—a journey from the head of the Gulf of Siam (a location most distant from his familiar waters) to England (his home) paralleled in some way by an action internal to the understanding of the captain. Once the reader realizes not only that the journey is a symbol but also that the anchored ship cannot get under way until the captain assumes full command of her and the wind rises, he will see emphatically how he must study even the action as symbol.

Importance of Exposition in a Complex Story

What the narrator does in the exposition is to prepare the reader to identify on four different levels the significance of each step of the voyage—a significance that the narrator himself did not recognize until the voyage with Leggatt was complete. Because he is a retrospective first-person narrator looking back at what he thought and felt at the beginning of his journey, he also can point out to the reader both the areas of his blindness then and the specific qualities of his mind and his situation that made the whole occurrence possible. One of his most useful devices is his stating so clearly what his attitudes are toward major symbols. By the time in the story that he takes the anchor watch but before he discovers the ladder, the narrator makes a number of extremely important statements about his attitude toward the sea, the land, the stars, his ship, his men, himself, and the journey. In some instances two or more statements are made. Occasionally, they even appear together with the second stated as an appositive. For example, in one of the first general philosophical statements, he says of himself and the ship that both seem to be "measuring our fitness for a long and arduous enterprise" and restates that enterprise as "the appointed task of both our existences." In that same sentence he tucks away a most important view of the sky and sea when he speaks of them as the sole "spectators" and "judges" of his fitness and that of his ship.

The Log: A Technique for Studying Complex Stories

Since the story moves simultaneously on the levels of *action, emotion, idea,* and *symbol,* the reader needs to keep an extremely accurate chronological log of their interrelationship. Probably the most effective form would be a literal parallel listing in four columns. The action begins with his assuming command of the anchored ship. Emotionally, he is enjoying the solitude, stillness, and silence. The major symbols are the anchored ship and the clear sea. His idea is that what lies partially revealed below its surface is mysterious and incomprehensible. The first expository action is his asking about the ship (the *Sephora*) which he had barely glimpsed at sunset. He describes himself as disturbed by the stars' staring at him, a feeling intensified by his belief that the second mate sneers at him. He makes clear that the symbols (stars and second mate) intensify his feelings of being alone and strange; and he points out his philosophical concern with how he will measure up to his own secret ideal of himself. His third action and his first assertion of command, the taking of the anchor watch, leads him to a feeling of great security. On the intellectual level he records with the irony of retrospection his appreciation that this life is an "untempted life presenting no disquieting problems, invested with an elementary moral beauty by the absolute straightforwardness of its appeal and by the singleness of its purpose." That idea he sees symbolized in what he calls here "the stable sea." When an introspective narrator relating his story in retrospect makes a philosophical statement knowing that the opposite is true, the reader may be certain that a major part of his intellectual job will be to learn precisely how the narrator's philosophical expectation is not fulfilled.

In addition to keeping a four-column log similar to the five-column lists for "The Beggar," keeping a simple action line in standard form will help the student keep a sense of the formal structure of the story and will serve as a ready index to his more complex log.

Character

The log system is an almost foolproof technique for commanding the facts on the four levels of the story. However, the reader also must study the character of the captain and of Leggatt if he is to share the captain's recognition of the meaning of his experience. In his study, the reader must never doubt that both men are real. Only once does the narrator record that "an irresistible doubt of his bodily existence flitted through my mind." Nevertheless, both Leggatt and the captain must be studied as symbolic as well as real persons. As a human man, Leggatt needs to share with an understanding listener his own experience so that he can understand it completely himself and can accept it and bear its cost responsibly. However, Leggatt personifies to an extent that must be determined by the reader "that ideal conception of his own personality" that the captain "sets up for himself secretly"—an ideal against which the captain measures his real self.

Leggatt first appears moments after the captain has taken the anchor watch—the action of a human being, not of an experienced captain. The captain, "agreeably at ease in his sleeping suit," hears "a deep, quiet, trustful sigh of some sleeper inside" and suddenly rejoices in "the great security of the sea..., in my choice of that untempted life presenting no disquieting problems...." When the captain discovers that the rope side ladder has not been hauled in, he questions with irritation "whether it was wise ever to interfere with the established routine of duties even from the kindest of motives." Seeing Leggatt's "headless corpse," the captain experiences first a "horrid, frostbound sensation" and "a moment of vain exclamations" never uttered. During that short interval, he is troubled by his intuition that Leggatt does not want to come aboard and that he is capable of deciding not to. As a consequence, the captain asks in an "ordinary tone, 'What's the matter?'" This question is no more an official question than was the order official which relieved the men from the anchor watch. Instead, it reveals the narrator's human concern. He does not want, by acting officially, to provoke a decision by Leggatt to swim away from a ship already five miles from land.

This meeting is possible for both men only because each is so concerned with his private individual need for communication with another self that the need of each overrides his immediate responsibility. In terms of the literal story, Leggatt would not have come on board had he met an official rather than a human being; his personal responsibilities to survive or to die independently would have kept him down. The captain could not have permitted Leggatt's secret boarding had he already fully accepted his responsibilities as a ship's officer rather than having come on deck to get better acquainted with his ship and himself. As Leggatt says later, "Your speaking to me so quietly—as if you expected me—made me hold on a little longer." On the symbolic level, Leggatt serves as the captain's secret self—his own self to which he feels himself a stranger and with whom he carries on whispered conversations. From Leggatt's point of view, however, the captain is the symbol. Immediately after Leggatt decides that he must be marooned, he speaks again of that first night: "You seemed to have been there on purpose." That purpose, from his point of view, is to get "somebody to understand."

Relation of Character to Major Decision

Regardless of what can be said of the two characters separately, what the reader must determine is the precise contribution that their interaction makes to every development in the narrative. Particularly, the reader must determine how the two men, through their relationship with each other, decide on the one hand that Leggatt must be marooned and never come to life again and, on the other, that the captain shall experience "the perfect communion of a seaman with his first command." Leggatt will be the primary focus of the study.

Leggatt shares with the captain his experience of killing the seaman, facing the legal consequences, refusing to escape at a time when any other person's life would be endangered, and deciding that he "was ready enough to go off wandering on the face of the earth—and that was price enough to pay for an Abel of that sort." What Leggatt needs is someone to understand his nature, his experience, and his final decision. What he shares exemplifies what the captain must evaluate as potential in himself before he can be free to assume command. To understand Leggatt, then, the reader should keep especially careful track, first, of Leggatt's own decisions about himself and his responsibilities and, second, of what the narrator finds most significant and impressive about him.

To study the narrator, the reader should gather three primary kinds of evidence. The first kind of information reveals the awareness of the narrator of some trait or reaction which he and Leggatt share. Obvious examples are "the mysterious communication ... established" between them by the time Leggatt had climbed on deck and the confidence with which the narrator suggests that the reason Leggatt killed a man was "fit of temper." The second kind of evidence involves Leggatt's influence on the behavior of the captain. An early example immediately follows Leggatt's announcing what his name is: "The voice was calm and resolute. A good voice. The self-possession of that man had somehow induced a corresponding state in myself." The third sort of evidence comprises the narrator's identification of ways in which he and Leggatt distinctly differ. One of the first major differences the narrator notes is in the midst of Leggatt's explanation of how he planned to escape in the Sunda Straits: "And I could imagine perfectly the manner of his thinking out—a stubborn if not steadfast operation; something of which I should have been perfectly incapable."

After such close study of character and of action, emotion, philosophical observations, and symbol in "The Secret Sharer," the reader should be prepared to say a number of very precise things about the captain's recognition of his relation to the ideal that he held for himself at the beginning of the voyage. Some of his most significant statements will relate to the climax of the story which is one both external in the action and internal in the captain's relationship to Leggatt. In the climax he should see that the risk of the ship to release Leggatt is the most vivid symbol of the captain's internal risk—the risk of insanity avoided only by his assuming command of his own ship and his release of Leggatt from his symbolic role as the captain's secret self. Just as the captain feels that he cannot know his ship unless he risks it in the nearness of his approach to Koh-ring, so he feels that he cannot know himself until he risks himself completely also. Once this internal journey of self-knowledge is completed, the captain is free to act responsibly in his official role without being obsessed by his human needs to understand himself completely. During the time of his entire relationship with Leggatt, his external journey has been halting and unsure. The internal inadequacy of the captain for his command has been symbolized externally by the persistent stillness. Although the ship has moved, almost no headway has been made on the voyage because there has been so little wind. Furthermore, what commands the captain has had to give have been of the most routine nature and hence have required no real capacity for decision. In the climax, both the internal and the external situations change. Not only to permit him to free Leggatt for his wandering but also to seek a land breeze, the captain deliberately now commands the approach of his ship to Koh-ring. Quite clearly, this is the test. This literal approach to potential disaster is the highest point of measuring the captain's and the ship's fitness for the voyage from the Gulf of Siam to London. Symbolically, however, it is the measure of their fitness for the "appointed task" of their existences. Only the captain, Leggatt, and the sky and sea are spectators and judges who comprehend the meaning of the test. That the reader should comprehend it too is the purpose of the story; and that comprehension is the final step of the reader's sharing the whole retrospective narrative. The reader must review once more all of the actions of the captain when he comes on deck for the last time in the story. As he reviews, he may be surprised that except for three moments, the captain thinks totally of the necessities of his command and not of Leggatt. Even as the captain continues to see symbols (the way he speaks of Koh-ring as like the "gateway of Erebus" and of his hat make them symbols), he uses them as literal marks by which to navigate. Though the symbolic world speaks with power to him, that power is under his control.

With the safe rounding of Koh-ring, the test of the ship and of the captain's readiness for command is over. He recognizes that "Nothing! no one in the world should stand now between us, throwing a shadow on the way of silent knowledge and mute affection, the perfect communion of a seaman with his first command." He recognizes his personal freedom from the paralysis of being a stranger to himself and hence sees Leggatt also as free. If the reader has shared the captain's recognition, he should be able to state now precisely what Joseph Conrad says about the relationship of risk to self-knowledge and of self-knowledge to one's fitness for his individual "appointed task" in the universe. When the reader recognizes both emotionally and intellectually those relationships in terms of his own journey toward self-understanding, he shares the recognition for which Conrad designed the story. Now, to complete his interpretation of the story, the reader need only state that recognition in universal terms as the story's theme.

Questions for Discussion and Writing

1. What is the evidence in the opening paragraph that Conrad's story is serious?
2. What is the evidence that Hawthorne's subject is serious?
3. What kinds of images does each of the two authors evoke in the first paragraph of his story? What is the atmosphere that each set of images evokes?
4. What are the differences in the reader's involvement that are dependent on point of view in "The Hollow of the Three Hills" and in "The Secret Sharer"?
5. How appropriate is the literal setting of "The Secret Sharer"?
6. Is the literal setting equally important in "The Hollow of the Three Hills" and in "The Secret Sharer"? If so, why? If not, why not?
7. Why does Conrad have the narrator explain his intellectual and emotional awareness of his past experience?
8. Why does Conrad provide some physical symbol for whatever

idea engrosses the narrator at the time of a particular action? What examples substantiate your answer?

9. In what way is the journey the key symbol of the story?

10. Point by point, what does each action of the story mean on the symbolic level?

11. Precisely in what ways does Leggatt personify "that ideal perception of his own personality" that the captain "set up for himself secretly"?

12. Precisely what does Leggatt need "somebody to understand"?

13. How does the captain symbolize the person whom Leggatt needs?

14. At the end of the story, what does the captain recognize about his relation to the ideal that he held for himself at the beginning of the story?

15. Why is it appropriate that only the captain, Leggatt, the sky, and the sea are "spectators and judges" who comprehend the meaning of bringing the ship so near to Koh-ring?

16. In what way is every man a captain who must risk his ship by coming into the shadow of his own particular Koh-ring?

The Champion of the World

ROALD DAHL

All day, in between serving customers, we had been crouching over the table in the office of my filling station, preparing the raisins. They were plump and soft from being soaked in water, and when you nicked them with a razor blade the skin sprang open and the jelly stuff inside squeezed out as easily as you could wish. But we had a hundred and ninety-six of them to do altogether, and the evening was nearly upon us before we had finished.

"Don't they look marvellous!" Claud cried, rubbing his hands together hard. "What time is it, Gordon?"

"Just after five."

Through the window, we could see a station wagon pulling up at the petrol pumps, with a woman at the wheel and about eight children in the back eating ice creams.

"We ought to be moving soon," Claud said. "The whole thing'll be a washout if we don't arrive before sunset, you realize that." He was getting twitchy now. His face had the same flushed and popeyed look it got before a dog race.

We both went outside, and Claud gave the woman the number of gallons she wanted. When she had gone, he remained standing in the middle of the driveway, squinting anxiously up at the sun, which was now only the width of a man's hand above the line of trees along the crest of the ridge on the far side of the valley.

"All right," I said. "Lock up."

He went quickly from pump to pump, securing each nozzle in its holder with a small padlock.

"You'd better take off that yellow pullover," he said.

"Why should I?"

"You'll be shining like a bloody beacon out there in the moonlight."

"I'll be all right."

"You will not," he said. "Take it off, Gordon, please. I'll see you in three minutes." He disappeared into his caravan behind the filling station, and I went indoors and changed my yellow pullover for a blue one.

When we met again outside, Claud was dressed in a pair of black trousers and a dark-green turtleneck sweater. On his head he wore a brown cloth cap with the peak pulled down low over his eyes, and he looked like an apache actor out of a night club.

"What's under there?" I asked, seeing the bulge at his waistline.

He pulled up his sweater and showed me two thin but very large white cotton sacks bound neat and tight around his belly. "To carry the stuff," he said.

"I see."

"Let's go," he said.

"I still think we ought to take the car."

"It's too risky. They'll see it parked."

"But it's over three miles up to that wood."

"Yes," he said. "And I suppose you realize we can get six months in the clink if they catch us."

"You never told me that."

"Didn't I?"

"I'm not coming," I said. "It's not worth it."

"The walk will do you good, Gordon. Come on."

It was a calm, sunny evening, with little wisps of brilliant white cloud hanging motionless in the sky, and the valley was cool and very quiet as the two of us began walking along the grass on the side of the road that ran between the hills toward Oxford.

"You got the raisins?" Claud asked.

"They're in my pocket."

"Good," he said. "Marvellous."

Ten minutes later, we turned left off the main road into a narrow lane with high hedges on either side, and from then on it was all uphill.

"How many keepers are there?" I asked.

"Three."

Claud threw away a half-finished cigarette. A minute later, he lit another. "It'll be a milestone in the history of poaching," he said. "But don't you go telling a single soul how we've done it, you understand? Because if this ever leaked out, we'd have every bloody fool in the district doing the same thing, and there wouldn't be a pheasant left."

"I won't say a word."

"You ought to be very proud of yourself," he went on. "There's been men with brains studying this problem for hundreds of years, and not one of them's ever come up with anything even a quarter as artful as you have. Why didn't you tell me about it before?"

"You never invited my opinion," I said.

And that was the truth. In fact, up until the day before, Claud had never even offered to discuss with me the sacred subject of poaching. Often enough, on a summer's evening when work was finished, I had seen him, with cap on head, sliding quietly out of his caravan and disappearing up the road toward the woods; and sometimes, watching him through the window of the filling station, I would find myself wondering exactly what he was going to do, what tricks he was going to practice all alone up there under the trees in the night. He seldom came back until very late, and never, absolutely never, did he bring any of the spoils with him on his return. But the following afternoon—I couldn't imagine how he did it—there would always be a pheasant or a hare or a brace of partridges hanging up in the shed behind the filling station.

This summer, he had been particularly active, and during the past couple of months he had stepped up the tempo to a point where he was going out four and sometimes five nights a week. But that was not all. It seemed to me that recently his whole attitude toward poaching had undergone a subtle and mysterious change. He was more purposeful about it now, more tight-lipped and intense than before, and I had formed the impression that this was not so much a game any longer as a sort of private war that he was waging against the famous Mr. Victor Hazel himself. Mr. Hazel was a pie and sausage manufacturer, with an unbelievably arrogant manner. He was rich beyond words, and his property stretched for miles along either side of the valley. He was a self-made man, with no charm at all and precious few virtues. He loathed all persons of humble station, having once been one of them himself, and he strove desperately to mingle with what he believed were the right kind of folk. He hunted with the hounds and gave shooting parties and wore fancy waistcoats, and every weekday he drove an enormous black Rolls-Royce past the filling station on his way to and from his factory. As he flashed by, we would sometimes catch a glimpse of his great, glistening butcher's face above the wheel, pink as a ham, all soft and inflamed from eating too much meat.

Anyway, the day before, which was Wednesday, Claud had suddenly said to me, right out of the blue, "I'll be going on up to Hazel's woods again tonight. Why don't you come along?"

"Who, me?"

"It's about the last chance this year for pheasants," he had said. "The shooting season opens Saturday, and the birds'll be scattered all over the place after that—if there's any left."

"Why the sudden invitation?" I had asked.

"No special reason, Gordon. No reason at all."

"I suppose you keep a gun or something hidden away up there?"

"A gun!" he cried, disgusted. "Nobody ever *shoots* pheasants, didn't you know that? You've only got to fire a *cap pistol* in Hazel's woods and the keepers'll be on you."

"Then how do you do it?"

"Ah," he said. There was a long pause. Then he said, "Do you think you could keep your mouth shut if I was to tell you a thing or two?"

"Definitely."

"I've never told this to anyone else in my whole life, Gordon."

"I am greatly honored," I said. "You can trust me completely."

He turned his head, fixing me with pale eyes. "I am now about to let you in on the three best ways in the world of poaching a pheasant," he said. "And, seeing that you're the guest on this little trip, I am going to give you the choice of which one you'd like us to use tonight. How's that?"

"There's a catch in this."

"There's no catch, Gordon. I swear it."

"All right, go on."

"Now, here's the thing," he said. "Here's the first big secret." He paused and took a long suck at his cigarette. "Pheasants," he whispered softly, "is *crazy* about raisins."

"Raisins?"

"Just ordinary raisins. It's like a *mania* with them. My dad discovered that more than forty years ago, just like he discovered all three of these methods."

"I thought you said your dad was a drunk."

"Maybe he was. But he was also a great poacher, Gordon. Possibly the greatest there's ever been in the history of England. My dad studied poaching like a scientist."

"Is that so?"

"I mean it. I really mean it."

"I believe you."

"Do you know," he said, "my dad used to keep a whole flock of prime cockerels in the back yard, purely for experimental purposes."

"Cockerels?"

"That's right. And whenever he thought up some new stunt for catching a pheasant, he'd try it out on a cockerel first, to see how it worked. That's how he discovered about raisins. It's also how he invented the horsehair method."

Claud paused and glanced over his shoulder, as though to make sure there was nobody listening. "Here's how it's done," he said. "First you take a few raisins and you soak them overnight in water to make them nice and plump and juicy. Then you get a bit of good stiff horsehair and you cut it up into half-inch lengths. Then you push one of these lengths of horsehair through the middle of each raisin, so that there's about an eighth of an inch of it sticking out on either side. You follow?"

"Yes."

"Now. The old pheasant comes along and eats one of these raisins. Right? And you're watching him from behind a tree. So, what then?"

"I imagine it sticks in his throat."

"That's obvious, Gordon. But here's the amazing thing. Here's what my dad discovered. The moment this happens, the bird *never moves his feet again!* He becomes absolutely rooted to the spot, and there he stands pumping his silly neck up and down, and all you've got to do is walk calmly out from the place where you're hiding and pick him up in your hands."

"I don't believe that."

"I swear it," he said. "Once a pheasant's had the horsehair, you can fire a rifle in his ear and he won't even jump. It's just one of these unexplainable little things. But it takes a genius to discover it."

He paused, and there was a gleam of pride in his eye as he dwelt for a moment upon the memory of his father, the great inventor.

"So that's Method Number One," he said. "Method Number Two is even more simple still. All you do is you have a fishing line. Then you bait the hook with a raisin, and you fish for the pheasant just like you fish for a fish. You pay out the line about fifty yards, and you lie there on your stomach in the bushes, waiting till you get a bite. Then you haul him in."

"I don't think your father was the first to invent that one."

"It's very popular with fishermen," he said, choosing not to hear me. "Keen fishermen who can't get down to the seaside as often as they want. It gives them a bit of the old thrill."

"What is Method Number Three?" I asked.

"Ah," he said. "Number Three's a real beauty. It was the last one my dad ever invented before he passed away."

"His final great work?"

"Exactly, Gordon. And I can even remember the very day it happened—a Sunday morning it was—and suddenly my dad comes into the kitchen holding a huge white cockerel in his hands, and he says, 'I think I've got it.' There's a little smile on his face and a shine of glory in his eyes, and he comes in very soft and quiet, and he puts the bird down right in the middle of the kitchen table, and he says, 'By God, I think I've got a good one this time.' 'A good what?' Mum says, looking up from the sink. 'Horace, take that filthy bird off my table.' The cockerel has a funny little paper hat over its head, like an ice-cream cone upside down, and my dad is pointing to it proudly. 'Stroke him,' he says. 'He won't move an inch.' The cockerel starts scratching away at the paper hat with one of its feet, but the hat seems to be stuck on with glue, and it won't come off. 'No bird in the world is going to run away once you cover up his eyes,' my dad says, and he starts poking the cockerel with his finger and pushing it around on the table, but it doesn't take the slightest bit of notice. And then straightaway he takes me by the arm and marches me quickly out the door, and off we go over the fields and up into the big forest the other side of Haddenham, which used to belong to the Duke of Buckingham, and in less than two hours we get five lovely fat pheasants with no more trouble than it takes to go out and buy them in a shop."

Claud paused for breath. His eyes were huge and moist and dreamy as they gazed back into the wonderful world of his youth.

"I don't quite follow this," I said. "How did he get the paper hats over the pheasants' heads up in the woods?"

"You'd never guess it."

"I'm sure I wouldn't."

"Then here it is. First of all you dig a little hole in the ground. Then you twist a piece of paper into the shape of a cone and you fit this into the hole, hollow end upward, like a cup. Then you smear the paper cup all around the inside with birdlime, and drop in a few raisins. At the same time, you lay a trail of raisins along the ground leading up to it. Now, the old pheasant comes pecking along the trail, and when he gets to the hole, he pops his head inside to gobble the raisins, and the next thing he knows he's got a paper hat stuck over his eyes and he can't see a thing. Isn't it marvellous what some people think of, Gordon? Don't you agree?"

"Your dad was a genius," I said.

"Then take your pick. Choose whichever one of the three methods you fancy, and we'll use it tonight."

"You don't think they're all just a trifle on the crude side, do you?"

"Crude!" he cried, aghast. "Oh, my God! And who's been having roasted pheasant in the house nearly every single day for the last six months and not a penny to pay?"

He walked away toward the door of the workshop. I could see that he was deeply pained by my remark.

"Wait a minute," I said. "Don't go."

"You want to come or don't you?"

"Yes, but let me ask you something first. I've just had a bit of an idea."

"Keep it," he said. "You are talking about a subject you don't know the first thing about."

"Do you remember that bottle of sleeping pills the doc gave me last month when I had a bad back?"

"What about them?"

"Is there any reason why those wouldn't work on a pheasant?"

Claud closed his eyes and shook his head pityingly.

"Wait," I said.

"It's not worth discussing," he said. "No pheasant in the world is going to swallow those lousy red capsules. Don't you know any better than that?"

"You are forgetting the raisins," I said. "Now listen to this. We take a raisin. Then we soak it till it swells. Then we make a tiny slit in one side of it with a razor blade. Then we hollow it out a little. Then we open up one of my red capsules and pour all the powder into the raisin. Then we get a needle and cotton, and very carefully we sew up the slit. Now . . ."

Out of the corner of my eye, I saw Claud's mouth slowly beginning to open.

"Now," I said. "We have a nice, clean-looking raisin with two and a half grains of seconal inside it, and let me tell *you* something now. That's enough dope to knock the average *man* unconscious, never mind about *birds!*"

I paused for ten seconds to allow the full impact of this to strike home.

"What's more, with this method we could operate on a really grand scale. We could prepare *twenty* raisins if we felt like it, and all we'd have to do is scatter them around the feeding grounds at sunset and then walk away. Half an hour later, we'd come back, and the pills would be beginning to work, and the pheasants would be up in the branches by then, roosting, and they'd be starting to feel groggy, and soon every pheasant that had eaten *one single raisin* would keel over unconscious and fall to the ground. My dear boy, they'd be dropping out of the trees like apples, and all we'd have to do is walk around picking them up!"

Claud was staring at me, rapt. "Oh, Christ," he said softly.

"And they'd never catch us, either. We'd simply stroll through the woods, dropping a few raisins here and there as we went, and even if the keepers were *watching* us, they wouldn't notice anything."

"Gordon," he said, laying a hand on my knee, "if this thing works, it will revolutionize poaching."

"I'm glad to hear it."

"How many pills have you got left?" he asked.

"Forty-nine. There were fifty in the bottle, and I've only used one."

"Forty-nine's not enough. We want at least two hundred."

"Are you mad!" I cried.

He walked slowly away and stood by the door with his back to me, gazing at the sky. "Two hundred's the bare minimum," he said quietly. "There's really not much point in doing it unless we have two hundred."

What is it now, I wondered. What the hell's he trying to do?

"This is almost the last chance we'll have before the season opens," he said.

"I couldn't possibly get any more."

"You wouldn't want us to come back empty-handed, would you?"

"But why so *many?*"

Claud looked at me with large, innocent eyes. "Why not?" he said gently. "Do you have any objection?"

My God, I thought suddenly. The crazy bastard is out to wreck Mr. Victor Hazel's opening-day shooting party.

Mr. Hazel's party took place on the first of October every year, and it was a very famous event. Debilitated gentlemen in tweed suits, some with titles and some who were merely rich, motored in from miles around, with their gunbearers and dogs and wives, and all day long the noise of shooting rolled across the valley. There were always enough pheasants to go around, for each summer the woods were methodically restocked with dozens and dozens of young birds, at incredible expense. I had heard it said that the cost of rearing and keeping each pheasant up to the time when it was ready to be shot was well over five pounds. But to Mr. Hazel it was worth every penny of it. He became, if only for a few hours, a big cheese in a little world, and even the Lord Lieutenant of the county slapped him on the back and tried to remember his first name when he said goodbye.

"You get us two hundred of those pills," Claud said, "and then it'll be worth doing."

"I can't."

"How would it be if we just reduced the dose?" he asked. "Why couldn't we divide the contents of one capsule among four raisins?"

"I suppose you could, if you wanted to."

"But would a quarter of a capsule be strong enough for each bird?"

One simply had to admire the man's nerve. It was dangerous enough to poach a single pheasant up in those woods at this time of year, and here he was planning to knock off the bloody lot.

"A quarter would be plenty," I said.

"You're sure of that?"

"Work it out for yourself. It's all done by body weight. You'd still be giving about twenty times more than is necessary."

"Then we'll quarter the dose," he said, rubbing his hands. He paused, and calculated for a moment. "We'll have one hundred and ninety-six raisins!"

"Do you realize what that involves?" I said. "They'll take hours to prepare."

"What of it!" he cried. "We'll go tomorrow instead. We'll soak the raisins overnight and then we'll have all morning and afternoon to get them ready."

And that was precisely what we did.

We had been walking steadily for about forty minutes, and we were nearing the point where the lane curved around to the right and ran along the crest of the hill toward the big wood where the pheasants lived. There was about a mile to go.

"I don't suppose by any chance these keepers might be carrying guns?" I asked.

"All keepers carry guns," Claud said.

I had been afraid of that.

"It's for the vermin mostly," he added.

"Ah."

"Of course, there's no guarantee they won't take a pot at a poacher now and again."

"You're joking."

"Not at all. But they only do it from behind—only when you're running away. They like to pepper you in the legs at about fifty yards."

"They can't do that!" I cried. "It's a criminal offense!"

"So is poaching," Claud said.

We walked on awhile in silence. The sun was below the high hedge on our right now, and the lane was in shadow.

"You can consider yourself lucky this isn't thirty years ago," he went on. "They used to shoot you on sight in those days."

"Do you believe that?"

"I know it," he said. "There wasn't a man in the whole village who didn't have a bit of shot in him. But my dad was the champion."

"Good luck to him," I said.

"I wish to hell he was here now," Claud said, wistful. "He'd have given anything in the world to be coming with us on this job tonight."

"He could take my place," I said. "Gladly."

We had reached the crest of the hill and now we could see the wood ahead of us, huge and dark, with the sun going down behind the trees and little sparks of gold shining through.

"You'd better let me have those raisins," Claud said.

I gave him the bag, and he slid it gently into a trouser pocket.

"No talking once we're inside," he said. "Just follow me, and try not to go snapping any branches."

Five minutes later, we were there. The lane ran right up to the wood itself and then skirted the edge of it for about three hundred yards, with only a little hedge between. Claud slipped through the hedge on all fours, and I followed.

It was cool and dark inside the wood. No sunlight came in at all.

"This is spooky," I said.

"Sh-h-h!"

Claud was very tense. He was walking just ahead of me, picking his feet up high and putting them down gently on the moist ground. He kept his head moving all the time, the eyes sweeping slowly from side to side, searching for danger. I tried doing the same, but soon I began to see a keeper behind every tree, so I gave it up.

Then a large patch of sky appeared ahead of us in the roof of the forest, and I knew that this must be the clearing. Claud had told me that the clearing was the place where the young birds were introduced into the woods in early July, where they were fed and watered and guarded by the keepers, and where many of them stayed, from force of habit, until the shooting began. "There's always plenty of pheasants in the clearing," he had said.

We were now advancing in a series of quick, crouching spurts, running from tree to tree and stopping and waiting and listening and running on again, and then at last we knelt safely behind a big clump of alder, right on the edge of the clearing, and Claud grinned and nudged me in the ribs and pointed through the branches at the pheasants.

The place was absolutely stiff with birds. There must have been two hundred of them, at least, strutting around among the tree stumps.

"You see what I mean?" Claud whispered.

It was an astonishing sight—a poacher's dream come true. And how close they were! Some of them were not more than ten paces from where we were kneeling. The hens were plump and creamy brown, and so fat that their breast feathers almost brushed the ground as they walked. The cocks were slim and beautiful, with long tails and brilliant red patches around the eyes, like scarlet spectacles. I glanced at Claud. His big oxlike face was transfigured with ecstasy. The mouth was slightly open, and the eyes had a kind of glazy look about them as they stared at the pheasants.

There was a long pause. The birds made a queer rustling noise as they moved about among the dead leaves in the clearing. "Ah-ha," Claud said softly a minute later. "You see the keeper?"

"Where?"

"Over the other side, standing by that big tree. Look carefully."

"My God!"

"It's all right. He can't see *us*."

We crouched close to the ground, watching the keeper. He was a smallish man with a cap on his head and a gun under one arm. He never moved. He was like a little post standing there.

"Let's go," I whispered.

The keeper's face was shadowed by the peak of his cap, but it seemed to me that he was looking directly at us.

"I'm not staying here," I said.

"Hush!" Claud said.

Slowly, never taking his eyes from the keeper, he reached into his pocket and brought out a single raisin. He placed it in the palm of his right hand, and then quickly, with a little flick of the wrist, he threw the raisin high into the air. I watched it as it went sailing over the bushes, and I saw it land within a yard or so of two hen birds standing together beside an old tree stump. Both birds turned their heads sharply at the drop of the raisin. Then one of them hopped over and made a quick peck at the ground.

I glanced up at the keeper. He hadn't moved.

Claud threw a second raisin into the clearing; then a third, and a fourth, and a fifth. At this point, I saw the keeper turn his head away to survey the woods behind him. Quick as a flash, Claud pulled the paper bag out of his pocket and tipped a huge pile of raisins into the cup of his right hand.

"Stop," I said.

But with a great sweep of the arm he flung the whole handful high over the bushes into the clearing. They fell with a soft little patter, like raindrops on dry leaves, and every single pheasant in the place must have heard them fall. There was a flurry of wings and a rush to find the treasure.

The keeper's head flicked round as though there were a spring inside his neck. The birds were all pecking away madly at the raisins. The keeper took two quick paces forward, and for a moment I thought he was going to investigate. But then he stopped, and his face came up, and his eyes began travelling slowly around the perimeter of the clearing.

"Follow me," Claud whispered. "And *keep down*." He started crawling away swiftly on all fours, under cover of the bushes.

I went after him, and we went along like this for about a hundred yards.

"Now run," Claud said.

We got to our feet and ran, and a few minutes later we emerged through the hedge into the lovely open safety of the lane.

"It went marvellous," Claud said, breathing heavily. "Didn't it go absolutely marvellous?" The big face was scarlet and glowing with triumph. "In another five minutes, it'll be pitch-dark inside the wood, and that keeper will be sloping off home to his supper."

"I think I'll join him," I said.

"You're a great poacher," Claud said. He sat down on the grassy bank under the hedge and lit a cigarette.

The sun had set now and the sky was a pale smoke-blue, faintly glazed with yellow. In the wood behind us, the shadows and the spaces in between the trees were turning from gray to black.

"How long does a sleeping pill take to work?" Claud asked.

"Look out!" I said. "There's someone coming."

The man had appeared suddenly and silently out of the dusk, and he was only thirty yards away when I saw him.

"Another bloody keeper," Claud said.

We both looked at the keeper as he came down the lane toward us. He had a shotgun under his arm, and there was a black Labrador walking at his heels. He stopped when he was a few paces away, and the dog stopped with him and stayed behind him, watching us through the keeper's legs.

"Good evening," Claud said, nice and friendly.

This one was a tall bony man of about forty, with a swift eye and a hard cheek and hard dangerous hands.

"I know you," he said softly, coming closer. "I know the both of you."

Claud didn't answer this.

"You're from the fillin' station. Right?" His lips were thin and dry. "You're Cubbage and Hawes, and you're from the fillin' station on the main road. Right?"

"What are we playing?" Claud said. "Twenty Questions?"

The keeper took a step forward. "Beat it," he said. "Go on. Get out."

Claud sat on the bank, smoking his cigarette and looking at the keeper's feet.

"Go on," the man said. "Get out." When he spoke, the upper lip lifted above the gum, and I could see a row of small discolored teeth, one of them black, the others quince and ochre.

"This happens to be a public highway," Claud said. "Kindly do not molest us."

The keeper shifted the gun from his left arm to his right. "You're loiterin'," he said, "with intent to commit a felony. I could run you in for that."

"No, you couldn't," Claud said.

All this made me rather nervous.

"I've had my eye on you for some time," the keeper said, looking at Claud.

"It's getting late," I said. "Shall we stroll on?"

Claud flipped away his cigarette and got slowly to his feet. "All right," he said. "Let's go."

We wandered off down the lane the way we had come, leaving him standing there, and soon the man was out of sight in the half darkness behind us.

"That's the head keeper," Claud said. "His name is Rabbetts."

"Let's get the hell out," I said.

"Come in here," Claud said.

There was a gate on our left leading into a field, and we climbed over it and sat down behind the hedge.

"Mr. Rabbetts is also due for his supper," Claud said. "You mustn't worry about him."

We sat quietly behind the hedge, waiting for the keeper to walk past us on his way home. A few stars were showing, and a bright three-quarter moon was coming up over the hills behind us in the east.

"Here he is," Claud whispered. "Don't move."

The keeper came loping softly up the lane with the dog padding quick and soft-footed at his heels, and we watched them through the hedge as they went by.

"He won't be coming back tonight," Claud said.

"How do you know that?"

"A keeper never waits for you in the wood if he knows where you live. He goes to your house and hides outside and watches for you to come back."

"That's worse."

"No, it isn't. Not if you dump the loot somewhere else before you go home. He can't touch you then."

"What about the other one—the one in the clearing?"

"He's gone, too."

"You can't be sure of that."

"I've been studying these bastards for months, Gordon. Honest I have. I know all their habits. There's no danger."

A few minutes later, I reluctantly followed Claud back into the wood. It was pitch-dark in there now, and very silent, and as we moved cautiously forward, the noise of our footsteps seemed to go echoing around the walls of the forest as though we were walking in a cathedral.

"Here's where we threw the raisins," Claud said.

I peered through the bushes. The clearing lay dim and milky in the moonlight.

"You're quite sure the keeper's gone?"

"I *know* he's gone."

I could just see Claud's face under the peak of his cap—the pale lips, the soft, pale cheeks, and the large eyes with a little spark of excitement dancing in each.

"Are they roosting?" I asked.

"Yes. In the branches."

"Whereabouts?"

"All around. They don't go far."

"What do we do next?"

"We stay here and wait. I brought you a light," he added, and he handed me one of those small pocket flashlights shaped like a fountain pen. "You may need it."

I was beginning to feel better. "Shall we see if we can spot some of them sitting in the trees?" I said.

"No."

"I should like to see how they look when they're roosting."

"This isn't a nature study," Claud said. "Please be quiet."

We stood there for a long time, waiting for something to happen.

"I've just had a nasty thought," I said. "If a bird can keep its balance on a branch when it's asleep, then surely there isn't any reason why the pills should make it fall down."

Claud looked at me quick.

"After all," I said, "it's not dead. It's still only sleeping."

"It's doped," Claud said.

"But that's just a *deeper* sort of sleep. Why should we expect it to fall down just because it's in a deeper sleep?"

There was a gloomy silence.

"We should've tried it with chickens," Claud said. "My dad would've done that."

"Your dad was a genius," I said.

At that moment, there came a soft thump from the wood behind us.

"Hey!" I said.

"Sh-h-h!"

We stood listening.

Thump!

"There's another!"

It was a deep, muffled sound, as though a small bag of sand had been dropped from about shoulder height.

Thump!

"They're pheasants!" I cried.

"Wait!"

"I'm sure they're pheasants!"

Thump! Thump!

"You're right!"

We ran back into the wood.

"Where were they?" I asked.

"Over here! Two of them were over here!"

"I thought they were this way."

"Keep looking!" Claud shouted. "They can't be far."

We searched for about a minute.

"Here's one!" he called.

When I got to him, he was holding a magnificent cockbird in both hands. We examined it closely with our flashlights.

"It's doped to the gills," Claud said. "It's still alive, I can feel its heart, but it's doped to the bloody gills."

Thump!

"There's another!" he cried.

Thump! Thump!

"Two more!"

Thump!

Thump! Thump! Thump!

"Jesus Christ!"

Thump! Thump! Thump! Thump!
Thump! Thump!

All around us, the pheasants were starting to rain down out of the trees. We began rushing around madly in the dark, sweeping the ground with our flashlights.

Thump! Thump! Thump! This lot fell almost on top of me. I was right under the tree as they came down, and I found all three of them immediately—two cocks and a hen. They were limp and warm, the feathers wonderfully soft in the hand.

"Where shall I put them?" I called out. I was holding them by the legs.

"Lay them here, Gordon! Just pile them up here where it's light!"

Claud was standing on the edge of the clearing with the moonlight streaming down all over him and a great bunch of pheasants in each hand. His face was bright, his eyes big and bright and wonderful, and he was staring around him like a child who has just discovered that the whole world is made of chocolate.

Thump!
Thump! Thump!

"I don't like it," I said. "It's too many."

"It's beautiful!" he cried, and he dumped the birds he was carrying and ran off to look for more.

Thump! Thump! Thump! Thump!
Thump!

It was easy to find them now. There were one or two lying under every tree. I quickly collected six more, three in each hand, and ran back and dumped them with the others. Then six more. Then six more after that. And still they kept falling.

Claud was in a whirl of ecstasy now, dashing about like a mad ghost under the trees. I could see the beam of his flashlight waving around in the dark, and each time he found a bird he gave a little yelp of triumph.

Thump! Thump! Thump!

"Mr. Victor Hazel ought to hear this!" he called out.

"Don't shout," I said. "It frightens me."

"What?"

"Don't *shout*. There might be keepers."

"To hell with the keepers!" he cried. "They're all eating!"

For three or four minutes, the pheasants kept on falling. Then suddenly they stopped.

"Keep searching!" Claud shouted. "There's plenty more on the ground!"

"Don't you think we ought to get out while the going's good?"

"No," he said.

We went on searching. Between us, we looked under every tree within a hundred yards of the clearing—north, south, east, and west—and I think we found most of them in the end. At the collecting point, there was a pile of pheasants as big as a bonfire.

"It's a miracle," Claud said. "It's a bloody miracle." He was staring at them in a kind of trance.

"We'd better just take half a dozen each and get out quick," I said.

"I would like to count them, Gordon."

"There's no time for that."

"I must count them."

"No," I said. "Come on."

"One. Two. Three. Four . . ." He began counting them very carefully, picking up each bird in turn and laying it gently to one side. The moon was directly overhead now, and the whole clearing was brilliantly illuminated.

"I'm not standing around here like this," I said. I walked back a few paces and hid myself in the shadows, waiting for him to finish.

"A hundred and seventeen, a hundred and eighteen, a hundred and nineteen, *a hundred and twenty!*" he cried. "*One hundred and twenty birds!* It's an all-time record!"

I didn't doubt it for a moment.

"The most my dad ever got in one night was fifteen, and he was drunk for a week afterward!"

"You're the champion of the world," I said. "Are you ready now?"

"One minute," he answered, and he pulled up his sweater and began to unwind the two big white cotton sacks from around his belly. "Here's yours," he said, handing one of them to me. "Fill it up quick."

The light of the moon was so strong that I could read the small print along the base of the sack. "J. W. Crump," it said. "Keston Flour Mills, London S.W. 17."

"You don't think that bastard with the brown teeth is watching us this very moment, from behind a tree?"

"There's no chance of that," Claud said. "He's down at the filling station, like I told you, waiting for us to come home."

We started loading the pheasants into the sacks. They were soft and floppy-necked, and the skin underneath the feathers was warm.

"There'll be a taxi waiting for us in the lane," Claud said.

"What?"

"I always go back in a taxi, Gordon. Didn't you know that? A taxi is anonymous. Nobody knows who's inside a taxi except the driver. My dad taught me that."

"Which driver?"

"Charlie Kinch. He's only too glad to oblige."

We finished loading the pheasants, and I tried to hump my bulging sack onto my shoulder. My sack had about sixty birds inside it, and it must have weighed a hundredweight and a half, at least. "I can't carry this," I said. "We'll have to leave some of them behind."

"Drag it," Claud said. "Just pull it behind you."

We started off through the pitch-black woods, pulling the pheasants behind us. "We'll never make it all the way back to the village like this," I said.

"Charlie's never let me down yet," Claud said.

We came to the margin of the wood and peered through the hedge into the lane. The taxi was there, not five yards away. Claud said, "Charlie boy," very softly, and the old man behind the wheel poked his head out into the moonlight and gave us a sly, toothless grin. We slid through the hedge, dragging the sacks after us.

"Hullo!" Charlie said. "What's this?"

"It's cabbages," Claud told him. "Open the door."

Two minutes later, we were safely inside the taxi, cruising slowly down the hill toward the village.

It was all over now bar the shouting. Claud was triumphant, bursting with pride and excitement, and he kept leaning forward and tapping Charlie Kinch on the shoulder and saying, "How about it, Charlie? How about this for a haul?," and Charlie kept glancing back popeyed at the huge, bulging sacks lying on the floor between us and saying, "Jesus Christ, man! How did you do it?"

"There's six brace of them for you, Charlie," Claud said.

Charlie said, "I reckon pheasants is going to be a bit scarce up at Mr. Victor Hazel's opening-day shoot this year," and Claud said, "I imagine they are, Charlie, I imagine they are."

"What in God's name are you going to do with a hundred and twenty pheasants?" I asked.

"Put them in cold storage for the winter," Claud said. "Put them in with the dog meat in the deep freeze at the filling station."

"Not tonight, I trust?"

"No, Gordon, not tonight. We leave them at Bessie's house tonight."

"Bessie who?"

"Bessie Organ."

"Bessie *Organ!*" I was completely stunned. Mrs. Organ was the wife of the Reverend Jack Organ, the local vicar.

"Bessie always delivers my game, didn't you know that?"

"I don't know anything," I said.

"Always choose a respectable woman to deliver your game," Claud announced. "That's correct, Charlie, isn't it?"

"Bessie's a right smart girl," Charlie said.

We were driving through the village now and the street lamps were still on and the men were wandering home from the pubs. I saw Will Prattley letting himself in quietly by the side door of his fishmonger's shop, and Mrs. Prattley's head was sticking out the window just above him, but he didn't know it.

"The vicar is very partial to roasted pheasant," Claud said.

"He hangs it eighteen days," Charlie said. "Then he gives it a couple of good shakes and all the feathers drop off."

The taxi turned left and swung in through the gates of the vicarage.

There were no lights on in the house, and nobody met us. Claud and I dumped the pheasants in the coal shed at the rear, and then we said goodbye to Charlie Kinch and walked back in the moonlight to the filling station, empty-handed. Whether or not Mr. Rabbetts was watching us as we went in, I do not know. We saw no sign of him.

"Here she comes," Claud said to me the next morning. He was looking through the window of the filling station.

"Who?"

"Bessie—Bessie Organ." He spoke the name proudly and with a slight proprietary air, as though he were a general referring to his bravest officer.

I followed him outside.

"Down there," he said, pointing.

Far away down the road, I could see a small female figure advancing toward us. "What's she pushing?" I asked.

Claud gave me a sly look. "There's only one safe way of delivering game," he announced, "and that's under a baby."

"Yes," I murmured. "Yes, of course."

"That'll be young Christopher Organ in the pram, aged one and a half. He's a lovely child, Gordon."

I could just make out the small dot of a baby sitting high up in the pram, which had its hood folded down.

"There's sixty or seventy pheasants at least under that little nipper," Claud said happily. "Just imagine that."

"You can't fit sixty or seventy pheasants into a pram," I said.

"You can if it's got a good deep well underneath it, and if you take out the mattress and pack them in tight, right up to the top. All you need then is a sheet. You'll be surprised how little room a pheasant takes up when it's limp."

We stood beside the pumps, waiting for Bessie Organ to arrive. It was one of those warm, windless September mornings, with a darkening sky and a smell of thunder in the air.

"Right through the village, bold as brass," Claud said. "Good old Bessie."

"She seems in rather a hurry to me."

Claud lit a new cigarette from the stub of the old one. "Bessie is never in a hurry," he said.

"She certainly isn't walking normal," I told him. "You look."

He squinted at her through the smoke of his cigarette. Then he took the cigarette out of his mouth and looked again.

"Well?" I said.

"She does seem to be going a tiny bit quick, doesn't she?" he said carefully.

"She's going damn quick."

There was a pause. Claud was beginning to stare hard at the approaching woman. "Perhaps she doesn't want to be caught in the rain, Gordon. I'll bet that's exactly what it is—she thinks it's going to rain, and she don't want the baby to get wet."

"She's *running!*" I cried. "Look!" Bessie had suddenly broken into a full sprint.

Claud stood very still, watching the woman; and in the silence that followed I fancied I could hear a baby screaming.

"There's something wrong with that baby," I said. "Listen."

At this point, Bessie was about two hundred yards away from us, but closing fast.

"Can you hear him now?" I said.

"Yes."

"He's yelling his head off."

The small shrill voice in the distance was growing louder every second—frantic, piercing, almost hysterical.

"He's having a fit," Claud announced.

"I think he must be."

"That's why she's running, Gordon. She wants to get him in here quick and put him under a cold tap."

"I'm sure you're right," I said.

Claud shifted his feet uneasily on the gravel of the driveway. "There's a thousand and one different things keep happening every day to little babies like that," he said.

"Of course."

"Whatever it is," Claud said, "I wish to Christ she'd stop running."

A long lorry loaded with bricks came up alongside of Bessie, and the driver slowed down and poked his head out the window to stare. Bessie flew on, and she was so close now that I could see her big red face, with the mouth wide open, panting for breath. I noticed she was wearing white gloves on her hands, very prim and dainty, and there was a funny little white hat to match perched right on the top of her head, like a mushroom.

Suddenly, out of the pram, straight up into the air, flew an enormous pheasant.

Claud let out a cry of horror.

The fool in the truck going along beside Bessie roared with laughter. The pheasant flapped around drunkenly for a few seconds, then it lost height and landed in the grass by the side of the road. Bessie kept on running.

Then—*whoosh!*—a second pheasant flew up out of the pram.

Then a third and a fourth. Then a fifth.

"My God!" I said. "It's the pills! They're wearing off!"

Bessie covered the last fifty yards at a tremendous pace, and she came swinging into the driveway of the filling station with birds flying up out of the pram in all directions.

"What the hell's going on?" she cried.

"Go round the back!" I shouted. "Go round the back!" But she pulled up sharp beside the first pump in the line, and before we could reach her, she had seized the screaming infant in her arms and dragged him clear.

"No! No!" Claud cried, racing toward her. "Don't lift the baby! Put him back! Hold down the sheet!" But she wasn't even listening, and with the weight of the child suddenly lifted away, a great cloud of pheasants rose up out of the pram—forty or fifty of them, at least—and the whole sky above us was filled with huge brown birds clapping their wings furiously to gain height.

Claud and I started running up and down the driveway, waving our arms to frighten them off the premises. "Go away!" we shouted. "Shoo! Go away!" But they were too dopey still to take any notice of us, and within half a minute down they came again and settled themselves like a swarm of locusts all over the front of my filling station. The place was covered with them. They sat wing to wing along the edges of the roof and on the concrete canopy that came out over the pumps, and a dozen, at least, were clinging to the sill of the office window. Some had flown down onto the rack that held the bottles of lubricating oil, and others were sliding about on the bonnets of my second-hand cars. One cockbird with a fine tail was perched superbly on top of a petrol pump, and quite a number simply squatted in the driveway at our feet, fluffing their feathers and blinking their small eyes.

Across the road, a line of cars had already started forming behind the brick lorry, and people were opening their doors and getting out and beginning to cross over to have a closer look. I glanced at my watch. It was twenty to nine. Any moment now, I thought, a large black car is going to come streaking along the road from the direction of the village, and the car will be a Rolls, and the face behind the wheel will be the great butcher's face of Mr. Victor Hazel, maker of sausages and pies.

"They near pecked him to pieces!" Bessie was shouting, clasping the screaming baby to her bosom.

"You go on home, Bessie," Claud said, white in the face.

"Lock up," I said. "Put out the sign. We've gone for the day."

Plot

"The Champion of the World" is an excellent story for the review of most of what the reader should now know about the formal short story. Much of that knowledge can now be summarized under the term **plot**. In general, plot describes whatever structure an author selects or designs to permit him to present with the most unified effect some view of the world and of human beings that he feels is interesting or significant. Therefore, a plot has to do only with structure, while style, tone, effect, and theme stem from but are not determined by that structure.

Kinds of Plot

A **formal plot** is the most established pattern: action in time and place is so arranged that characters are revealed in a conflict that is introduced, complicated, and resolved. The action line is the basic diagram of a formal plot. To see the necessity not to oversimplify what the term formal plot covers requires only that the reader test various stories by the definition. The structures of "The Schartz-Metterklume Method," "Hop-Frog," and "The Unicorn in the Garden" are clearly formal. "The Beggar," however, is concerned with internal, not external action, although its pattern involves action arranged in time and place so that characters are revealed in a conflict that is introduced and complicated, though in this case not resolved. The action line of "The Beggar" is diagrammatic of its plot only if it is accompanied by a parallel development of Skvortsoff's internal reactions and motives. Again, in "The Secret Sharer," the plot is formal because action orders the story's development. However, in "The Secret Sharer" the reader must simultaneously maintain his awareness of three progressions parallel to the action: from emotion through symbol to philosophy.

"Bartleby" and "The Hollow of the Three Hills" illustrate another variation on the formal plot. They are formal in that their action is chronological and that a conflict is presented in order. However, the action is not continuous but episodic, with each episode having its own inciting action, rising action, and climax. Even though both stories can be called episodic formal plots, even they differ greatly. A reader explaining their structure would have to deal quite specifically with how flashbacks to a former time, internal action, and symbols alter structure.

The so-called **stream-of-consciousness plot** is often an episodic story like "The Crumbs of One Man's Year," which is aimed at the emotions to help the reader recognize the theme. The organization of individual episodes has little relation to action, though it may trace chronologically emotional responses to symbols. However, a stream-of-consciousness story may be only an extended single episode or a fragment of reverie. The usual order of materials in stream-of-consciousness episodes is first a flood of concrete details, largely sensory, that act as symbols to produce emotional responses in the reader. The emotional climax of the episode is a response usually to a single symbol of some universal trait of human beings. Therefore, the unity of a stream-of-consciousness plot is thematic rather than structural. A stream-of-consciousness episode is an illustration from life, not a conflict.

Symbol is often the clearest clue to the complication of structure. The more intellectual the detachment from the symbols, the more formal the story. Conversely, the more personal the emotions fired by symbols, the more likely either a stream-of-consciousness plot or a radial plot becomes. In the absence of symbols, the plot usually is simple and uncomplicatedly formal. With the presence of internal action, the external action usually assumes a symbolic function.

The central-symbol story may have a superficially formal external action or a stream-of-consciousness episodic structure. Chronological external action may order the presentation of episodes, but the material flows into sentences structured by the logic of stream-of-consciousness. Because stream of consciousness logic is characterized by the multiplication of symbols and the consequent multiplication of emotional responses, each symbol seems to lead off in all directions with a resulting apparent fragmentation of plot. However, at the climax of the minimal external action, there almost always appears in such stories a single unifying symbol that both draws to itself and radiates from it the multiple meanings that seem fragmented. In some episodic stories the same symbol is simply repeated. In either case, one may well say that such distantly formal, stream-of-consciousness, central-symbol stories have **radial plots.** "A Country Doctor" illustrates the radial plot. Unlike a stream-of-consciousness plot, one that is radial may involve a conflict.

Steps in Analyzing "The Champion of the World"

To determine the plot of "The Champion of the World," the reader needs first to study the actions, second to determine who is the protagonist and who or what is the antagonist, third to examine what in the natures of the protagonist and the antagonist cause them to be in conflict, and fourth to analyze the steps by which the conflict moves to a resolution. Since the reader knows that plot does not include a number of the important elements of the short story, he should proceed to study these elements also.

Once more the reader's study of character is dependent on his recognition of the point of view. Therefore, he must study carefully who the narrator is, what his intelligence and personal qualifications are, and what his interest in the conflict is. His study of point of view should involve the reader almost immediately in atmosphere. Since it influences the emotional effect of the story, the reader should wait to study effect until the rest of his basic analysis is completed. Assessing the intellectual effect of a story such as "The Champion of the World" throws the reader into a consideration of the nature of humor. For that study, the reader should pick perhaps five places in the action that appeal to his own personal sense of humor and should determine in each whether the humor is in the situation or the characters or the vocabulary. Obviously, whatever humor is inherent in how Roald Dahl writes requires that the reader determine what unique combination of devices of style characterize his writing. Despite the fact that this is a humorous story, the intention of which clearly is to entertain, the author has presented the story in the context of his own basic view of what human beings and the human condition are like. As in all stories, the reader's understanding of theme depends primarily on his ability to experience and to see beyond the emotional and intellectual effect of the story. When the reader has arrived at the theme of "The Champion of the World," he may wish to compare or contrast the techniques or the views of Mr. Dahl with those of other authors.

The Crumbs of One Man's Year

DYLAN THOMAS

Slung as though in a hammock, or a lull, between one Christmas forever over and a New Year nearing full of relentless surprises, waywardly and gladly I pry back at those wizening twelve months and see only a waltzing snippet of the tipsy-turvy times, flickers of vistas, flashes of queer fishes, patches and checquers of a bard's-eye view.

Of what is coming in the New Year I know nothing except that all that is certain will come like thunderclaps or like comets in the shape of four-leaved clovers, and that all that is unforeseen will appear with the certainty of the sun who every morning shakes a leg in the sky. And of what has gone I know only shilly-shally snatches and freckled plaids, flecks and dabs, dazzle and froth; a simple second caught in coursing snow-light; an instant, gay or sorry, struck motionless in the curve of flight like a bird or a scythe; the spindrift leaf and stray-paper whirl, canter, quarrel and people-chase of everybody's street; suddenly the way the grotesque wind slashes and freezes at a corner the clothes of a passerby so that she stays remembered, cold and still until the world like a night light in a nursery goes out; and a waddling couple of the small occurrences, comic as ducks, that quack their way through our calamitous days; whits and dots and tittles.

"Look back, back," the big voices clarion, "look back at the black colossal year," while the rich music fanfares and dead-marches.

I can give you only a scattering of some of the crumbs of one man's year, and the penny music whistles.

Any memory, of the long, revolving year, will do, to begin with.

I was walking, one afternoon in August, along a riverbank, thinking the same thoughts that I always think when I walk along a riverbank in August. As I was walking, I was thinking—now it is August and I am walking along a riverbank. I do not think I was thinking of anything else. I should have been thinking of what I should have been doing, but I was thinking only of what I was doing then and it was all right: it was good, and ordinary, and slow, and idle, and old, and sure, and what I was doing I could have been doing a thousand years before, had I been alive then and myself or any other man. You could have thought the river was ringing—almost you could hear the green, rapid bells sing in it: it could have been the River Elusina, "that dances at the noise of Musick, for with Musick it bubbles, dances and grows sandy, and so continues til the musick ceases..."; or it could have been the River "in Judea that runs swiftly all the six dayes of the week, and stands still and rests all their Sabbath." There were trees blowing, standing still, growing, knowing, whose names I never knew. (Once, indeed, with a friend I wrote a poem beginning, "All trees are oaks, except fir trees.") There were birds being busy, or sleep-flying, in the sky. (The poem had continued, "All birds are robins, except crows, or rooks.") Nature was doing what it was doing, and thinking just that. And I was walking and thinking that I was walking, and for August it was not such a cold day. And then I saw, drifting along the water, a piece of paper, and I thought: something wonderful may be written on this paper. I was alone on the gooseberry earth, or alone for two green miles, and a message drifted towards me on that tabby-coloured water that ran through the middle of the cow-patched, mooing fields. It was a message from multitudinous nowhere to my solitary self. I put out my stick and caught the piece of paper and held it close to the riverbank. It was a page torn from a very old periodical. That I could see. I leant over and read, through water, the message on the rippling page. I made out, with difficulty, only one sentence:

it commemorated the fact that, over a hundred years ago, a man in Worcester had, for a bet, eaten at one sitting fifty-two pounds of plums.

And any other memory, of the long evolving year, will do, to go on with.

Here now, to my memory, come peaceful blitz and pieces of the Fifth of November, guys in the streets and forks in the sky, when Catherine wheels and Jacky jumps and good bombs burst in the blistered areas. The rockets are few but they star between roofs and up to the wall of the warless night. "A penny for the Guy?" "No, that's my father." The great joke brocks and sizzles. Sirius explodes in the back yard by the shelter. Timorous ladies sit in their back rooms, with the eighth programme on very loud. Retiring men snarl under their blankets. In the unkempt gardens of the very rich, the second butler lights a squib. In everybody's street the fearless children shout, under the little, homely raids. But I was standing on a signalling country hill where they fed a hungry bonfire Guy with brushwood, sticks and crackerjacks; the bonfire Guy whooped for more; small sulphurous puddings banged in his burning belly, and his thorned hair caught. He lurched, and made common noises. He was a long time dying on the hill over the starlit fields where the tabby river, without a message, ran on, with bells and trout and tins and bangles and literature and cats in it, to the sea never out of sound.

And on one occasion, in this long dissolving year, I remember that I boarded a London bus from a district I have forgotten, and where I certainly could have been up to little good, to an appointment that I did not want to keep.

It was a shooting green spring morning, nimble and crocus, with all the young women treading on naked flower-stalks, the metropolitan sward, swinging their milkpail handbags, gentle, fickle, inviting, accessible, forgiving each robustly abandoned gesture of salutation before it was made or imagined, assenting, as they revelled demurely towards the manicure salon or the typewriting office, to all the ardent unspoken endearments of shaggy strangers and the winks and pipes of cloven-footed sandwichmen. The sun shrilled, the buses gambolled, policemen and daffodils bowed in the breeze that tasted of buttermilk. Delicate carousal plashed and babbled from the public houses which were not yet open. I felt like a young god. I removed my collar studs and opened my shirt. I tossed back my hair. There was an aviary in my heart but without any owls or eagles. My cheeks were cherried warm, I smelt, I thought, of sea pinks. To the sound of madrigals sung by slim sopranos in waterfalled valleys where I was the only tenor, I leapt on to a bus. The bus was full. Carefree, open-collared, my eyes alight, my veins full of the spring as a dancer's shoe should be full of champagne, I stood, in love and at ease and always young, on the packed lower deck. And a man of exactly my own age—or perhaps he was a little older—got up and offered me his seat. He said, in a respectful voice, as though to an old justice of the peace, "Please, won't you take my seat?" and then he added—"Sir."

How many variegations of inconsiderable defeats and disillusionments I have forgotten! How many shades and shapes from the polychromatic zebra house! How many Joseph's coats I have left uncalled for in the Gentlemen's Cloakrooms of the year!

And one man's year is like the country of a cloud, mapped on the sky, that soon will vanish into the watery, ordered wastes, into the spinning rule, into the dark which is light. Now the cloud is flying very slowly, out of sight, and I can remember of all that voyaging geography, no palaced morning hills or huge plush valleys in the downing sun, forests simmering with birds, stagged moors, merry legendary meadowland, bullish plains, but only—the street near Waterloo Station where a small boy, wearing cutdown khaki and a steel helmet, pushed a pram full of firewood and shouted, in a dispassionate voice, after each passer-by, "Where's your tail?"

The estuary pool under the collapsed castle, where the July children rolled together in original mud, skreaking and yauping, and low life, long before newts, twitched on their hands.

The crisp path through the field in this December snow, in the deep dark, where we trod the buried grass like ghosts on dry toast.

The single-line run along the spring-green riverbank where watervoles went Indian file to work, and where the young impatient voles, in their sleek vests, always in a hurry, jumped over the threadbare backs of the old ones.

The razor-scarred back-street café bar where a man with cut cheeks and chewed ears, huskily and furiously complained, over tarry tea, that the new baby panda in the Zoo was not floodlit.

The gully sands in March, under the flayed and flailing cliff-top trees, when the wind played old Harry, or old Thomas, with me, and cormorants, far off, sped like motorboats across the bay, as I weaved towards the toppling town and the black, loud Lion where the cat, who purred like a fire, looked out of two cinders at the gently swilling retired sea-captains in the snug-as-a-bug back bar.

And the basement kitchen in nipping February, with napkins on the line slung across from door to chockablock corner, and a bicycle by the larder very much down at wheels, and hats and toy engines and bottles and spanners on the broken rocking chair, and billowing papers and half-finished crosswords stacked on the radio always turned full tilt, and the fire smoking, and onions peeling, and chips always spitting on the stove, and small men in their overcoats talking of self-discipline and the ascetic life until the air grew woodbine-blue and the clock choked and the traffic died.

And then the moment of a night in that cavorting spring, rare and unforgettable as a bicycle clip found in the middle of the desert. The lane was long and soused and dark that led to the house I helped to fill and bedraggle.

"Who's left this in this corner?"

"What, where?"

"Here, this."

A doll's arm, the chitterlings of a clock, a saucepan full of hat-bands.

The lane was rutted as though by bosky water carts, and so dark you couldn't see your front in spite of you. Rain barrelled down. On one side you couldn't hear the deer that lived there, and on the other side—voices began to whisper, muffled in the midnight sack. A man's voice and a woman's voice. "Lovers," I said to myself. For at night the heart comes out, like a cat on the tiles. Discourteously I shone my torch. There, in the thick rain, a young man and a young woman stood, very close together, near the hedge that whirred in the wind. And a yard from them, another young man sat staidly, on the grass verge, holding an open book from which he appeared to read. And in the very rutted and puddly middle of the lane, two dogs were fighting, with brutish concentration and in absolute silence.

Story Title as a Clue to Interpretation

Sometimes the title of a story centers attention on a character ("Hop-Frog," "Bartleby," "The Beggar") either because he is the subject of study or is the provocative force for the revelation of a narrator. Other stories are recalled for a significant symbol ("The Unicorn in the Garden"), a setting essential to atmosphere ("The Hollow of the Three Hills"), or a phrase that recalls a particularly effective episode or irony ("The Schartz-Metterklume Method").

Examination of the title of a story for clues to the author's emphasis and perhaps organization is almost always profitable. In "The Crumbs of One Man's Year," that inquiry is imperative. The implication of the metaphorical title clearly is that the story's author presents not the major loaf of the narrator's life—which must have been digested and is gone—but the crumbs that presumably have fallen almost without notice. Even if they are noticed, crumbs are seldom worth gathering because they permit such an elusive taste of what the whole loaf is like. However, if the crumbs do convey the flavor of the whole, the crumbs of a year's living may well be worth sampling.

If the reader will allow two or three random but quite concrete pictures to float up from his own last year, he may be able to see more sympathetically what the author has chosen. He may be startled to realize that what he recalls is both inconsequential and far distant from what he would assert to be his major interest in life. Yet, if he examines them closely, he most probably will find them directly related to what he values most. His identification of crumbs from his own year, therefore, should help the reader to seek sympathetically the significance of those crumbs that Thomas chooses. The apparent randomness of organization by a common value indicates also a lack of action and conflict that suggests a new sort of narrative. "The Crumbs of One Man's Year" is ideal as a title for a story of the type called stream-of-consciousness.

Stream-of-Consciousness

A New Form for the Short Story

The term **stream-of-consciousness** is a figurative way of describing the flow of ideas through the mind. As with water in a stream, the flow of the whole stream is continuous in a single direction, but pools and rapids or falls can interrupt or change that flow. A single picture may splash into a fine spray of pictures, each prompted by some small concrete detail in the first. Similarly, ideas conveyed by words, particularly abstractions like love, may be diverted through a whole line of synonyms or connotations, each with its own memories and pictures. Therefore, though the leap of ideas may seem completely random, an emotional or intellectual connection is always present.

If for about a minute the reader will jot down in order every thought, however random, that comes to his mind, he will have a rough idea how stream-of-consciousness works. If he begins thinking, for example, of how much paper he uses making all these notes, he may next write something about how small his allowance is, and then another note about how angry his parents can get. To anyone else looking at the list, there might seem to be no connections. However, if his parents provide his allowance (and think it is already generous) and a great deal of it is being spent for paper, there are indeed very clear personal links. In well-written stream-of-consciousness literature, the connection between a series of ideas must be universal rather than private so that any competent reader can follow them. The story may be episodic or continuous.

There are paragraphs of very good stream-of-consciousness writing in "The Crumbs of One Man's Year." One of the best examples begins with the narrator's recollection of a walk along a river bank in August. From thinking of his walking only as itself and pleasant, he moves to "what I was doing I could have been doing a thousand years before." The distance in time makes him consider how universal such walking is, since had he been alive then, he might have been "myself or any other man." Next, he remembers that the river seemed to be ringing, a sound that reminds him of what he imagined when he read about two other rivers. The combination of thoughts about reading and walking by a river makes him recall the trees there and then his not knowing all their names. The combination of his not knowing them and his thinking about the works of other writers brings to mind a childhood poem of his about trees—a poem that also included birds. The birds of his poem bring his attention back to the birds beside this river and again to the waters of the river itself. In this mood of awareness of things as they are and as he thought them to be when he was a child and as they must have been for an age, he sees a piece of paper in the water. Aware of the universality of his simple experience, he feels that somehow this occasion is momentous not only for him but also for the universe. He thinks that he of all the people of the world is destined to be there ready to receive what someone else who writes has valued enough to wish to share. Instead of the momentous insight he expected, the message "commemorated the fact that, over a hundred years ago, a man in Worcester had, for a bet, eaten at one sitting fifty-two pounds of plums."

Irony and Symbol

The reader must see that the narrator records the discrepancy between his great expectation in that frame of mind and the inconsequential fulfillment. That moment of awareness of the irony of life is a crumb worthy to be recorded from this year. Because every reader has experienced a similar disillusionment, he identifies with the narrator and so shares the episode personally and directly even more than intellectually. In other words, the key to stream-of-consciousness literature is that it communicates directly with symbolic rather than logical power. Each reader transforms symbolically the narrator's walking by the river into whatever solitary journey is meaningful to him—an excursion from his own life when he recognized a gap between what he had hoped for and the disappointment of what really happened. The author provides a symbol; the reader intuitively apprehends its analogy to his personal experience, different in its details but similar in its irony. If a writer wishes to communicate with the contemporary reader through the short story, he may find the stream-of-consciousness plot far more suitable than the formal one. Intelligent, logical analysis can heighten tremendously the reader's intuitive understanding.

Three Steps for the Reader

If the reader wishes to heighten his intuitive response to stream-of-consciousness, he may profitably study in detail almost any episode in "The Crumbs of One Man's Year." There are three steps usual to such writing. First, the writer prepares the attitude of the reader so that he may respond in precisely the same way as the narrator to a multitude of primarily sensory details most often presented by poetic techniques. Having established the overall attitude, the author secondly describes, as he would in a lyric poem, both what his senses tell him and what his response to each sensation is. Sometimes he describes his mental world as if it were concrete. Third, he brings the reader through some climax of his emotional experience. That climax provides the symbol with which he intends to share some universal human situation.

An enjoyable episode to study begins, "And on one occasion in this long, dissolving year, I remember that I boarded a London bus. . . ." Thomas carefully prepares the reader to share the narrator's attitude. With precise details he identifies his attitude as carefree and irresponsible, first noting that he has forgotten the district from which he took the bus, and second, by stating confidently that though he cannot remember where he was, he is sure that he "could have been up to little good...." To intensify that attitude, he says that though he had an appointment, he did not wish to keep it. That universal wish every reader sometimes shares.

In the second step, he communicates the details of what he feels or hears or tastes on such a day in such a frame of mind. No reader can fail to respond to the emotional power of his description, hence to share his view of himself at the moment that he leapt onto the bus. Given that happily carefree youthful assurance, one experiences also the jolts, first of being deferred to respectfully "as though to an old justice of the peace," and finally as a last deference to his advancing age, of being addressed as "Sir." In that third step, Thomas has, through the narrator, presented once more a universal emotional experience of disillusionment. This time the reader shares the moment when the narrator sees the discrepancy between his view of himself as like a young god and the realistic view of others who see only his appearance. Thomas' reaction here parallels his humorous acceptance of the irony that the immortal message that he had dragged from the river told him a mundane fact that he had no wish to know.

Source of Reader Involvement in Stream-of-Consciousness

If only because he has been caught up so well into the mood of the narrator, the reader recognizes, probably, that these two examples of stream-of-consciousness are well written. If he wishes to praise these two passages, however, he must be prepared to show where his involvement comes from. That explanation involves him in the interpretation of detail. What he must do is to show how each figure of speech, each set of adjectives, each special change of phrase from normal usage contributes to what the writer wishes to share with the reader. For example, the reader should explain that the bowing of daffodils on a beautiful spring day is a rather conventional description. However, when Thomas has daffodils *and* policemen bow in response to the same breeze, something special enters the story. The reader should examine the apparently incongruous combination until he can see that though the motions of both can be described with the same word, the bowing of the flower is merely the natural response of a slender stem before the pressure of air, while the bending of the policemen is a voluntary human response that shows the power of the beauty of the day. Thomas' ability to combine the incongruous believably is one of the most delightfully successful elements of his writing.

Unfortunately, there are many times in "The Crumbs of One Man's Year" that Thomas' writing annoys rather than delights. Perhaps the most obvious occurrence of flawed writing in the story is the first cluttered and overly clever sentence. Because Thomas is attempting to establish an attitude that he wants the reader to hold throughout the story, the failure is quite serious. If one is to criticize negatively a writer, particularly one of the poetic power of Dylan Thomas, he must be willing to examine minutely what he has written, what his intention seems to have been, and specifically how he fails. Much of this study involves close attention to the poet's **diction**—the effectiveness of the connotations and denotations of his vocabulary.

"Slung as though in a hammock," the narrator begins. What is a hammock? Where is one ordinarily hung? When is one usually in a hammock? What is his habitual attitude there? But is a person, rather than a hammock, ever slung? With this stretching of the first-person narrator between a past Christmas and an approaching New Year, Thomas has transferred the hammock state of mind to the narrator and the reader. Next the reader is given a choice: if not in a hammock, the narrator is slung "in a lull." Clearly, this is not a possible real action, yet the word *lull* fits even more accurately than *hammock* the suspension in time and reinforces the relaxed attitude in the first phrase. The narrator is slung "between one Christmas forever over and a New Year nearing, full of relentless surprises." Why not use the natural order "over forever"? In Thomas' phrase, the two-syllable rime draws attention to the sense of stillness of things past, particularly since they never will recur. The unaccented second syllable and the feminine rime also weaken the motion. The sounds of the vowels and the *r*'s particularly reinforce the uninterruptedness of "forever." Thomas uses rime again immediately with an opposite effect achieved by the same devices. In "a New Year nearing," the one-syllable strong masculine rime makes the New Year seem to move while the sounds of the *v*'s of "forever over" staple Christmas firmly in place. Of course, *-ing* verbs also make the most active adjectives. There is a third rime in this single prose sentence. "Full" is an approximate rime with "lull." As eye rime it is identical, but the vowel sounds are different. "Relentless surprises" carries in its repeated *s*'s a continuous, perhaps slightly ominous hiss that underlines the oppositeness of the two words. "Relentless" usually implies a pressure that one would prefer to have relieved while "surprises" are thought of primarily as pleasant. "Relentless" reinforces, too, the idea of how the New Year approaches and how all time becomes "forever over." So far the reader has examined closely only the long adjective phrase preceding the subject.

Before the subject Thomas moves two adverbs out of natural order to emphasize that the narrator's activity in the hammock-like existence is attempted "waywardly and gladly"—deliberately straying from main paths and with pleasure rather than reluctance. He chooses to "pry back at those wizening twelve months"—months that are already drying and hardening because they have been cut off from what gave them life—months that now must be pried into, both in the sense of forced open as with a lever and peered at nosily.

Through the crack that he pries into his past year, the narrator sees three kinds of pictures whose motion makes their close examination impossible. He sees first a snippet (an edge or scrap) clipped from something "of the tipsy-turvy times," deliberately changing the cliché "topsy-turvy" (upside down) to "tipsy-turvy," suggesting both alcoholic exhilaration and the unsteadiness of anything too heavy for its base. The narrator sees only a small clip of these turned-about exuberant times, and that snippet he sees in a free-swinging dance. There can be no doubt of the gaiety and joy and abandon of that particular figure nor of its suitability to the unusual brief experiences of unusual emotions. In contrast to the snippets that are in motion, the second picture is of vistas that are still while the viewer moves. A vista is a distant view unlimited in depth but restricted on the sides—like a view seen at the end of a street lined on both sides by tall buildings. For vistas to "flicker," then, the viewer must see them while he is in motion so rapid that the separations between vistas are not seen for themselves at all. The third picture, "flashes of queer fishes," can either imply a continuation of the viewer's movement or the viewer's watching fish dart momentarily out of obscurity. Calling them "queer fish" permits the author the use of the whole water world for its variety of connotations while at the same time the reader knows that he means odd people. The final pictures—"patches and chequers," both square, but one placed erratically and the other regularly patterned—are now seen from high above, first from the traditional "bird's eye view," then from the narrator's "bard's eye view." While a bird sees precisely but does not reason about the facts of the world below him, the poet with his perspective selects and interprets, often by reproducing the emotion with which he sees the literal contents of the patches and chequers.

Despite the fact that this first sentence is interesting and original, the reader can scarcely respond with the emotion Thomas wants. The reader willingly gives himself to the feeling of relaxation and receptiveness suggested by the hammock and the lull, and he joins the narrator "waywardly and gladly" that far. Even the lover of words must admit, however, that the differences between a snippet and a vista or a flash and a chequer are not sufficient reward for his mental effort in recognizing them. Furthermore, though one clever play on familiar words may not distract the reader too much, having both "tipsy-turvy times" and a "bard's eye view" in a single sentence is at least annoying. Thomas' riming of the prose here compounds the annoyance. The reader might accept the difficulty of saying "forever over" for what the rime and order of sounds adds to the suspension of time, but he will not willingly pronounce three words later "New Year nearing." Instead of delighting the reader with his poetic amalgamation of opposites, Thomas has alienated him with clutter and cleverness. The reader may even suspect that Thomas plays with the language for his own pleasure without proper regard for whether his reader understands or not.

The Author's Contract with the Reader

Every author has an unwritten contract with the reader that, because he respects him, he will make the reader's effort worthwhile. The contract includes the writer's promise to provide every detail that a reader needs to understand the story. Thus, the author guarantees his intellectual and emotional honesty in handling both the characters and their actions. For example, he may never resolve a conflict by an act not in keeping with the nature of the characters or by introducing some external force not prepared for. Nor will he deliberately withhold information necessary for the reader's understanding. Neither will he make the reading any more difficult than is absolutely necessary for the reader to experience the full emotional and intellectual effect of the story. Therefore, he will include no sentence that is not necessary for his intended effect.

> A skilful literary artist has constructed a tale. If wise, he has not fashioned his thoughts to accommodate his incidents; but having conceived, with deliberate care, a certain unique or single effect to be wrought out, he then invents such incidents—he then combines such events as may best aid him in establishing this preconceived effect. If his very initial sentence tend not to be out-bringing of this effect, then he has failed in his first step. In the whole composition there should be no word written, of which the tendency, direct or indirect, is not to the one preestablished design. And by such means, with such care and skill, a picture is at length painted which leaves in the mind of him who contemplates it with a kindred art, a sense of the fullest satisfaction.[1]

The author promises also that the reader who permits himself to experience the effect will be able to understand what the author says about the human condition. Obviously the reader's part of the contract is an acceptance of the necessity to recreate in his own mind whatever the author gives him words for. Any violation by the au-

---

[1] Edgar Allan Poe, "Review of Nathaniel Hawthorne's *Twice-Told Tales*," revision published in *Godey's Lady's Book*, 1847, together with a review of *Mosses from an Old Manse;* original version published in *Graham's Lady's and Gentleman's Magazine*, 1842.

thor of any part of this contract will result in a break of tone. A break in tone signals to the reader a fault in characterization, development of action, or style.

Tone

The **tone** of a story exists intangibly somewhere between an author's sentence structure, the sound of his words, and their sense. The tone is what the reader recognizes to be the author's attitude toward his materials and toward the reader. Ideally, a reader should be able to assume that an author writes what he wants to in a way that he chooses but always for some purpose that he personally thinks is important. Therefore, tone is apparent first in the subject matter that interests the author because his vehicle for saying particularly what he values in life is his characters and their conflict. More precisely, the part of tone that depends on the facts of the story is closely tied to the theme or idea that interests him. For example, Hawthorne chose to write a story about a woman overcome by grief for her guilt in the presence of a witch. He made that choice so that he could say very seriously that all men should see their own sinfulness rather than judge others. A major part of the tone of "The Hollow of the Three Hills" clearly is inherent in the choice of subject regardless of how it is written about. How he chooses to express himself in structure and sound is more of a technical question of style. Style certainly determines tone to a great extent.

Style

Style is essentially a matter of how an author uses language. In what sort of sentences and paragraphs, made up of what sort of words, are his stories written? Are his sentences long, complex grammatical structures requiring that the reader understand very fine points of meaning? Do they move smoothly and rhythmically? Are most of his words concrete, hence dependent upon the sharpness of the reader's five senses, or are they frequently abstract words that convey ideas rather than sensations? How frequently does he present pictures to the reader? How often do his pictures involve literal details of landscape or appearance? How often are his pictures instead figurative so that the reader must imagine what a thing is like rather than simply to be told what it is? All these and many other questions about an author's use of language will identify his style. If a story's tone is to be consistent, there must be nothing in the author's style that violates his contract with his reader. However, a fault in style almost never represents a deliberate default on his contract. Usually, it represents, instead, an author's inability to make the language behave as he tries to make it.

Identifying Thomas' Style

The reader undoubtedly recognizes that the long analysis of the first sentence of "The Crumbs of One Man's Year" is essentially a study of Thomas' style there. Applying the questions given not only to that first paragraph but also to the two other sections studied in depth, what may a reader say of his style? He uses long, complicated sentences that require considerable grammatical unwinding. He deliberately puts words out of their expected order. He uses words in most unconventional meanings or as unexpected parts of speech, and sometimes he calls for a word to carry two or three meanings simultaneously. Most of his sentences are very rhythmical. A great many of his words are concrete sense words describing literal physical detail, but almost always these are mixed with figures of speech. His writing can hardly be understood at all if the reader cannot translate metaphors, similes, metonymies, and paradoxes. The total combination of facts of structure, diction, verbal imagination and usage compiled here identifies Dylan Thomas' style as distinct from that of any other author. Every author of ability has his own unique combination of stylistic elements. Even a writer of formula fiction makes some personal imprint on his materials.

No matter how carefully one may analyze elements of any author's style, actually there is only one pertinent question to ask: does his style permit that author to say what he wants to say with the effect that he intends? If his writing in no way violates his contract with the reader, his style is effective no matter what unexpected or unorthodox elements may be combined in it. In fact, if his style is effective, to change it would then be a violation of the contract. The pertinent question to ask about "The Crumbs of One Man's Year," therefore, is: is Thomas' style effective? Certainly the answer is "no" for too many parts of the story. Because of Thomas' imperfect command of his style, he seems neither to respect the reader's right to have every sentence lead toward the intended effect nor to give the reader all of the information necessary to understand the story. Even if the reader enjoys the forced play with words in the first sentence, he is watching the author write rather than responding to a single effect. With the first complete episode—the walking by the river—the reader may begin to experience the intended effect of relaxed openness to all experience. But jarringly clever puns like "blitz and pieces" and too many private connections with Guy Fawkes Day may destroy this attitude completely. Nevertheless, Thomas' writing is effective enough to regain periodically the reader's sympathy—an amazing tribute to an imperfect style.

Since Thomas defaults stylistically on his contract with the reader, the reader certainly has a right to reject the story. However, because some of the episodes in "The Crumbs of One Man's Year" are so excellent, the reader may find ample reward for overlooking the flaws and compensating with his own mental effort for Thomas' failures.

Using Effect, Recognition, and Theme to Compensate for a Failure in Tone

In this particular story, that compensation requires first the reader's deliberate adoption of the carefree exuberant tone that Thomas apparently intended to create consistently. That first step will facilitate the reader's second one: seeing whether or not the effect that he can recognize in one episode is potential in the others. To the two episodes already closely analyzed, the reader probably responded by sharing both the narrator's amusement at the deflation of his ego and his intellectual awareness that his high expectations were so ridiculously fulfilled. That dual emotional and intellectual response identifies the effect of the episodes. If the reader recognizes that the same irony typifies his own life, he can say with assurance that the theme of these episodes first identifies what life is like and then suggests how best to live. Life, suggests the narrator, is ironic. What we get from life is always far different from and less significant than what we expect. The narrator demonstrates by his own attitude and action that life is appreciated most fully if it is lived not only with high hope but also with an acuteness of observation and a completeness of response that permits life's ironies to be recognized and enjoyed, not suffered. Such an argument for effect, recognition, and theme is possible from two fragments of the story. Next the reader should determine whether other episodes ratify or destroy this interpretation.

For close study of "The Crumbs of One Man's Year," the reader had best ignore the annoying puns and too extravagant figures of speech. He need not struggle too long either with passages where the stream-of-consciousness connections are obscure. An example is the transitional paragraph between someone's giving him a seat on the bus and his imagining his life to be like a cloud country. All of the allusions and metaphors and personifications stem from connotation of "variegations," some so obscure that they require research as well as thought. Pursuing all of the possibilities proves that the passage is purposeful, but time spent elsewhere will be better rewarded.

There are several paragraphs, however, that deserve as much attention as time will permit a reader to spend. Despite the average American reader's lack of acquaintance with Guy Fawkes, the paragraph describing Guy Fawkes' Day deserves the reader's attention primarily for the contrast between the fireworks and the huge fire with the last sentence. Another of the paragraphs where his effect comes through is the one in which he imagines the year first as "the country of a cloud" with all of its usual romantic associations and then focuses on one extremely realistic scene that is tremendous in its contrast with the imaginary. For the effect here the reader must interpret extremely carefully the significance of the boy's clothing, his job, and his shout. The key to the irony in this passage is in the contrast between the "dispassionate voice" of this child and the spirit with which most children make that inquiry at that age. The last two episodes well worth the reader's analysis begin with the street brawler in the café bar furious that "the new baby panda in the Zoo was not floodlit." The second of those two episodes, and the story, ends with the two dogs "fighting with brutish concentration and in absolute silence."

If the reader studies each episode carefully, particularly by allowing himself to respond emotionally to the sense details, he will recognize that there is indeed a very strong, very consistent emotional effect in the story paralleled by an equally consistent intellectual focus on the author's ironic view of the human condition. Despite its inconsistency in tone, "The Crumbs of One Man's Year" contains all of the clues that a reader needs to understand the story in considerable depth. A great deal more skill in reading is required to appreciate the beauties of an imperfect story than to read one which is consistently excellent. However, the reward for studying a flawed story may more than compensate for the extra effort expended.

Questions for Discussion and Writing

1. How many "crumbs" of his year does Dylan Thomas treat?
2. What is the specific subject content of each crumb?
3. What is the author's view of the human condition? How is that view shown in each episode.
4. What are the three stream-of-consciousness steps for the reader in the paragraph describing Guy Fawkes Day? in the paragraph in which the little boy shouts "Where's your tail?" in the last paragraph of the story?
5. What does each word, each phrase, and each mark of punctuation contribute to the picture in the almost-sentence: "The razor-scarred back-street café bar where a man with cut cheeks and chewed

ears, huskily and furiously complained, over tarry tea, that the new baby panda in the Zoo was not floodlit"? What are the ironies in it? What are the symbols? Why does Thomas here take only the first step of communication by stream-of-consciousness logic? What is the precise logic of the sentence order: place, man, emotion, drink, complaint?

6. What part of the effect of "The crisp path through the field in this December show, in the deep dark, where we trod the buried grass like ghosts on dry toast" comes from poetic devices?

7. What similarities are there between Hawthorne's style and Conrad's?

8. What is Dahl's tone in "The Champion of the World"? Hawthorne's in "The Hollow of the Three Hills"? Saki's in "The Schartz-Metterklume Method"? Chekov's in "The Beggar"?

9. How does the structure of "Hop-Frog" unify the story?

10. How does the theme unify "The Crumbs of One Man's Year"?

Fable, Parable, and Allegory

Four stories remain to be studied before the reader has a command of the primary techniques and terms that will guide him in understanding short stories of whatever complexity of plot, symbol, or style. The first three—"The Prodigal Son," "Couriers," and "The Other Side of the Hedge"—are included primarily to make possible an intelligent study of the fourth: "A Country Doctor." Because the three stories are illustrations, they are explained more fully than usual, and therefore no questions are appended for their further study. The reader who studies "A Country Doctor" must do so with the full understanding that Kafka's writing is among the most complex of modern literature and that it will strain—even exhaust—the patience and the skill of most students. For those who persist in studying "A Country Doctor," possible methods of attack and sometimes illustrations of the methods or indications of their products are provided under familiar terms: action, character, setting, etc. However, although even closer study by the student will be rewarding, the commentary beginning with the heading "Allegory" is increasingly complete in itself.

A secondary purpose for including the first three stories is to teach both allusion—how references to other works of art or literature and to biography and history enrich a student's reading—and literary forms. Until the reader has developed techniques for reading independently, knowledge of allusions and of genre forms are not of great importance. Now, however, a reader's understanding of short stories should be expanded particularly by his learning to recognize the debt of modern stories to older forms. Primarily, the forms he needs to study are those intended for practical or moral instruction: the fable, the parable, the allegory. James Thurber's "The Unicorn in the Garden" is a modern fable kin to but different from the fables of Aesop. Kafka's parable "Couriers" must be studied in much the same way that one examines the New Testament parable "The Prodigal Son." E. M. Forster's "The Other Side of the Hedge" is an allegory related to major works like Dante's *Divine Comedy*. A story like "A Country Doctor" contains elements of all these forms.

Fable

The majority of Aesop's **fables,** the oldest of so-called moral tales, are beast fables: that is, animals, such as the fox, undergo human experiences like reaching unsuccessfully for grapes. Then the animals rationalize their experiences—the fox, for example, concluding that the grapes are sour anyway. Whether fables have human or animal actors, they are predominantly about accepting and adjusting to life, not about right and wrong. Only when Aesop's fables were collected were morals added, and then only to facilitate grouping them into subject categories. Although many Thurber fables are beast fables, "The Unicorn in the Garden" obviously concerns human beings involved in human experiences. Nevertheless, an animal, the unicorn, is a symbol central to the human experience, and the verb "hatch" has both animal and human connotations in the moral. Furthermore, the advice not to count one's boobies before they are hatched clearly is more practical than moral.

Parable

Whereas the fable is often erroneously thought of as a moral tale, in the sense of a story teaching right and wrong behavior, the parable should seldom be thought of as anything else. The prime purpose of a **parable** is to illustrate a right relationship to a supreme being.

Therefore, to read a parable as if it were merely practical advice is to misread it. Though a reader can study the content of a parable with the same techniques that he uses on any other story, he has an intellectual responsibility to discover the moral context of the parable before he attempts to interpret it. Certainly the reader need not believe what the parable teaches, but he must not distort its message by ignoring the restrictions of its historical or religious setting or by examining its details except as they contribute to a general lesson. Therefore, the proper understanding of a parable requires that the reader do some research about its background.

The biblical parable included here speaks of the relationship of two Jewish sons to their father. Since this parable is a teaching story attributed to Jesus, it must be read in the Christian frame so that the father represents God. Biographical research will verify that Kafka was intensely concerned with the alienation of man from the Judeo-Christian God. Therefore, the reader can do justice to "Couriers" only if he thinks of God as the king who permitted the children the choice of being couriers or kings. He will do the parable an injustice if he reads it as purely psychological, for example.

Allegory

Like the parable, the allegory is intended to teach the reader a lesson about how to live. However, the allegory must be studied in as much detail as the parable should not be. The parable is an illustration, not a metaphor; that is, it has only a literal level, which as a whole can be used as an example. An **allegory** is an extended metaphor: every detail of its literal level must also be read as a part of a consistent figurative whole.

In Dante's great Catholic allegory, *The Divine Comedy,* the man Dante takes a literal physical trip down into the Inferno (hell), up to the Mount of Purgatory, through the planets, and to the Mystic Rose. His allegorical trip is Dante's view of the spiritual journey of all mankind. In that figurative journey, Mankind comes to himself by the grace of Light given by Mercy, and he then turns to Reason. Reason and Philosophy prepare him to see the results of sin and the purpose of repentance so that he finally is ready to be guided by Divine Revelation into the very presence of God. At every point in the spiritual journey there is a literal detail that makes the spiritual level concrete.

Forster's allegory, too, is concerned with values and uses a literal physical trip to provide metaphysical detail for a whole manner of living. However, the value in the Forster story is human rather than religious, although his allusions include both Biblical and pagan religious references. The other side of the hedge is called a "park or garden" and clearly is a paradise like the Biblical Garden of Eden. However, the gates of horn and of ivory are a direct allusion to Penelope's statement in *The Odyssey* that dreams that reach us through an ivory gate are empty dreams while those that come through gates of horn will really happen.

"A Country Doctor" is distantly like the fable because it requires (but does not permit) a practical rationalization of a frustrating situation. As parable, it raises the question of how a man should live, not in the presence of but in the absence of a meaningful relationship with a supreme being. It comments clearly on the impotent inaction of modern man, but it offers no solution. Certainly it is no simple teaching illustration. However, it can be an allegory only if the story is structurally ironic—that is, if Kafka has used every convention of allegory for a purpose opposite to the conventional. Without question "A Country Doctor" is similar to an allegory in its representation of the life journey of a doctor who in many ways is Modern Man.

Differentiation of Fable, Parable, Allegory

The fable, the parable, and the allegory differ primarily in intention, in complexity, and in the knowledge required to understand each. The fable is a primarily realistic experience told in simple narrative form to teach expedient action. Often the actors in a fable are people thinly disguised as animals. The parable also often is a common experience told in simple story form, but always with human actors. However, its intention is to teach moral rather than expedient action, particularly the action appropriate to a man in relation to a supreme being. The characters in a parable usually represent man and God, but their actions are a part of the whole illustration and should not be examined apart from that whole. The allegory is usually a long segment of human experience (often a journey) outside the real world. The actors may be human and animal, but each represents a single quality or person on the figurative level. Not only are the actors representational. In an allegory every step of action has a precise one-to-one metaphorical meaning as well. To understand a fable, the reader needs only his own experience. To understand a parable, he needs not only to study the story but also to learn who tells it with what intention. To understand an allegory, he must be able to follow perfectly a complete action on a literal level, to see every character and every single action as metaphors, and to construct a complete figurative story parallel in every smallest feature to the literal one. In modern short stories, any one of the forms may also involve allusions, though they are most likely to be found in allegories.

The Prodigal Son

LUKE 15: 11–32

11   And he said, A certain man had two sons:
12   And the younger of them said to his father, Father, give me the portion of goods that falleth to me. And he divided unto them his living.
13   And not many days after, the younger son gathered all together, and took his journey into a far country, and there wasted his substance with riotous living.
14   And when he had spent all, there arose a mighty famine in that land; and he began to be in want.
15   And he went and joined himself to a citizen of that country; and he sent him into his fields to feed swine.
16   And he would fain have filled his belly with the husks that the swine did eat: and no man gave unto him.
17   And when he came to himself, he said, How many hired servants of my father's have bread enough and to spare, and I perish with hunger!
18   I will arise and go to my father, and will say unto him, Father, I have sinned against heaven, and before thee,
19   And am no more worthy to be called thy son: make me as one of thy hired servants.
20   And he arose, and came to his father. But when he was yet a great way off, his father saw him, and had compassion, and ran, and fell on his neck, and kissed him.
21   And the son said unto him, Father, I have sinned against

heaven, and in thy sight, and am no more worthy to be called thy son.
22   But the father said to his servants, Bring forth the best robe, and put it on him; and put a ring on his hand, and shoes on his feet:
23   And bring hither the fatted calf, and kill it; and let us eat, and be merry:
24   For this my son was dead, and is alive again; he was lost, and is found, and they began to be merry.
25   Now his elder son was in the field: and as he came and drew nigh to the house, he heard musick and dancing.
26   And he called one of the servants, and asked what these things meant.
27   And he said unto him, Thy brother is come; and thy father hath killed the fatted calf, because he hath received him safe and sound.
28   And he was angry, and would not go in: therefore came his father out, and intreated him.
29   And he answering said to his father, Lo, these many years do I serve thee, neither transgressed I at any time thy commandment: and yet thou never gavest me a kid, that I might make merry with my friends:
30   But as soon as this thy son was come, which hath devoured thy living with harlots, thou hast killed for him the fatted calf.
31   And he said unto him, Son, thou art ever with me, and all that I have is thine.
32   It was meet that we should make merry, and be glad: for this thy brother was dead, and is alive again; and was lost, and is found.

Action, Conflict, and Character

Because a parable is a teaching story which must be used in its entirety as an illustration, the reader must understand it first in terms of the simple facts of action and what these actions show of character. A brief action line shows clearly that the protagonist is the father, not the prodigal son. The younger son's asking for his share of his father's property is the inciting action. It is unexpected, first, because a son seldom receives a portion of an estate until a father's death, and, second, because of the very strong family ties which kept the usual Jewish family in the same household through the father's lifetime. The response of the father is equally unexpected: he immediately gives the son the third of the property which would be a second son's portion. His action frees the son to use his resources in any way he chooses. Whatever are the precise details of his "riotous living," the son exhausts his funds and falls into such financial need that he takes a job feeding pigs. For a Jewish boy, a job tending animals that his religion proscribed as food must have been absolutely a last resort. The reader learns also that he is hungry enough to eat the food provided for the pigs and that he is completely alone, apparently abandoned by all those with whom he spent his money. To this point in the story all of the actions of the young man reveal his nature, his habits, and his emotions. Naturally self-centered, he has asked for what he considered to be his (though his father need not have given it to him) and has spent it completely according to his wishes and desires. Only when he has no resources to indulge his emotions does he think. His first deliberation is expedient: he recognizes that even as a servant in his father's house, his circumstances would be better and his life more human. Therefore, he determines to return home. He deliberates morally also, for he recognizes that he has "sinned against heaven" and "before" his father—that his selfish wasting of himself and his resources has been basically wrong and furthermore a wrong recognized and permitted by his father. Consequently, he accepts that he in no way merits the relationship of a son to a father nor has any right to expect to be hired as a servant. With this speech of confession prepared, he sets out for home as quickly as possible. Before he reaches home and before he can say anything, the father takes command of the action. He sees the son "a great way off" and has compassion and runs and falls on his neck and kisses him—actions revealing the nature of the father and dependent in no way on the son's decision, except that he waits for the son to decide to return. As soon as he can speak, the son confesses his sin and his unworthiness to be called a son—his attempt to resolve the conflict which he set in motion by asking for his portion of the property. It is the father, however, who resolves it by restoring him instead to a position of honor and full restoration as a son, though not to more property. The restoration is spiritual, not material.

The Teachings of the Parable

Because the father is the protagonist responding to the inciting action of his son and acting to resolve the conflict, the teaching purpose of the parable clearly concerns primarily the nature of the father. The roles of the father and the sons are representative as in an allegory, but the details of the story are examples, not parts of an extended metaphor. The parable should be understood as an illustration of how the son (mankind)—no matter how complete his abuse of his relationship to the father (God)—can be restored if the son "comes to himself"—recognizes his sin against heaven and before his father—and returns in repentance. However, the resolution contains a further insight into the nature of the father.

The first-born son, whose portion of the estate is the remaining two-thirds when his father chooses to give it to him, never asks for his portion, stays at home, and presumably runs the estate exactly according to his father's direction. When this elder son returns from his fields and discovers the celebration in his brother's honor, he becomes angry and refuses to go in. Because of the father's nature, the father responds to the son's refusal by entreating the son to join them. This new conflict grows out of the original one and hence is a necessary part of the resolution if both brothers are to be at home as they were at the beginning of the story. The nature of this conflict becomes clear in the son's response that his perfect service has never been rewarded while his brother's return from his dissipation is celebrated. The climax of the elder son's argument is his refusing to call the prodigal "brother," bitterly referring to him instead as "this thy son." The father's resolution of this conflict is not an action but a speech. He reminds the son that he now is his sole heir and has had his complete attention in the absence of the prodigal. His final rebuke of the son is his emphatic reference to "this thy brother" whose return he describes as a greater source of joy than if the son had returned after death. What the older son's response is is not recorded, but the teaching intention of the parable is clear. This son (also mankind), without repentance for his proud assumption of spiritual superiority demonstrated in his expectation to be rewarded for his legal obedience to his father, no more deserves his relationship with the father than did his prodigal brother.

Although the parable could be read as a statement of the ideal nature of parental love and could be spoken of in humanistic terms only, the reader who does not consider it in its Christian context will not have understood it fully. He need not be a Christian himself to be an accurate reader of Christian materials, but if he chooses to read them well he must accept their context.

Understanding and Using Allusions

Once read and understood, a biblical story or any other literary or historical material is available to the reader for purposes of allusion. In such a reference, the narrow sense may be dropped and only the universality of the experience referred to. However, a reference should recall to a careful reader the context as well as the material. For example, a writer can refer to a person as a "prodigal" or say of a character that "he wasted his substance in riotous living." The character called a "prodigal" would most probably be thought of as someone with considerable means who had wasted them foolishly. The other focus would cause most readers to think of the acts of fruitless self-indulgence that brought the son to loneliness and near starvation. Either allusion should carry with it the possibility that the person can be restored to meaningful existence. References by authors to other works of literature, art, or history—**allusions**—enrich the greater part of modern, particularly symbolic, literature. Understanding allusions requires that the reader know them as nearly as possible in their original context. That is not to say that a reader who understands biblical allusions is a man of faith nor to imply that a man of faith need write evangelistic literature. Two important allusions in "The Other Side of the Hedge" illustrate how the reader must learn to read such references sympathetically. Forster's calling the green side of the hedge a park or paradise should call to the reader's mind the biblical stories of the perfect relationship of Adam and Eve and the other creatures to the Hebrew God who walked with them in the Garden of Eden. For Forster's purposes, however, the reader must accept equally solemnly Penelope's ancient Greek faith that the gods had spoken truly to her about the gates of horn and ivory through which dreams come. That these references occur in a story whose values are humanistic and which is written by an Englishman does not require that the reader be either a Jewish or a Greek humanist with English sympathies. What is required is the reader's recognition that allusions permit a writer to borrow in capsule form any fact of theme, experience, or revelation recorded in art, literature, or history. This unique ability of allusions to assist a reader in seeing universal themes makes understanding allusions vital to the reader's recognition of the personal relevance of any story, but particularly of symbolic stories.

Couriers

FRANZ KAFKA

They were offered the choice between becoming kings or the couriers of kings. The way children would, they all wanted to be couriers. Therefore there are only couriers who hurry about the world, shouting to each other—since there are no kings—messages that have become meaningless. They would like to put an end to this miserable life of theirs but they dare not because of their oaths of service.

A Technique for Studying Parables

Kafka's parable "Couriers," like "The Prodigal Son," is intended as an illustration, not a metaphor. That it is an illustration concerned with the meaning of life—even with how life should be lived—is equally clear. Moreover, it is a moral statement of the proper relationship of a man to a supreme being even though it is pessimistic about the possibility of such a relationship. The major difficulty for the reader in this, or any other Kafka story, is in sorting out all the apparently ambiguous possibilities that Kafka deliberately sets up.

Many questions need to be raised. What, precisely, is the difference between a king and a courier in the context of this parable? A courier is a messenger who vows to his king a lifetime of faithfully carrying messages from his king to other kings. He does not know the meaning of the messages he carries, nor can any other courier understand him. Therefore, meaningful life for a courier requires that he receive and successfully deliver messages from his king and return to him replies to those messages. A king, on the other hand, has the power to make and to understand messages. To choose to be a king is to accept the responsibility for sending meaningful messages and for thinking seriously about messages that he receives from other kings. To decide to be a courier seems to be to choose to associate oneself with ideas of importance but to remove oneself from the responsibility for understanding, for decision, or for decisive action.

Who is the king? It is he to whom the couriers have sworn their oaths of service. It is he who has given them messages. Since there are only couriers, it must be he who offered them the choice of being kings like him, who could give and receive messages, or of being only couriers with messages that they could not understand.

What sort of king has the power, on the one hand, to limit a person's choice of lives to two and, on the other, to guarantee the permanence of his choice? What sort of king would permit absolute freedom of choice and bind himself to that choice? Particularly, what sort of king would bind himself to that choice if it eliminated the possibility of there being kings with whom he might himself communicate?

Why do "they" (the couriers) make so important a choice in "the way children would"? Are they, in fact, the king's children, hence eligible by birth to become kings? Or do they make their individual decisions on childish grounds? Do they not recognize the necessity for the existence of kings, or do they simply assume that enough others will make that more difficult choice? Their choice was permanent and universal: now "there are only couriers," no kings. Why do they hurry about the world? Why do they shout? What has caused the originally worthy messages to "become meaningless"? The meaninglessness to them of the messages they carry to no one is what makes their lives so miserable that they would like to commit suicide. However, "none dares end his misery" since death would deny his faithfulness. Is this offer of the choice between becoming couriers or kings never to be made again? The answer to that question will take the reader into an examination of what view of man and the universe the parable illustrates.

"Couriers" is a traditional parable in its concern with the proper relationship of man to a supreme being. However, Kafka uses it to show that man, in Kafka's view, has by his own free choice cut himself off eternally from God. This concern with the loss of the Judeo-Christian metaphysic is a recurrent theme of Kafka's.

The Other Side of the Hedge

E. M. FORSTER

My pedometer told me that I was twenty-five; and, though it is a shocking thing to stop walking, I was so tired that I sat down on a milestone to rest. People outstripped me, jeering as they did so, but I was too apathetic to feel resentful, and even when Miss Eliza Dimbleby, the great educationist, swept past, exhorting me to persevere I only smiled and raised my hat.

At first I thought I was going to be like my brother, whom I had had to leave by the roadside a year or two round the corner. He had wasted his breath on singing, and his strength on helping others. But I had travelled more wisely, and now it was only the monotony of the highway that oppressed me—dust under foot and brown crackling hedges on either side, ever since I could remember.

And I had already dropped several things—indeed, the road behind was strewn with the things we all had dropped; and the white dust was settling down on them, so that already they looked no better than stones. My muscles were so weary that I could not even bear the weight of those things I still carried. I slid off the milestone into the road, and lay there prostrate, with my face to the great parched hedge, praying that I might give up.

A little puff of air revived me. It seemed to come from the hedge; and, when I opened my eyes, there was a glint of light through the tangle of boughs and dead leaves. The hedge could not be as thick as usual. In my weak, morbid state, I longed to force my way in, and see what was on the other side. No one was in sight, or I should not have dared to try. For we of the road do not admit in conversation that there is another side at all.

I yielded to the temptation, saying to myself that I would come back in a minute. The thorns scratched my face, and I had to use my arms as a shield, depending on my feet alone to push me forward. Halfway through I would have gone back, for in the passage all the things I was carrying were scraped off me, and my clothes were torn. But I was so wedged that return was impossible, and I had to wriggle blindly forward, expecting every moment that my strength would fail me, and that I should perish in the undergrowth.

Suddenly cold water closed round my head, and I seemed sinking down for ever. I had fallen out of the hedge into a deep pool. I rose to the surface at last, crying for help, and I heard someone on the opposite bank laugh and say: "Another!" And then I was twitched out and laid panting on the dry ground.

Even when the water was out of my eyes, I was still dazed, for I had never been in so large a space, nor seen such grass and sunshine. The blue sky was no longer a strip, and beneath it the earth had risen gradually into hills—clean, bare buttresses, with beech trees in their folds, and meadows and clear pools at their feet. But the hills were not high, and there was in the landscape a sense of human occupation—so that one might have called it a park, or garden, if the words did not imply a certain triviality and constraint.

As soon as I got my breath, I turned to my rescuer and said: "Where does this place lead to?"

"Nowhere, thank the Lord!" said he, and laughed. He was a man of fifty or sixty—just the kind of age we mistrust on the road—but there was no anxiety in his manner, and his voice was that of a boy of eighteen.

"But it must lead somewhere!" I cried, too much surprised at his answer to thank him for saving my life.

"He wants to know where it leads!" he shouted to some men on the hill side, and they laughed back, and waved their caps.

I noticed then that the pool into which I had fallen was really a moat which bent round to the left and to the right, and that the hedge followed it continually. The hedge was green on this side—its roots showed through the clear water, and fish swam about in them—and it was wreathed over with dog-roses and Traveller's Joy. But it was a barrier, and in a moment I lost all pleasure in the grass, the sky, the trees, the happy men and women, and realized that the place was but a prison, for all its beauty and extent.

We moved away from the boundary, and then followed a path almost parallel to it, across the meadows. I found it difficult walking, for I was always trying to out-distance my companion, and there was no advantage in doing this if the place led nowhere. I had never kept step with anyone since I left my brother.

I amused him by stopping suddenly and saying disconsolately, "This is perfectly terrible. One cannot advance: one cannot progress. Now we of the road——"

"Yes. I know."

"I was going to say, we advance continually."

"I know."

"We are always learning, expanding, developing. Why, even in my short life I have seen a great deal of advance—the Transvaal War, the Fiscal Question, Christian Science, Radium. Here for example——"

I took out my pedometer, but it still marked twenty-five, not a degree more.

"Oh, it's stopped! I meant to show you. It should have registered all the time I was walking with you. But it makes me only twenty-five."

"Many things don't work in here," he said. "One day a man brought in a Lee-Metford, and that wouldn't work."

"The laws of science are universal in their application. It must be the water in the moat that has injured the machinery. In normal conditions everything works. Science and the spirit of emulation—those are the forces that have made us what we are."

I had to break off and acknowledge the pleasant greetings of people whom we passed. Some of them were singing, some talking, some engaged in gardening, hay-making, or other rudimentary industries. They all seemed happy; and I might have been happy too, if I could have forgotten that the place led nowhere.

I was startled by a young man who came sprinting across our path, took a little fence in fine style, and went tearing over a ploughed field till he plunged into a lake, across which he began to swim. Here was true energy, and I exclaimed: "A cross-country race! Where are the others?"

"There are no others," my companion replied; and, later on, when we passed some long grass from which came the voice of a girl singing exquisitely to herself, he said again: "There are no others." I was bewildered at the waste in production, and murmured to myself, "What does it all mean?"

He said: "It means nothing but itself"—and he repeated the words slowly, as if I were a child.

"I understand," I said quietly, "but I do not agree. Every achievement is worthless unless it is a link in the chain of development. And I must not trespass on your kindness any longer. I must get back somehow to the road, and have my pedometer mended."

"First, you must see the gates," he replied, "for we have gates, though we never use them."

I yielded politely, and before long we reached the moat again, at a point where it was spanned by a bridge. Over the bridge was a big gate, as white as ivory, which was fitted into a gap in the boundary hedge. The gate opened outwards, and I exclaimed in amazement, for from it ran a road—just such a road as I had left—dusty under foot, with brown crackling hedges on either side as far as the eye could reach.

"That's my road!" I cried.

He shut the gate and said: "But not your part of the road. It is through this gate that humanity went out countless ages ago, when it was first seized with the desire to walk."

I denied this, observing that the part of the road I myself had left was not more than two miles off. But with the obstinacy of his years he repeated: "It is the same road. This is the beginning, and though it seems to run straight away from us, it doubles so often, that it is never far from our boundary and sometimes touches it." He stooped down by the moat, and traced on its moist margin an absurd figure like a maze. As we walked back through the meadows, I tried to convince him of his mistake.

"The road sometimes doubles, to be sure, but that is part of our discipline. Who can doubt that its general tendency is onward? To what goal we know not—it may be to some mountain where we shall touch the sky, it may be over precipices into the sea. But that it goes forward—who can doubt that? It is the thought of that that makes us strive to excel, each in his own way, and gives us an impetus which is lacking with you. Now that man who passed us—it's true that he ran well, and jumped well, and swam well; but we have men who can run better, and men who can jump better, and who can swim better. Specialization has produced results which would surprise you. Similarly, that girl———"

Here I interrupted myself to exclaim: "Good gracious me! I could have sworn it was Miss Eliza Dimbleby over there, with her feet in the fountain!"

He believed that it was.

"Impossible! I left her on the road, and she is due to lecture this evening at Tunbridge Wells. Why, her train leaves Cannon Street in —of course my watch has stopped like everything else. She is the last person to be here."

"People always are astonished at meeting each other. All kinds come through the hedge, and come at all times—when they are drawing ahead in the race, when they are lagging behind, when they are left for dead. I often stand near the boundary listening to the sounds of the road—you know what they are—and wonder if anyone will turn aside. It is my great happiness to help someone out of the moat, as I helped you. For our country fills up slowly, though it was meant for all mankind."

"Mankind have other aims," I said gently, for I thought him well-meaning; "and I must join them." I bade him good evening, for the sun was declining, and I wished to be on the road by nightfall. To my alarm, he caught hold of me, crying: "You are not to go yet!" I tried to shake him off, for we had no interests in common, and his civility was becoming irksome to me. But for all my struggles the tiresome old man would not let go; and, as wrestling is not my specialty, I was obliged to follow him.

It was true that I could have never found alone the place where I came in, and I hoped that, when I had seen the other sights about which he was worrying, he would take me back to it. But I was determined not to sleep in the country, for I mistrusted it, and the people too, for all their friendliness. Hungry though I was, I would not join them in their evening meals of milk and fruit, and, when they gave me flowers, I flung them away as soon as I could do so unobserved. Already they were lying down for the night like cattle—some out on the bare hillside, others in groups under the beeches. In the light of an orange sunset I hurried on with my unwelcome guide, dead tired, faint for want of food, but murmuring indomitably: "Give me life, with its struggles and victories, with its failures and hatreds, with its deep moral meaning and its unknown goal!"

At last we came to a place where the encircling moat was spanned by another bridge, and where another gate interrupted the line of the boundary hedge. It was different from the first gate; for it was half transparent like horn, and opened inwards. But through it, in the waning light, I saw again just such a road as I had left—monotonous, dusty, with brown crackling hedges on either side, as far as the eye could reach.

I was strangely disquieted at the sight, which seemed to deprive me of all self-control. A man was passing us, returning for the night to the hills, with a scythe over his shoulder and a can of some liquid in his hand. I forgot the destiny of our race. I forgot the road that lay before by eyes and I sprang at him, wrenched the can out of his hand, and began to drink.

It was nothing stronger than beer, but in my exhausted state it overcame me in a moment. As in a dream, I saw the old man shut the gate, and heard him say: "This is where your road ends, and through this gate humanity—all that is left of it—will come in to us."

Though my senses were sinking into oblivion, they seemed to expand ere they reached it. They perceived the magic song of nightingales, and the odour of invisible hay, and stars piercing the fading sky. The man whose beer I had stolen lowered me down gently to sleep off its effects, and, as he did so, I saw that he was my brother.

The Literal Level of Allegory

To understand an allegory properly, a reader should establish firmly the literal level, taking especial pains to define and examine fully the factual details that are given. For example, the narrator reports that his pedometer (an instrument for measuring distance walked) registered, instead of distance, his age. When he sits down to rest, his seat is a milestone (a marker set at absolutely regular intervals and numbered in order from the point of origin to the end of a particular roadway). Clearly, this is no ordinary road if time is measured in distance walked. However, even this much precision of detail disappears almost immediately when the narrator begins to speak of all instruments and objects of man's scientific invention as "things"—things whose weight is so great that the travelers drop them, only to have them be covered by the dust of the road until they looked "no better than stones." The reader must very precisely identify and examine every concrete possibility in this story (the dust, the brown crackling hedge), and he must also identify both who travels on the road and what actions are appropriate to those travelers.

Obviously the narrator is the major character. At twenty-five he stops walking because he is so tired and sits down to rest on a milestone off which he slides because the weight of the things he carries is so great. He himself finds his stopping "a shocking thing" and therefore is "too apathetic to feel resentful" when people pass him, jeering. Apparently he has been a model walker before, for he "had traveled more wisely" than his brother, whom he "had to leave by the roadside a year or two around the corner." His wisdom in living on the road is that he has not "wasted his breath on singing, and his strength on helping others." He is concerned that he "had already dropped several things" and is disconcerted that his remaining things pull him from the milestone into the dust of the road. There, contrary to every demand of the road, he prays not for strength to go on walking, but to give up.

The other people on the road continue to act properly: they jeer as they outstrip him. For example, Miss Eliza Dimbleby, an authority on educational theory ("educationist" also has connotations of inflexibility, antitraditionalism, and intellectual limitation), does not even slow down as she passes him, though she does exhort him "to persevere." The persistence of the other people's walking with their burden of things constitutes their superiority to him. In contrast both to the narrator and to the people of the road, the narrator's brother acted in a most improper manner. He used to sing and help people. That wasteful behavior made the narrator's leaving correct. Presumably he jeered as he outstripped his brother.

On a literal level, then, the narrator has been vigorously walking for twenty-five years down a dusty road lined closely by dry, brittle hedges, in the company of people like himself who value the things that they carry and the distance that they travel, and who despise those who spend any strength on activity not directly productive of progress in walking. Suddenly, oppressed by "the monotony of the highway" and "the weight of the things . . . still carried," he stops to rest, falls into the dust of the road with his "face to the great parched hedge," and prays to give up. Had anyone been in sight he would not have dared to try to escape, "For we of the road do not admit in conversation that there is any other side at all." On impulse he begins to push his way through the hedge, then attempts to turn back, "for in the passage, all the things I was carrying were scraped off me. . . ." The hedge marks the boundary at which things stop.

The simplest way to study what he finds on the other side of the hedge is to note the direct literal contrasts between what he finds there and on the road. Having lost all the "things" that had dragged him to the dust in the road, the narrator is light enough to be "twitched out" of the deep pool into which he had fallen from the hedge. This rescue is a laughing response to his cry for help. The narrator remarks: "I had never been in so large a space or seen such grass and sunshine. The blue sky was no longer a strip . . . and there was in the landscape a sense of human occupation. . . ." The narrator marks this contrast more sharply by keeping the attitude of the road that restrains him from calling the area "a park, or garden," which words he says "imply a certain triviality and constraint." His first question is " 'Where does this place lead to?' " His rescuer is "just the kind of age we mistrust on the road." He loses his "pleasure in the grass, the sky, the trees, the happy men and women" when he sees the moat as "a barrier" to the dry side of the hedge. He finds walking with someone difficult both because there is no advantage to outdistancing his companion and particularly because he "had never kept step with anyone since [he] left [his] brother."

The rest of the story should be observed for literal significance: "things" like the Lee-Metford gun and the pedometer do not work; actions mean nothing but themselves; the gate of ivory—the gate through which come empty dreams—marks the beginning of the road on which the narrator has traveled for twenty-five years; when the road reaches the gate of horn—through which come dreams that will really happen—all mankind will reenter the "park." By clear implication, the dream that led mankind out of the park through the gates of ivory was an empty dream, and those who come through the hedge return to the proper life.

The Metaphorical Level of Allegory

The reader's problem is to interpret the literal level of "The Other Side of the Hedge" to arrive accurately at the allegorical level. In that process, he must remember that in an allegory the literal details are not symbolic but **metaphorical.** That is, a literal fact does not ray out multiple possibilities of meaning (as does a symbol) but instead is restricted by its content to a single figurative equivalent (as is a metaphor). However, literal detail in an allegory does have representative power. Allegorical details tend to stand for whole classes of similar objects, roles, or actions: the narrator represents mankind; the pedometer, all sorts of invented devices to serve men; the gun, inventions used for destructive purposes, etc. The symbol differs because it is able to represent simultaneously totally different things. Since, then, every fact should have only one consistent figurative possibility in an allegory, the reader should translate literal details into as restricted but complete figures as possible. Take for examples the pedometer and what is apparently the narrator's age, though improperly recorded by the pedometer.

The pedometer is a scientific instrument designed by man. For that design he depends upon the exercise of his reason about the laws of nature, turning the truth that he finds into a concrete thing. He designs the pedometer to measure distance walked. In the apparent absence of the scientist's continued definition of it and his lack of supervision of its operation (presumably because his energies are expended on designing more things), the pedometer is put to a use for which it was not intended and that it cannot fulfill: measuring life. Yet, the misused pedometer becomes for those on the road the most important "thing" in their lives, determining their whole expenditure of energy rather than being subject to their use. Quite literally, no one stops to think about the meaning of the pedometer or of the race measured by it. The significance of the pedometer on the figurative level is tightly confined. Representing as it does all scientific invention, the pedometer permits the author to criticize: (1) the reason of men when turned toward the devising of things rather than to the search for truth, (2) the tendency of science to assume no responsibility for the proper use of its discoveries, (3) the tendency of a scientific society to focus so much on what it owns that it comes to value the increase of material things over human beings, and (4) the insidious fashion in which material things, elevated to highest value, become tyrants over the men whom they were intended to serve.

Since the pedometer takes on the function of measuring life in terms of progress on the road, the reader must assume that age here equals the history of man on the road—the time since he was led by empty dreams out of paradise onto the dusty road. Consequently, the reader can logically arrive at the fact that the twenty-five registered by the pedometer is somehow reinforced by the presence of a milestone at the precise point where the narrator, mankind in general, faltered in his journey for the first time in his life. That life began twenty-five units of something ago. Presumably that unit is one of time, as the milestone should be of distance. To discover precisely what natural time that twenty-five represents, the reader needs to speculate about what occurrence in history launched mankind on the road to scientific, materialist thought, and produced mankind's first pedometer. Because that kind of thought depends upon belief that man's reason can discover all truth, the reader must with patience uncover the fact that modern, scientific thought is considered to have its origins in the Greek philosophy of twenty-five centuries ago. How especially appropriate is Forster's allusion to Penelope's statement about dreams in *The Odyssey* by the Greeks' earliest author!

The prime point for this particular study is that "The Other Side of the Hedge" is a literal story with a second very carefully controlled figurative meaning. Its details are metaphorical, not symbolic. They do not ray out multiple meanings all attached to a single theme. Instead, the theme of the story can be told simply by converting the literal level to its single consistent allegorical sense.

A Country Doctor

FRANZ KAFKA

I was in great perplexity; I had to start on an urgent journey; a seriously ill patient was waiting for me in a village ten miles off; a thick blizzard of snow filled all the wide spaces between him and me; I had a gig, a light gig with big wheels, exactly right for our country roads; muffled in furs, my bag of instruments in my hand, I was in the courtyard all ready for the journey; but there was no horse to be had, no horse. My own horse had died in the night, worn out by the fatigues of this icy winter; my servant girl was now running round the village trying to borrow a horse; but it was hopeless, I knew it, and I stood there forlornly, with the snow gathering more and more thickly upon me, more and more unable to move. In the gateway the girl appeared, alone, and waved the lantern; of course, who would lend a horse at this time for such a journey? I strode through the courtyard once more; I could see no way out; in my confused distress I kicked at the dilapidated door of the year-long uninhabited pigsty. It flew open and flapped to and fro on its hinges. A steam and smell as of horses came out from it. A dim stable lantern was swinging inside from a rope. A man, crouching on his hams in that low space, showed an open blue-eyed face. "Shall I yoke up?" he asked, crawling out on all fours. I did not know what to say and merely stooped down to see what else was in the sty. The servant girl was standing beside me. "You never know what you're going to find in your own house," she said, and we both laughed. "Hey there, Brother, hey there, Sister!" called the groom, and two horses, enormous creatures with powerful flanks, one after the other, their legs tucked close to their bodies, each well-shaped head lowered like a camel's, by sheer strength of buttocking squeezed out through the door hole which they filled entirely. But at once they were standing up, their legs long and their bodies steaming thickly. "Give him a hand," I said, and the willing girl hurried to help the groom with the harnessing. Yet hardly was she beside him when the groom clipped hold of her and pushed his face against hers. She screamed and fled back to me; on her cheek stood out in red the marks of two rows of teeth. "You brute," I yelled in fury, "do you want a whipping?" but in the same moment reflected that the man was a stranger; that I did not know where he came from, and that of his own free will he was helping me out when everyone else had failed me. As if he knew my thoughts he took no offense at my threat but, still busied with the horses, only turned round once towards me. "Get in," he said then, and indeed: everything was ready. A magnificent pair of horses, I observed, such as I had never sat behind, and I climbed in happily. "But I'll drive, you don't know the way," I said. "Of course," said he, "I'm not coming with you anyway, I'm staying with Rose." "No," shrieked Rose, fleeing into the house with a justified presentiment that her fate was inescapable; I heard the door chain rattle as she put it up; I heard the key turn in the lock; I could see, moreover, how she put out the lights in the entrance hall and in further flight all through the rooms to keep herself from being discovered. "You're coming with me," I said to the groom, "or I won't go, urgent as my journey is. I'm not thinking of paying for it by handing the girl over to you." "Gee up!" he said; clapped his hands; the gig whirled off like a log in a freshet; I could just hear the door of my house splitting and bursting as the groom charged at it and then I was deafened and blinded by a storming rush that steadily buffeted all my senses. But this only for a moment, since, as if my patient's farmyard had opened out just before my courtyard gate, I was already there; the horses had come quietly to a standstill; the blizzard had stopped; moonlight all around; my patient's parents hurried out of the house, his sister behind them;

I was almost lifted out of the gig; from their confused ejaculations I gathered not a word; in the sickroom the air was almost unbreathable; the neglected stove was smoking; I wanted to push open a window; but first I had to look at my patient. Gaunt, without any fever, not cold, not warm, with vacant eyes, without a shirt, the youngster heaved himself up from under the feather bedding, threw his arms round my neck, and whispered in my ear: "Doctor, let me die." I glanced round the room; no one had heard it; the parents were leaning forward in silence waiting for my verdict; the sister had set a chair for my handbag; I opened the bag and hunted among my instruments; the boy kept clutching at me from his bed to remind me of his entreaty; I picked up a pair of tweezers, examined them in the candlelight and laid them down again. "Yes," I thought blasphemously, "in cases like this the gods are helpful, send the missing horse, add to it a second because of the urgency, and to crown everything bestow even a groom—" And only now did I remember Rose again; what was I to do, how could I rescue her, how could I pull her away from under that groom at ten miles' distance, with a team of horses I couldn't control. These horses, now, they had somehow slipped the reins loose, pushed the windows open from the outside, I did not know how; each of them had stuck a head in at a window and, quite unmoved by the startled cries of the family, stood eyeing the patient. "Better go back at once," I thought, as if the horses were summoning me to the return journey, yet I permitted the patient's sister, who fancied that I was dazed by the heat, to take my fur coat from me. A glass of rum was poured out for me, the old man clapped me on the shoulder, a familiarity justified by this offer of his treasure. I shook my head; in the narrow confines of the old man's thoughts I felt ill; that was my only reason for refusing the drink. The mother stood by the bedside and cajoled me towards it; I yielded, and, while one of the horses whinnied loudly to the ceiling, laid my head to the boy's breast, which shivered under my wet beard. I confirmed what I already knew; the boy was quite sound, something a little wrong with his circulation, saturated with coffee by his solicitous mother, but sound and best turned out of bed with one shove. I am no world reformer and so I let him lie. I was the district doctor and did my duty to the uttermost, to the point where it became almost too much. I was badly paid and yet generous and helpful to the poor. I had still to see that Rose was all right, and then the boy might have his way and I wanted to die too. What was I doing there in that endless winter! My horse was dead, and not a single person in the village would lend me another. I had to get my team out of the pigsty; if they hadn't chanced to be horses I should have had to travel with swine. That was how it was. And I nodded to the family. They knew nothing about it, and, had they known, would not have believed it. To write prescriptions is easy, but to come to an understanding with people is hard. Well, this should be the end of my visit, I had once more been called out needlessly, I was used to that, the whole district made my life a torment with my night bell, but that I should have to sacrifice Rose this time as well, the pretty girl who had lived in my house for years almost without my noticing her—that sacrifice was too much to ask, and I had somehow to get it reasoned out in my head with the help of what craft I could muster, in order not to let fly at this family, which with the best will in the world could not restore Rose to me. But as I shut my bag and put an arm out for my fur coat, the family meanwhile standing together, the father sniffing at the glass of rum in his hand, the mother, apparently disappointed in me—why, what do people expect?—biting her lips with tears in her eyes, the sister fluttering a blood-soaked towel, I was somehow ready to admit conditionally that the boy might be ill after all. I went towards him, he welcomed me smiling as if I were bringing him the most nourishing invalid broth—ah, now both horses were whinnying together; the noise, I suppose, was ordained by heaven to assist my examination of the patient—and this time I discovered that the boy was indeed ill. In his right side, near the hip, was an open wound as big as the palm of my hand. Rose-red, in many variations of shade, dark in the hollows, lighter at the edges, softly granulated, with irregular clots of blood, open as a surface mine to the daylight. That was how it looked from a distance. But on a closer inspection there was another complication. I could not help a low whistle of surprise. Worms, as thick and as long as my little finger, themselves rose-red and blood-spotted as well, were wriggling from their fastness in the interior of the wound towards the light, with small white heads and many little legs. Poor boy, you were past helping. I had discovered your great wound; this blossom in your side was destroying you. The family was pleased; they saw me busying myself; the sister told the mother, the mother the father, the father told several guests who were coming in, through the moonlight at the open door, walking on tiptoe, keeping their balance with outstretched arms. "Will you save me?" whispered the boy with a sob, quite blinded by the life within his wound. That is what people are like in my district. Always expecting the impossible from the doctor. They have lost their ancient beliefs; the parson sits at home and unravels his vestments, one after another; but the doctor is supposed to be omnipotent with his merciful surgeon's hand. Well, as it pleases them; I have not thrust my services on them; if they misuse me for sacred ends, I let that happen to me too; what better do I want, old country doctor that I am, bereft of my servant girl! And so they came, the family and the village elders, and stripped my clothes off me; a school choir with the teacher at the head of it stood before the house and sang these words to an utterly simple tune:

> Strip his clothes off, then he'll heal us,
> If he doesn't, kill him dead!
> Only a doctor, only a doctor.

Then my clothes were off and I looked at the people quietly, my fingers in my beard and my head cocked to one side. I was altogether composed and equal to the situation and remained so, although it was no help to me, since they now took me by the head and feet and carried me to the bed. They laid me down in it next to the wall, on the side of the wound. Then they all left the room; the door was shut; the singing stopped; clouds covered the moon; the bedding was warm around me; the horses' heads in the open windows wavered like shadows. "Do you know," said a voice in my ear, "I have very little confidence in you. Why, you were only blown in here, you didn't come on your own feet. Instead of helping me, you're cramping me on my deathbed. What I'd like best is to scratch your eyes out." "Right," I said, "it is a shame. And yet I am a doctor. What am I to do? Believe me, it is not too easy for me either." "Am I supposed to be content with this apology? Oh, I must be, I can't help it. I always have to put up with things. A fine wound is all I brought into the world; that was my sole endowment." "My young friend," said I, "your mistake is: you have not a wide enough view. I have been in all the sickrooms, far and wide, and I tell you: your wound is not so bad. Done in a tight corner with two strokes of the ax. Many a one proffers his side and can hardly hear the ax in the forest, far less that it is coming nearer to him." "Is that really so, or are you deluding me in my fever?" "It is really so, take the word of honor of an official doctor." And he took it and lay still. But now it was time for me to think of escaping. The horses were still standing faithfully in their places. My clothes, my fur coat, my bag were quickly collected; I didn't want to waste time dressing; if the horses raced home as they had come, I should only be springing, as it were, out of this bed into my own. Obediently a horse backed away from the window; I threw my bundle into the gig; the fur coat missed its mark and was caught on a hook only by the sleeve. Good enough. I swung myself onto the horse. With the reins loosely trailing, one horse barely fastened to the other, the gig swaying behind, my fur coat last of all in the snow. "Gee up!" I said, but there was no galloping; slowly, like old men, we crawled through the snowy wastes; a long time echoed behind us the new but faulty song of the children:

> O be joyful, all you patients,
> The doctor's laid in bed beside you!

Never shall I reach home at this rate; my flourishing practice is done for; my successor is robbing me, but in vain, for he cannot take my place; in my house the disgusting groom is raging; Rose is his victim; I do not want to think about it any more. Naked, exposed to the frost of this most unhappy of ages, with an earthly vehicle, unearthly horses, old man that I am, I wander astray. My fur coat is hanging from the back of the gig, but I cannot reach it, and none of my limber pack of patients lifts a finger. Betrayed! Betrayed! A false alarm on the night bell once answered—it cannot be made good, not ever.

Action

In a story as symbolic as "A Country Doctor," the action line is essential to identifying major actions that help to establish who the protagonist and the antagonist are, what their conflict is, and what in their basic natures makes that conflict inevitable. When interpretations, thoughts, and decisions are omitted, the extreme lack of importance of the external action becomes dramatically clear, but its unimportance does not remove the necessity for an action line. Understanding precisely what external actions the narrator does perform on the few occasions when he does act clarifies both the doctor's character and the point of view of the story. Perhaps the most significant revelation of the action line will be that the doctor is a reactor, not an actor, and that even when he reacts, as a rule, he acts on the least demanding level: the verbal.

A study allied to the action line is an analysis in chronological order of all of the verbs in "A Country Doctor" of which the narrator is the subject. Primarily, they fall into five classes: verbs of possession ("I had a...") ; verbs of obligation ("I had to...") ; passive-voice verbs from which, as the subject, the narrator receives action; linking verbs followed primarily by nouns that name him in some facet of his role of doctor or by adjectives that describe his emotions; and verbs that show action but have no object. Those few verbs that do show his action on an object deserve particular attention. When all of the evidence from the study of verbs is gathered, the reader will see a definite pattern greatly revealing of the narrator's selfish nature whether as passive receiver of action, as reactor rather than actor, as possessor of persons and objects, or as an enjoyer of the suffering caused him by his duties in his chosen occupation. A similar analysis of pronouns referring to the doctor helps to clarify the interpretation of the end of the story.

Point of View

Point of view in "A Country Doctor" is most unusual in respect to the time when the narrator tells his story. The story opens with the narrator speaking of himself in the past tense: "I was in great perplexity." Antecedent action is in the perfect of that same tense: "My own horse had died in the night." In the last six sentences of the story, however, the narrator speaks of all actions either in the present ("I wander astray...") or in the future ("Never shall I reach home..."). Some actions of others are in progressive form ("My successor is robbing me..."; "the disgusting groom is raging"). Other of his verbs are potential forms, all in the negative: his successor "cannot take [his] place"; he himself "cannot reach" his fur coat; and "A false alarm on the night bell once answered—it cannot be made good, not ever."

The reader needs to look first at these verbs in their functional arrangement from past to present to future. Then he needs to project the death of the narrator, summarize the narrator's position at the time when he uses the present tense, and then look back on the narrator's past action. The second order permits the reader to study the narrator's living out his mature life in "this most unhappy of ages" in this nightmare. The logical support for that study can be found by analyzing very closely the actions continuing in the present in the last six sentences. Logic will demand also that these actions be seen continuing into the future. If "at this rate" the narrator never will reach home, logically, he—exposed and naked to the frost of his times—must review continually in his own mind the past action that he narrates.

Character

Biological Trait

Despite its apparent simplicity, the question of why Kafka chose a male doctor as his protagonist is one of the most complex potential in the story because it requires a discussion of theme.

Physical Traits

The absence of detail relevant to a particular trait always must be seen as significant. To what extent are the beard, the coat, and the bag of implements the man? When he is stripped of his clothes, "my fingers in my beard," can it be an accident that the doctor emphasizes the only cover that remains to him? His physical traits are most important on the symbolic level.

Natural and Habitual Traits

The reader searching for evidence of habits and of nature must remember that the character's disposition will determine to a great extent the habits that he acquires. To prove the existence of an habitual action, locate every reference to it and define precisely what aspect of the action is emphasized. Understanding the reason for that emphasis requires seeing the connection between the character's pattern of thinking about an habitual response and the character's basic nature. The reader should remember, however, that repetition is as often an indication of a symbol as it is of a habit.

The study of action reveals clearly, for example, that it is the doctor's habit to answer the night bell or it would not have become a torment to him. Also, he considers his horse and his servant equally agents of his will and accepts uncritically, as he does from the groom, whatever others do to facilitate his wishes. These few habits establish his basically selfish nature emphasized throughout the story in every kind of action that he performs or receives. Here, the doctor's habit of answering the night bell also is a major factor in identifying the doctor as a man of duty; but a closer look at the manner and the spirit in which he performs his duty shows clearly that his belief in his duty helps him to evade unselfish involvement. Particularly, the symbolic power of the night bell is important in the last sentence.

One of the most subtle problems in studying this doctor is identifying emotional habits. For example, when the narrator is stripped, he displays not the least embarrassment, shock, or surprise—all of which most readers would expect. The inference demanded by the narrator's composure under these circumstances is that he has developed a pose with which he habitually meets such personal indignities. Once his action becomes a pattern, it is habit, not emotion. For an understanding of habits developed because of emotional needs, the reader must examine the doctor's strange ritual with his instruments in response to his patient's whispering, "Doctor, let me die." How typical are the doctor's thinking of himself rather than of his patient and his using his instruments for nonmedical purposes?

The reader can prove also that even most of the doctor's deliberation is habitual and stems from his self-centered nature. For example, though for an instant the doctor is furious with the groom for biting Rose, he never thinks of her real situation until he is at the patient's house. Rather, he responds habitually by letting nothing precede his duty. The fact that the doctor believes that he acts from a sense of duty can be used to focus on the discrepancy between what the doctor thinks his motives are and what they really are—part of the central irony of the story.

Emotional Traits

A number of emotional traits either are asserted by the doctor or are readily identified. That he is perplexed, forlorn, confused, and distressed he states and demonstrates clearly at the beginning of the story. By the end of the study of the first page the reader can see that the doctor's emotional condition has reduced him to impotence. That interpretation is reinforced throughout the story by the random quality of the few specific but futile acts that he does perform and of the way that he permits himself to be treated by the groom, the patient's family, the townspeople, and even the horses. The analysis of verbs suggested in the study of action will be of significant help here. His emotional incapacity is emphasized further by a number of the major symbols of the story.

Unexpected actions, of course, reveal emotional traits. The doctor's "confused distress" leads him to kick the pigsty; his surprise keeps him from answering when the groom crawls out asking, "Shall I yoke up?" When Rose flees to him with the teeth marks on her cheek, he yells furiously at the groom. This sort of catalogue of unexpected actions needs to be made for the whole story. Then the reader can understand adequately all of the doctor's specific emotions and can see that they are elements of an overriding anxiety. That anxiety is rooted in the doctor's sense that his commitment to his duty as a doctor is futile—as are his individual actions done presumably in fulfillment of that duty. Whenever the doctor substitutes what he thinks is his duty for what his medical or human duty really is, the reader can identify a point where the doctor's anxiety about the meaninglessness of his life is intensified.

Probably the most overt statement of the doctor's sense of futility follows his finding the boy quite sound and "best turned out of bed with one shove."

> I am no world reformer and so I let him lie. I was the district doctor and did my duty to the uttermost, to the point where it became almost too much. I was badly paid and yet generous and helpful to the poor. I had still to see that Rose was all right, and then the boy might have his way and I wanted to die too. What was I doing there in that endless winter! My horse was dead, and not a single person in the village would lend me another. I had to get my team out of the pigsty; if they hadn't chanced to be horses I should have had to travel with swine. That was how it was.

Because this passage is central to the identification of the doctor's emotional traits (hence his anxiety), the reader must see both the literal level of the doctor's action and what the doctor conceives his action's relationship to duty to be. This kind of thinking demands of the reader the most rigorous kind of fidelity to the objective level of the doctor's statements. (1) Despite a blizzard, the doctor prepares to travel ten miles in answer to the night bell. (2) Having no horse, he waits, although without real hope, for his servant girl to try to borrow one. (3) When his hopelessness is justified, he kicks the pigsty in the anguish of finding himself to be right about the selfishness of others that interferes with his duty. (4) Though he is surprised that horses and a groom emerge from the pigsty, he accepts without question that they are to assist him in carrying out his duty. (5) Made by the groom to choose between defending Rose—an object in his household—and beginning his journey, he chooses his duty. (6) Arrived at the patient's, he participates in a ritual conducted by the family that concludes with only a cursory contact with the patient. (7) That contact confirms what apparently the doctor believed even while he sacrificed Rose: the call that it was his duty to answer would be a false alarm.

What the doctor thinks of as his duty he considers to be a continuously empty gesture; yet he deliberately chooses that empty gesture over actions that might give his life meaning. The reader must become aware that the doctor's false sense of duty permits him not only to consider his life one prolonged self-sacrifice but also to use that sacrifice to indulge himself in demoralizing self-pity. In his view, his horse's dying seems almost intentional interference. The failure of the townspeople to place his need for a horse ahead of whatever their needs might be, he considers a personal affront. In fact, he is so busy pitying himself that he never sees that, were he dependent on what he could find in his pigsty by his personal effort, there would have been neither swine nor supernatural horses. When he says, "That is how it was," he thinks of his life as a selfless sacrifice to a duty that others have emptied of meaning.

What the reader must see is the doctor's emotional need to pity himself so that he need not see the real possibilities open to him for action. Also the reader must see the irony that it is the doctor himself who empties his duty of meaning. Essentially, the doctor pictures himself as the only person with a proper sense of duty; and a great part of his sense of futility comes from his belief that people expect him to do far more than his duty. That expectation added to the exhaustion produced simply by his duty itself is so overpowering that he exaggerates turning the boy out of bed until it seems to him world reform. The only emotion of the doctor that is ever satisfied fully is self-pity. The more the events of the story fulfill his desire to be misused, the more he pities himself. Ironically, the greater his self-pity, the greater also his anxiety about the meaning of his life. Testing the validity of such an interpretation requires that the reader study very carefully the stream-of-consciousness logic of the doctor's habitual deliberations in the manner illustrated here with the numbered steps and in the two succeeding paragraphs.

Deliberative Traits

Fear is an entirely different matter from anxiety. An understanding of that difference is essential for any student of modern literature. Fear has an object: that is, fear is a specific emotion provoked by a specific cause. Therefore, once the object of fear is identified, appropriate expedient action can overcome it. When the school choir sings for the community, "Strip his clothes off, then he'll heal us./If he doesn't, kill him dead!" the doctor believes the song, knows that he cannot cure the boy, fears death at the hands of the community, and, as soon as possible, escapes. Faced with a real threat, he can act—deliberately and effectively. However, escaping the townspeople in no way helps him to escape his anxiety.

Anxiety is the manifestation of mankind's modern concern with whether or not life is meaningful. Because meaninglessness is not a tangible object that can be removed or destroyed, there can be no satisfactory expedient deliberation about it. Therefore, the only persons who can act under the burden of anxiety are those who, because of radical commitment either to faith or to existential courage, can accept and tolerate meaninglessness as the nature of the human condition. Neither choice is possible for the doctor because he is too absorbed in himself.

Radical commitment to faith requires selflessness because faith submits all decisions to judgment against a value outside one's self. Because such values usually are systematized, a value system structures reality for the believer and hence often relieves him completely of anxiety. The radical man of faith considers all of his actions moral in that he constantly decides what to do on the basis of what he believes is right. Such a man of faith bears personal responsibility for the results of his actions; but his load is lightened because he believes that his value system gives meaning to all of his actions and their consequences, however painful those actions or their consequences are to him personally.

A false faith permits the pseudo-believer to act as he wishes, blaming all consequences on his faith. If the doctor is the man of true commitment to his duty, he must make no other test of any action but whether he believes it to be his duty or not. Therefore, if he believes that it is his duty to comfort his patient, he must not concentrate on saving himself. His attempting to save himself while claiming to be doing his duty identifies him most clearly as a man of false faith.

The purely existential commitment is different from that of the radical commitment to faith. If there is no meaning in existence, no action can have more meaning than another: no action is either prohibited or preferred; no action is either right or wrong. However, this absolute freedom confers on the existentialist total responsibility for the consequences of any action. That is, the existentialist has an unlimited choice of actions; but he must never presume that any power other than himself willed an action, he must never ask that his action be understood, and he must never complain about the intensity or the effect of responses that his actions provoke. However, the existential man is capable of reasoning about consequences and of choosing among actions. Therefore, duty is as good a reason for action as any other. Were the doctor an existentialist who had chosen duty as a reason for acting, each decision would have been checked against his concept of duty much as if duty had been his faith or a result of his faith. He would not have claimed duty as the ground for his action, however, and then have appealed to the world to understand and appreciate him as his patients did not.

As a pure existentialist, the doctor might deliberately choose, on the other hand, the direct fulfillment of his emotions as a guide to his action. Were his selfishness existential, however, the doctor scarcely would have chosen to be a doctor; he certainly would not have answered a call in the midst of a blizzard unless he had wanted to, had he been a selfish doctor, and he never would have pitied himself for the results of his actions. Nor would he have cared what others thought of his performance.

A third kind of commitment—half existential, half religious—is potential for the doctor and bears particularly on the parable of the woodsman. It is possible for an existentialist to find the human condition without discernable meaning and yet to believe, completely by faith, that there is a God who makes meaning of it. Were the doctor such a man, he could accept the anxiety of his existence with courage. Furthermore, he could continue to base his decisions on his best estimate of what he deems to be the will of God at the same time that he feels the existentialist's freedom to value all experience equally. He then could bear the consequences of his actions (even the necessity to die) alone but believing that his suffering is meaningful to God, hence to be valued.

The doctor is not a religious existentialist either. Because he is blind to his selfish nature, he thinks himself committed to duty, apparently because of religious faith. (He thinks his statement that the gods send horses and a groom is blasphemous; and blasphemy is possible only to a person who believes in what he is irreverent about.) However, that duty cannot help being false because it derives from a set of values that he holds in name only. The proof that he is suspended between a nominal faith and an unrecognized hence unaccepted selfishness is central in the study of the story. The evidence of his dilemma is the same that proves most clearly that his thoughts are habitual, not genuinely deliberative.

Even the doctor's few deliberations that are not habitual show that he is expedient in the service of his selfishness—a complete contradiction of what he believes to be the grounds on which he acts. At the beginning of the story, the doctor believes that it is his duty that compels him to answer the night bell and that restrains him from whipping the groom. Yet there is a gap in his logic. He is preserving his image, not serving his patient. He sees the "seriously ill patient" not as a person needing medical attention but as "waiting for me." He clearly believes also that what the groom is helping him to do is get to the patient, but his focus is that "everyone else had failed me"—a failure to him personally. The most dramatic example of the irony is his thinking that the "sacrifice" of Rose, in addition to his habitual sacrifice of himself, is "too much to ask." Even while he tries to talk himself into believing that she is important to him, he identifies her as "the pretty girl who had lived in my house for years almost without my noticing her." In fact, the only reason that he seems roused to care about her is that someone else, the groom, is taking her from him. That single sentence carefully examined for all of its implications is adequate proof that the narrator of "A Country Doctor" does not see the discrepancy between what he thinks he is and what he is.

The conclusions that the doctor reaches as a result of what he believes is deliberation all deserve study. A number of his conclusions are general statements about the meaninglessness of his life, usually with the indefinite pronoun "it." At the beginning of the story, for example, he says more about life than about the girl's borrowing the horse: "It was hopeless. I knew it." At the end of the story he announces, "I do not want to think about it any more." Almost always the reader's understanding of why the doctor cannot accept the apparent meaninglessness of his life hinges on how the doctor avoids commitment by avoiding action. Other significant conclusions reached after deliberation concern the doctor's view of himself, of other people, and of human relationships. Understanding them is primarily a matter of examining how the doctor's own selfcenteredness blinds him. Particularly, the reader should become aware of how little the doctor is even aware of the efforts of others to communicate with him.

Setting

The use of specific concrete and historical detail gives reality to "A Country Doctor" and makes it believable at the same time that distortion in time and place makes the story universal though fantastic. This distortion is what makes a nightmare of reality. In what way is modern historical time seen by Kafka's doctor as "this most unhappy of ages"? In what way is "his icy winter" also "endless"? How long does the story take? When does the narrator tell the first of the story? The action line provides this answer, and point of view extends it. Need the country in which the story takes place be Kafka's? If not, what is the effect of there being in that universal country a village in which there is a specific courtyard with a clearly described pigsty and a house whose rooms and door are identified concretely? What happens in the reader's mind when the literal ten miles between the doctor's courtyard and the patient's farmyard (1) is regarded as filled with snow as if it were a container, yet (2) is covered as real distance but in unreal time, and (3) becomes finally "the snowy wastes" through which the doctor will never reach home? Since literal elements of the story become distorted ingredients of the doctor's nightmare, the reader can trace their evolution from the concrete to the symbolic by listing chronologically any changes in their form or effect and discovering what in the doctor's internal or external action produces each change. For example, the reader can discover quickly that it is the frustration of the doctor exhibited in the literal kicking of a literal door of a literal pigsty that transforms the sty into the stables of the supernatural. Any literal object, even the doctor's coat, offers practice in tracing the evolution from reality to nightmare. The steps in the coat's removal from reality have discoverable causes that will lead the reader to understand later the nightmare distorting of relationships, values, actions, and conventions of society.

Atmosphere

Since the emotional climate is the doctor's, the reader must seek the atmosphere in the characters themselves, in the nature of the doctor's conflict, and especially in details of time, place, and space as they relate to the doctor. Especially in so symbolic a story, study of the atmosphere requires the reader to suspend his disbelief sufficiently to react to the blizzard, the gig, the horses, the groom, and even the wound as real even if supernatural. Nor must the reader falter in seeing the gathering of the elders and hearing both the singing of the children and the whispering of the doctor and his patient.

Effect

A chronological examination of the steps by which the reader comes to share the anxiety and the sense of futility of the narrator is probably his best approach to the study of emotional effect. Most crucially, the reader must share with the boy and the doctor the womb-like warmth of the feather bed. If the reader permits himself to respond fully, he will discover how near the truth the doctor really is. However, the reader may not fully experience the emotional effect until he understands the doctor's parable of the woodsman and shares the doctor's despair that his escape from death brings him no nearer to meaning in his life.

Studying the intellectual effect of the story primarily involves identifying the central irony of the story: the discrepancy between what the narrator believes his commitment to be and what it really is. The irony can be studied anywhere that a reader contrasts how the doctor acts with what a genuine commitment to the unselfish service of humanity would require of him. However, speculation about what true duty might have permitted is useful only when it clarifies what false duty allows the doctor to substitute. For example, had the doctor been concerned with the patient and not with his own image, he might have found the wound. Had his instruments been more than props for his role as doctor, he might have believed that they could help and have used them—at least the tweezers to remove the worms. Acting differently would have meant being a different character, however, so such a possibility must not be a point for discussion. The reader may now be thoroughly aware intellectually of the doctor's failure to recognize his duty not only as a doctor but also as a human being.

Recognition

Even though the doctor tells the story in retrospect, he never sees that in so selfishly saving himself he becomes lost forever. Neither does he see conversely that he need not have wandered alone forever had he lived his whole lifetime without trying to save himself. Therefore, the recognition in "A Country Doctor" has to be, of course, the reader's, not the doctor's. The paradox that the doctor's death could give meaning to his life probably cannot be understood fully either emotionally or intellectually until the reader studies the wound as a multiple symbol dependent in part on biblical allusions. When the reader can recognize fully what he shares of the doctor's self-centeredness, of his rationalizations to avoid involvement, of his anxiety over the meaning of his life, and of his final avoidance of action that would commit him—then the reader can generalize his recognition in this story to a universal theme. Several kinds of understanding must precede the completion of effect and recognition, hence of theme.

Style and Tone

Kafka's style in "A Country Doctor" probably has to be examined before a student understands the story thoroughly. Four major stylistic facts are clear: the story is a single unbroken paragraph; its individual sentences are primarily very complex; their clauses belong together only because of stream-of-consciousness logic; and almost every noun is a symbol. The only legitimate question about style is whether it is effective—whether it permits an author to say what he wants with the effect that he intends. Therefore, as a reader determines how Kafka writes, he must judge also the effectiveness—the tone—of his writing.

Detailed stylistic studies of individual sentences both permit evaluation of stylistic effect and yield important insights into the presentation of character and theme. Analysis of the first two sentences of the story demonstrate the stream-of-consciousness logic that needs study in every sentence of the whole. The first clause announces the doctor's perplexity and sets in motion two streams of thought. The first leads him to a statement that his journey is urgent, which urgency he identifies as a serious illness in a patient. The location of the patient at ten miles' distance compounds the perplexity. So far he has identified the literal need that he must meet. When he sees those ten miles filled with snow in the face of his urgency, instead of being baffled by it, he thinks of the readiness and appropriateness of the gig and of the readiness and appropriateness of its potential content: himself, muffled in furs, bag in hand, standing in the courtyard. The need and his competence to meet it with the things in his possession yield to the second stream of thought that flows from his perplexity: there was no horse. Before the conjunction *but,* the narrator establishes himself as central. After the conjunction, he makes clear that he is powerless despite a need and his readiness. The repetition of "no horse" establishes a tone of hopelessness as if it were a wail. The thought that there is no horse to be had leads him to remember that his horse has died in this night, an event so recent that he has had no opportunity to provide another. Since a horse is standard transportation for a country doctor of this era, the doctor's saying that the horse has been "worn out by the fatigues of this icy winter" establishes the doctor's own weariness—fatigue intensified by iciness. Despite his earlier assertion that there was no horse to be had, the doctor explains that his servant girl is seeking to borrow another. The slenderness of his hope of her success is emphasized by his focus on the random way that she is "now running around the village." Again he uses the negative conjunction "but," this time to compound the death of his horse and his knowledge that makes him feel his powerlessness to move as palpably as he feels the snow "gathering more thickly" upon him.

    The complex sentence structure reflects the complexity of circumstances that immobilize him. The sense of the clauses establishes both the urgency of his need to move if his life is to be meaningful and his complete inability to move because of factors that he believes to be completely beyond his control. In terms of the theme, then, these first sentences establish clearly that he has taken upon himself more weight than he can carry alone and that the hopelessness of his performing has immobilized him. Carefully examined, Kafka's sentences reveal also that the greatest weight that the doctor carries is the sense of himself as the center of the universe. As that center, he must give the universe meaning by his actions. That the reader feels the weight of hopelessness after only two literal statements suggests that Kafka's style is indeed effective. And the weight of style and content increases as the literal level of the story disappears.

Stylistic analysis of any complex sentence in the story will permit the reader to see the dramatic difference between the reality represented at the first of the story and the pure nightmare at the end. Without doubt "A Country Doctor" records a gradual descent from physical reality, each level exhibiting a different quality of consciousness, each closer to what the doctor's internal life is really like. Stylistically, Kafka parallels the progressive descent into the doctor's mind with the gradual removal of the literal level. The horses, his servant, his coat, the rest of his clothes—all either disappear or are transformed into symbols so pure that they bear little but the name of the objects or persons on the literal level. The reader's stylistic analysis of the present tense ending of the story will reveal as pure symbol intensified but unresolved what is established as literal in the first two sentences.

Allegory

An allegory affirms a value system and shows with simple characters how its values give life meaning. "A Country Doctor" demonstrates without system and primarily with a complex character that values have no meaning because they do not bear on life. The protagonist of an allegory personifies some virtue under attack or humanity simplified. The doctor not only symbolizes complex humanity but also permits and abets the destruction of the few characters (Rose, the boy, the boy's sister) who exhibit virtues. In an allegory, the major character surmounts obstacles that strengthen his faith or his virtue by their opposition. The obstacles for the doctor are symbolic opportunities for him to find a faith or the courage to replace his willfulness and self-pity at the same time that they are opportunities for him to become more selfish, hence more lost. The decisions of a traditional allegorical protagonist are moral and lead him from temptation or selfishness to triumph and moral purity. The decisions of the doctor appear moral, but they are expedient and plunge him deeper and deeper into selfishness, anxiety, and despair.

If the multitude of symbolic details of "A Country Doctor" do indeed form a negative allegorical pattern, Kafka perhaps has utilized **irony of structure:** the use of a traditional literary form for a purpose opposite to the conventional. Certainly "A Country Doctor" seems to be structurally an allegory of meaninglessness in which no value or logic or form is permitted to operate.

The values of duty, service, loyalty, and love do not operate. No one will lend the doctor a horse, "especially for such a journey"— a trip perhaps to save the life of a human being—because the horse might be lost. Science operates no more than values, for time and space defy measurement and what can be known by observation changes even while it is being observed. The year-long-uninhabited pigsty houses horses and a groom. A wound the size of the palm of a hand cannot at first be seen at all. A fatal illness has no observable symptoms. Roles are as jumbled as values and science. The parson sits at home and unravels his vestments while the doctor conducts medical services for the village elders as the secular school choir sings a hymn of faith threatening the doctor's life if he cannot perform a miracle of healing without his scientific aids. Relationships also are askew. Horses are named Brother and Sister. A groom gives his master orders. Paradox marks even the theme: the doctor who saves his life loses permanently what could make living meaningful. As the naked doctor's gig creeps with him away to the snowy wastes, the children sing a "new but faulty" song—a song of faith in the doctor deprived of his science: "O be joyful, all you patients,/The doctor's laid in bed beside you!" Even biblical allusions reinforce a loss of faith, not faith.

The structural irony extends even to the line of the plot itself. An allegory traditionally has a formal plot: action in time and place so arranged that characters are revealed in a conflict that is introduced, complicated, and resolved. "A Country Doctor" appears to have that arrangement, yet permits the narrator to resolve nothing because his continuous retelling of his story is its never-ended resolution. Each time the narrator completes his story, he finds himself wandering astray, and by implication, in his search for a reason for his being lost must tell himself the story again and again. Furthermore, the apparently formal plot depends completely on stream-of-consciousness logic, not formal logic. Therefore, the internal action is what matters, not what happens in the action structured formally. In fact, the action line is the list of the most meaningless actions of the entire story. The structural irony is greater yet: what seems total disunity is tightly structured by a symbol in a new kind of plot.

Symbols

Whether or not "A Country Doctor" is ironic allegory must be debated. That it is a symbolic story is certain. The only limit to the complexity of what can be understood in Kafka's symbols seems to be the reader's ability to imagine their reference to "this most unhappy of ages."

For example, snow is one of the most persistent symbols of the story. As literal snow, it is an obstacle to be overcome by a suitable vehicle, the gig; its coldness yields to a good fur coat. As a symbol it contributes to an understanding of the internal conflict: the snow makes the journey impossible if the doctor has no power beyond himself. In world literature a blizzard sometimes connotes the loss of metaphysical meaning—a loss of faith that there is a transcendent reality, power beyond the physical or material world. Therefore, the snow, gathering more and more thickly upon the doctor, can be seen to symbolize the anxiety that accompanies loss of metaphysical faith. Certainly the weight of the snow as the kinetic effect of anxiety immobilizes the doctor. However, snow need not be read only as a symbol of a loss of faith. As a solid barrier filling the space between the patient and the doctor, the snow isolates him from his practice—from meaningful activity. The snow's coldness, a major constituent of "this iciest of winters," is paralleled by the doctor's inability to experience human relationships. Additionally, snow's covering quality makes wastes around, behind, and before him in his attempted journey home.

Another important symbol is identified by the title. This is not "the" but "a" country doctor—an example, not a specific noun. As a representative of the scientifically trained mind, why is he especially suitable as a character who would take upon himself responsibilities once held to be the exclusive province of religious faith?

Without doubt, the servant girl whose name is Rose and a wound that is rose-like and has rose-red worms must be associated on a symbolic level. Much of their significance depends upon biblical allusions and an understanding of paradox that are more appropriately studied later. However, study of the literal wound as a symbol yields valuable insight into the levels of the doctor's consciousness and the distance of the symbol from reality at various points in the story. Moments before the doctor finds the wound, he is preparing to leave, pronouncing the boy well. Then, for only an instant, each member of the family impresses the doctor with his individual need for the doctor's medical skill and both of the horses whinny. For that instant the doctor is "somehow ready to admit conditionally that the boy might be ill after all." It is then that he sees for the first time "an open wound as big as the palm of my hand." In medical practice in the real world rather than in a nightmare, had a doctor discovered that he had overlooked such a wound, he would have been appalled. Instead, he admires the beauty of the wound and is fascinated, not repulsed, by his discovery of the worms. The paradoxical nature of truth as Kafka sees it is perhaps most clearly evidenced by the wound and the worms. That the wound is indeed the most multiple symbol of the story will be even more clear when the reader learns how many different allusions and paradoxes the wound unifies.

The symbolic functions of the horses and the groom each time that they appear in the story need to be studied with care equal to that given the wound, the doctor, and the snow. The student must remember that the sequence of symbols in this story represents an increasing distance from reality. Does the doctor will the horses and the groom into existence, or have they been in his house unbeknownst to him all along? What alternatives did the groom's asking if he should yoke up offer the doctor? What is the difference between his relationship to his dead horse and these? At what cost to himself and to Rose does he obtain their power? What desire or need of his own permits him to accept the command of the groom that he "Get in" after the team has been harnessed and Rose has been bitten and has fled futilely to him for help? Does the doctor realize that the urgency of the journey to which he responds is his own impatience to get on with his supposed duty, not the need of his patient? And precisely what value has Rose to him at this point?

What in the nature of the horses is represented by the speed by which they cover the ten miles from the doctor's to the patient's, their opening a window, their attention to the patient? Do the actions of the horses reinforce or contradict the doctor's? Do the horses appear at the window because he remembers Rose again, or does he remember Rose again because the horses appear at the window, or is their appearance at that moment a coincidence? Are the horses summoning him to the return journey or to examine the patient? Does the whinnying of both horses influence the doctor's tentative admission of the extreme possibility that the boy might be ill or his discovery that the boy was "indeed ill"?

When the doctor decides to escape rather than to stay and face possible death because he cannot cure his patient, the horses stand faithfully in their places. Why does the horse obey and back away from the window? Why is the horse only in this single instance under the command of the doctor? Why does the doctor swing onto the horse rather than into the gig? What is the significance of his being naked when he is first in direct contact with either horse? What does it mean that the reins trail and the gig "sways behind" the horses who are barely fastened together? Is the gig, "exactly right for our country roads," appropriate to the snowy wastes? Why do the horses and the doctor "crawl through the snowy wastes"? Why is the last view of the horses a view of the "naked man with an earthly vehicle, unearthly horses," wandering astray?

Any person, object, or action that the reader feels to be symbolic can be explored with a series of questions similar to but much more exhaustive than those about the horses and groom.

Conflict

One of the most provocative ways of looking at "A Country Doctor" is in terms of the doctor's relationship to power on three levels. Rose's statement: "You never know what you're going to find in your own house" is an ironic clue to the doctor's ignorance about power of all kinds. The doctor's horse, his bag of medical instruments, his gig, his pigsty, and one of the two lanterns are objects owned by the doctor with his knowledge and used or not used by him or at his command. What the doctor thinks he knows best are these objects. That he understands neither their proper use nor the responsibility for his power over them is clear both in his ritual rather than medical use of his instruments and in his accidental discovery that his year-long-uninhabited pigsty is not only occupied but also occupied by the supernatural. The doctor's abuse of his real horse also is willful. The clear inference is that the horse was driven to death. That abuse particularly cannot be condoned since apparently the death occurred as a result of routine practice, not because of an emergency in which the doctor had to choose between killing his horse by overuse or risking the life of a patient. By using the horse according to his will, the doctor himself, therefore, became responsible for having no horse when the night bell called him to this case at the most critical point in his personal life.

The doctor attempts to use both persons and the supernatural precisely as he uses things and drives himself as irrationally as he drove his horse. The doctor's lack of a proper understanding that Rose permits him power over her is a preview for the reader of the doctor's failure in every other human relationship in the story. The most important failure of relationship is of course to the boy when the doctor assumes that he can exercise the powers of God.

The doctor's relationship to the third level of power—the supernatural—helps most to define the conflict in "A Country Doctor." To understand it fully, the reader must study first the doctor's lack of awareness that the supernatural exists in his own house; second, how the doctor's failure to recognize the dual nature of the supernatural keeps him from recognizing his own potential for good and evil; and third, the results of the doctor's mistaken belief that his will directs the supernatural when, instead, it operates independently of him.

The conflict clearly involves the doctor's erroneous belief that he exercises power as he wills—an error that stems from his despairing belief that he alone and by his action alone can give meaning to an otherwise meaningless universe. The doctor's most fatal misuse not only of the boy's faith but also of himself begins with the boy's question: "Will you save me?" The doctor recognizes both that the question involves him as if he were "omnipotent with his merciful surgeon's hands" and that there is a difference between the boy's asking the medical and the theological questions. What will become increasingly clear is that the doctor as scientist considers the case hopeless yet, or perhaps therefore, accepts that he is to be "misused for sacred ends." That he wishes to act as if he were God is less obvious but still evident. If he does not wish the role, how can he be "altogether composed" stripped not only of his clothes but also of his instruments and his science? If he does not feel himself omnipotent, how can he stand before the people nothing more than a naked man, yet claim to be "altogether... equal to the situation"? Clearly, his retrospective view is that "he remained so." Therefore, the reader can see that the doctor's acting as if he were God is deliberate and, furthermore, that his assuming omnipotence is the highest development of his false sense of duty. The people exit, shut the door, and stop singing; the moonlight dims; and the feather bed envelops the doctor as well as the patient. Interestingly, when the doctor assumes omnipotence, the heads of the supernatural horses "wavered like shadows." The doctor and the patient are at this moment only themselves, and even the doctor is briefly honest. The boy recognizes that the doctor is without power of his own—"you were only blown in here"—and justly has no confidence in him. The doctor's response is genuine, though his concern is for himself, not the boy. Obviously, there is a difference in tone between the doctor's saying fairly honestly: "Believe me, it is not too easy for me either," and his later pompous response: "My young friend, . . . your mistake is: you have not a wide enough view."

What is there in the boy's rejection of the doctor's momentary admission of human fallibility that prompts the doctor to reassume his role as man of faith? It is not in the doctor's nature for him to tell the story for the sake of the boy. Therefore, the reader must assume that the doctor cannot tolerate the boy's loss of faith in him as a doctor and so deliberately becomes what the boy will have faith in. He says that he has been "in all the sickrooms, far and wide"—something only a god could have done—and hence can tell the boy with assurance: "your wound is not so bad."

Parable

Only when he knows without question that there is nothing that he can or will do to help his patient, the doctor tells the parable to calm the boy, not to save him.

> "My young friend," said I, "your mistake is: you have not a wide enough view. I have been in all the sickrooms, far and wide, and I tell you: your wound is not so bad. Done in a tight corner with two strokes of the ax. Many a one proffers his side and can hardly hear the ax in the forest, far less that it is coming nearer to him."

If the boy can believe that others think him fortunate to bear a supernatural wound, he can accept it gratefully because of the meaning that it bestows on his life and the honor it brings to his death. To understand the irony of the doctor's telling the boy the parable, the reader must interpret what the literal details of the doctor's parable say of the proper relationship of man to the woodsman. Since the parable is told at a point in the story where all things are almost pure symbol, there can be no doubt that the only woodsman capable of inflicting a supernatural wound is God.

Many people desire precisely the sort of wound with which the boy was born. They desire it because it is a mark of direct contact with the woodsman. Yet all that they can do is wait in hope that the woodsman will accept their proffered sides and wound them. Their faith, evident in their readiness to be wounded, cannot compel the woodsman to choose them. He elects whom he chooses; and, the doctor implies, the highest election is to be born with the wound. They must be content if their closest contact with the woodsman is hearing his ax distantly without the sound ever even moving toward them. By extention, their faith should sustain their readiness to receive a wound should they hear no sound at all to prove even the existence of a woodsman and should they never see a person with a symbolic wound.

When the doctor finishes telling the parable, the boy asks: "Is that really so, or are you deluding me in my fever?" Stripped of his science, the doctor pronounces "as an official doctor" on the reliability of his theology. Simultaneously, he remembers that "now it was time for me to think of escaping." The highest irony of the story, the explanation of why the doctor wanders forever in a life without meaning, and the climax of the formal action are the doctor's escape without understanding his own parable. The song of the people promises him death if he remains with the patient but does not cure him. His remaining in the face of that probability would have sustained the boy until his wound killed him. By staying, the doctor figuratively would have bared his side to the woodsman. The boy's saving wound would have become the doctor's. He would have died, but by his own decision to do his duty as a human being in the face of a supernatural wound beyond the power of his science. He chose to save his life, though he did not intend to wander astray never recognizing why his life of duty lacked meaning.

Allusions

Most students who have studied "A Country Doctor" as closely as they have been asked to, have a thorough and unified knowledge of it. However, at least three biblical references need to be understood before the story can be explored in full depth. One allusion establishes the Old Testament concept of the Messiah as a suffering servant. A second refers to the crucifixion of Jesus—the man Christians believe to be the suffering servant—whose final wound was in the side. The third passage describes what will happen when the Messiah comes for the second, and last, time. There also is a long secular literary tradition of referring to Jesus' mother Mary as the Rose of Sharon. The name derives from a verse in The Song of Songs, a book in the Apochrypha rather than the Old or New Testaments.

The Old Testament description in Isaiah of the savior of mankind as a suffering servant is central to the Jewish expectation of the Messiah not yet come; and New Testament writers use the same passage as proof that Jesus was that Messiah. Critics of modern literature often argue that any character whose suffering is redemptive is a Christ figure. The writer of Second Isaiah prophesies the manner in which the Christ will be caused to suffer when he comes as a servant to save man:

3 He is despised and rejected of men; a man of sorrows, and acquainted with grief: and we hid as it were our faces from him; he was despised and we esteemed him not.

4 Surely he hath borne our griefs, and carried our sorrows: yet we did esteem him stricken, smitten of God, and afflicted.

5 But he was wounded for our transgressions, he was bruised for our iniquities: the chastisement of our peace was upon him; and with his stripes we are healed.

6 All we like sheep have gone astray; we have turned every one to his own way; and the Lord hath laid on him the iniquity of us all.

Isaiah 54: 3–6

The theological concept of the suffering servant definitely enriches the reader's understanding of Rose's servant relationship to the doctor. Her willingness to serve the doctor beyond any normal duty is clear from the beginning. The doctor knows that she is "running" to try to find a horse; and long before she is near enough to speak, she signals with the lantern even though she returns without a horse. She stands beside him, obviously prepared to serve him more when the groom and horses emerge from the pigsty. It is she who says what might have made him rethink his situation and perhaps act differently: "You never know what you're going to find in your own house." When the doctor orders her to help the groom, "the willing girl hurried" to serve him. To understand what Rose symbolizes, the reader needs to see how Rose herself is a suffering servant "wounded" for the doctor's "transgressions," "bruised" for his "iniquities." Furthermore, the reader needs to discover how the doctor might have been saved by Rose's suffering either then or later when he remembers that she is suffering the obviously unwanted sexual attack of the groom. In that light, Rose's first suffering is a call to the doctor to accept responsibility for what is potential or present in his own house. His sheeplike, purposeless straying "to his own way" permits, even requires, her suffering. She flees to him when the groom bites her—an action that is possible by the groom only because she carried out the doctor's order to help hitch up the team. Her turning to him offers two kinds of salvation to the doctor—self-knowledge and human relationship. If he could act in her defense, he could accept that his distressed kicking of the pigsty, an expression of his own selfish and frustrated will, called the evil groom as well as the horses into their lives. Therefore, he also might come to accept himself as both good and evil. Beyond that, had he seen Rose as a person, not as a servant, and had he subordinated his wishes and needs to hers, he could have been saved to a human relationship that would have brought warmth and meaning to his icy life. In his blindness, however, the doctor leaves Rose to her own defenses, believing that going to his patient is a duty that justifies whatever sacrifices other people must make in his behalf. The doctor esteemed Rose not and deliberately sacrificed her to his duty.

Rose's second suffering also symbolizes the evil potential in any man who acts wholly as he chooses. Particularly it symbolizes evil hidden from a man by a false conception of moral necessity. In the midst of his ritual examination of the tweezers, the doctor remembers Rose's frantic flight from the sexual intentions of the groom and presumes that she has been raped. Simultaneously, he notices that the horses have opened the windows and are eying the patient. Although the doctor remembers Rose too late to save her from the groom's assault, had his remembering led him to accept that she was "bruised" for his "iniquities" (raped because he had abandoned her to the groom for a duty he believed to be empty), he might have been "healed" by her "stripes" (brought to a recognition of the evil and the goodness in his nature and hence a recognition also of his true responsibility). That recognition might have called him from his long-suffering condescension to the boy's family and to a sound medical attitude toward the boy. The irony is, of course, that her suffering does not permit the doctor to save the boy and cannot save him to self-knowledge, human relationship, or professional competence. Instead of thinking of her pain, he lapses into his habitual self-pity, complaining that his loss of her was one sacrifice that was "too much to ask."

The allusion from Isaiah to the Christ as suffering servant also applies to the parable of the wound, to the boy, and to the wound itself. Kafka's parable of the woodsman suggests that to be wounded is an honor accorded only to a few who have direct contact with the woodsman. Yet, the doctor does not really consider the boy honored by the privilege of suffering. He thinks of the boy only as "stricken" and "afflicted"—hopelessly ill of an infested wound, cause unknown. Ironically, he does not think him "smitten by God," though in the parable that he then makes up, the doctor implies that his is a wound bestowed by the supernatural woodsman. Like Rose, the boy with the wound has the potential to save the doctor from going further "astray" into selfishness. Where Rose calls him to human relationship, however, the relationship to which the boy's wound calls the doctor is to the supernatural that caused the wound as well as to the human boy who needs him more as a man than as a doctor.

The boy's wound is wholly supernatural. It has no medical symptoms like fever or coldness and is not, in fact, visible to the doctor until both horses whinny after the sister's "fluttering a blood-soaked towel." The only literal symptom that the doctor notes in his first examination is "something a little wrong with his circulation." The boy has had the wound since he was born (his "sole endowment"). The knowledge that he has the wound makes him want to die; then, seeing the life in it, he wishes to be saved. The boy's wound and his and the doctor's consequent discussion of the relation of the wound to faith offers the doctor his final chance to commit himself to a value beyond himself—an opportunity reinforced by the horses whenever he might "return from his own way."

Full understanding of the symbolism of the boy's wound depends on recognizing that almost universally an allusion to a wound in the side is considered a reference to the New Testament record of the wound in the side of Jesus after his crucifixion. One reference (John 19: 31–37) explains that the Roman soldiers came to hasten the deaths of the three persons crucified that Friday by breaking their legs. Since that particular Friday was Preparation day before the Passover, the haste was necessary if that most holy sabbath not be defiled by criminals not buried. One of the soldiers, believing that Jesus was already dead, did not break his legs but instead pierced his side with a spear. The wound in Jesus' side became for Christians a prime proof that Jesus died a human death. However, in traditional Christian interpretation the presence of the wound in the side verifies that Jesus rose from the dead. John 20: 24–29 records that eight days after his death Jesus presented his wounded side and hands to Thomas, one of his disciples who had doubted reports of Jesus' resurrection. Upon that proof, Thomas confessed his restored faith and Jesus responded: "Thomas, because thou hast seen me, thou hast believed: blessed are they that have not seen, and yet have believed."

The analogy of those who, in "A Country Doctor," offer their sides to the woodsman whose ax may never even be heard in the forest and those who have never seen yet believe in Jesus seems clear. The second analogy is between the wound of the boy that the doctor says is "not so bad" and the wound of Jesus. Although contrasts can be made between even minor actions of the doctor and of Jesus, such detailed allusion probably was not intended. In fact, on minor points, any number of literary or historical figures would offer almost equally valid contrasts. The major evidence that "A Country Doctor" alludes to Jesus is the direct oppositeness of the commitments and the lives of the doctor and of Jesus despite the similarity of their situations.

The doctor identifies himself as "I was the district doctor and did my duty to the uttermost, to the point where it became almost too much." Part of what makes him say that he "wanted to die too" is his feeling that "the whole district made my life a torment with my night bell" and that he is constantly asked to sacrifice too much—even "the pretty girl who had lived in my house for years almost without my noticing her." As part of the duty that the doctor bears so heavily, he accedes to whatever "pleases" the people of his district—people whom he recognizes "have lost their ancient beliefs" so that "the parson sits at home" while "the doctor is supposed to be omnipotent."

Jesus also chose to serve others, believing that those who saw him saw God more clearly. Jesus insisted always that his duty was to God and refused to meet the demands of his hearers, knowing with increasing certainty that that refusal meant his eventual death. In contrast to the members of the doctor's district, Jesus hearers often held their ancient beliefs so strongly that they thought Jesus blasphemous (John 8). For the country doctor, blasphemy is thinking that the supernatural is potentially helpful.

Enough of the doctor's ancient belief remains for him to know that part of the demands on him are "misuse ... for sacred ends," yet he makes no protest for he thinks self-pityingly: "what better do I want, old country doctor that I am, bereft of my servant girl!" He even suspects that his thought is blasphemous that only in false alarms "like this the gods are helpful, send the missing horse, add to it a second because of the urgency, and to crown everything bestow even a groom—" The irony that prompts his calling this circumstance urgent now that he has gone through his ritual with his instruments is nostalgic. The same nostalgic irony that the gods are not indeed available to offer help echoes in his saying as he discovers the boy's wound: "ah, now both horses were whinnying together; the noise, I suppose was ordained by heaven to assist my examination of the patient...."

The greatest contrast between Jesus and the doctor is related to the appropriateness of the boy's faith that the doctor has the power to save him. The fact of the boy's faith can be deduced from his asking the doctor "Will you save me?" rather than "Can you?" The doctor, though "only a doctor," willingly pretends to know saving spiritual truths—truths whose validity he assures to the boy by giving his "word as an official doctor." That is, the doctor uses his authority as a representative of the government and as a man of science (a student of objective proof) to validate a statement of faith in a metaphysical woodsman. In fact, he makes his validation seem both more scientific and more omniscient by referring to his personal observation of all the sickrooms of the world. Therefore, it is the boy's faith in the doctor, not in the woodsman, that lets him "lie still," assured that the wound that will cause his death makes his life meaningful.

Not merely an observer, Jesus, whose death Christians believe validates his life, made his claims for God by faith, knowing that keeping his faith meant his death. The doctor, to save his life, gives his word of honor as an official doctor in support of what he believes to be a lie. Were the doctor committed either to the woodsman or to his duty as a doctor, he should have remained to comfort his patient and, if necessary, to accept his death rather than deny what he believed. When the real test comes, the doctor chooses to save his life by denying his duty and lying about his lack of faith. He has not the least recognition that his ultimate concern is himself and that it is the boy who is "Betrayed! Betrayed!"

The doctor's choosing to save his life rather than risk it by staying with the boy suggests another biblical allusion. At its heart is a **paradox:** two diametrically opposite statements, each of which somehow is nevertheless true. The author of Luke describes what is known to theologians as the Second Coming of the Messiah—"the day when the Son of Man is revealed":

> 33 Whosoever shall seek to save his life shall lose it; and whosoever shall lose his life shall preserve it.
>
> 34 I tell you, in that night there shall be two men in one bed; the one shall be taken, and the other shall be left.
>
> Luke 17: 33–34

Biblical scholars differ on the meaning of the second verse although they agree that it implies that judgment will be made even between the closest associates. In the Kafka parable, the one who is taken is the one who is wounded at the hands of the woodsman. The doctor, who is left, unwounded, wanders astray.

Unity in Complexity: The Radial Plot

The symbol of the wound—the center of the radial plot—simultaneously unifies the major allusions, the major paradoxes, and the other major symbols of "A Country Doctor." The wound's raying out so many coexistent meanings makes the symbol infinitely complex and overwhelmingly effective. The wound combines Rose the servant, the wounded boy, and the worms that are the life in the wound. The parable of the woodsman adds the wound as a mark of faith. Allusions add the Suffering Servant to Rose and the boy and make the idea potential for the doctor; the crucifixion adds the wound and the parable to all three; the Second Coming of the Messiah adds them all to the scene in the feather bed. The flower aspect of the wound and of Rose as the beautiful flower in the doctor's house suggests the Rose of Sharon which adds Mary, the mother of Jesus. Her son Jesus' death on the cross, necessary to his resurrection, is roughly analagous to the fatal wound's producing the worms that symbolize life. That ability of the wound to produce life suggests the beauty of even ugly things that potentially yield life: a pigsty gives birth to horses and a groom; a servant girl could provide relationship and produce children; the doctor's parable, told as a lie in the feather bed, could give meaning to his life; the supernatural horses that transport the doctor endlessly through meaninglessness could have brought the doctor to responsibility. To complicate the symbol more, there is a symbol producing a symbol stated as a paradox: a wound yields death that promises life.

A major part of the complexity of the wound derives from the paradoxes inherent in it. The wound is simultaneously beautiful and ugly. Yet its hideousness produces repulsion and fascination in the reader at the same time, and the wound's beauty makes the doctor express feeling for another person for the only time in the story. The wound is a fatal flower, yet it produces life both in the form of worms and in the form of faith expressed in the parable of the woodsman.

The effect on the reader of so complex a symbol unifying such diverse meanings is overwhelming. Paradoxically, the more meanings a reader sees in the wound, the more impossible it is for him to know precisely what the wound means. Ironically, that intellectual effect produces an emotional paralysis in the reader quite like that which the doctor's perplexity produces in him at the beginning of the story. Yet the effect on the reader and the effect on the doctor come from opposite causes. The reader is overwhelmed by the fantastic quantity of isolated meanings unified by a single symbol. The doctor suffers emotionally under complexity, but he is overwhelmed intellectually by a complete lack of recognition of any relationship between events, persons, or decisions. The reader sees so much that meaning is lost in the complexity. The doctor sees so little (and that in isolation) that he cannot believe that meaning exists. Unable to recognize the complexity of his life, the doctor suffers under the emotions that denote a response to complexity; yet, he thinks so simply (and only of himself) that he has no hope of understanding these emotions or coping with them. By reducing complexity to singleness, the doctor rejects reality and is overwhelmed by isolation.

By rejecting reality the doctor makes the recognition and acceptance of the meaninglessness of his life impossible. However, the recognition that the doctor willfully refuses is possible for the reader. Seeing the meanings unified by the wound as a symbol, the reader senses the existence of a single universal meaning behind the multiplicity of the doctor's life.

Theme

Kafka suggests that acting faithfully according to some commitment makes possible the acceptance of meaninglessness.

Questions for Discussion and Writing

1. What is the conflict of "A Country Doctor"?
2. What do verbs show of the doctor as passive receiver of action, as reactor rather than actor, as possessor of persons and objects, and as an enjoyer of the suffering caused by his duties in his chosen profession?
3. When does the doctor narrate his story?
4. Is the narrator his own audience? If not, who is?
5. Why does the doctor tell his story at all?
6. In the last six sentences of the story, what is the significance of the actions of the doctor's successor and the groom being in the most active form of the present tense while the doctor's verbs primarily show his potential actions, all negated?
7. Why is it appropriate that the major character is a man?
8. To what extent are the doctor's beard, his coat, and his bag the man?
9. What in the doctor's nature has caused him to develop the habit of answering the night bell? of considering all things and persons agents of his will? of using his instruments for ritual purposes? of meeting personal indignities with composure? of rationalizing away the need for unselfish action?
10. What is the irony in the doctor's referring at the end of the story to his fur coat, his patients, his practice, and his house as his possessions?
11. How does the way in which the doctor acts reveal the discrepancy between what the doctor thinks his motives are and what they really are?

12. In the course of the story, what emotions does the doctor state and demonstrate?

13. Why does the doctor's emotional condition make him unable to act?

14. Why does the doctor deliberately choose to act according to his duty even though he thinks of those actions as empty gestures? Are they empty? If so, why?

15. To what need, value, or potential in each character does the doctor's self-pity blind him?

16. How does self-pity keep the doctor from seeing himself?

17. Why does self-pity increase his anxiety about the meaning of his life?

18. How does the doctor use his false faith to appeal from the consequences of his own actions?

19. How do the doctor's general statements with the indefinite pronoun "it" reveal that the doctor cannot accept the apparent meaninglessness of his life?

20. What is the relation of the doctor's assertion—"To write prescriptions is easy, but to come to an understanding with people is hard"—to the doctor's choosing empty duty over involvement with people?

21. How does the concrete detail of the doctor's courtyard, the horses, the patient's home and family, and the wound allow the distortions of the nightmare to seem real?

22. How do such literal objects as the coat, the lantern, the horses, the night bell, and the wound evolve into pure symbols?

23. To what extent do Rose, the groom, the patient and his family, the choir, and the elders become symbols as well as concrete people?

24. What details of setting establish the atmosphere in the scene in the feather bed?

25. Why is it ironic that the doctor's horse had died at all? that it had died on the very night that this story begins? that the doctor considers his inability to obtain a horse the failure of the townspeople to recognize their duty? that the doctor tells the groom that he himself will drive? that the doctor tells the groom that he knows the way?

26. Is Kafka's style effective?

27. How does the opening sentence of this one-paragraph story establish both the content subject and the logic for the whole story?

28. In what ways is the problem of the first two sentences the same as that in the last six sentences? In what ways is it different?

29. In what respects is "A Country Doctor" an allegory? A parable? A fable?

30. What do the reversals of the reader's expectations (example: the doctor's conducting services for the townspeople while the parson sits at home) add to the reader's understanding of the doctor's perplexity?

31. What are the conditions that immediately precede the doctor's discovery of the wound? How does each element lead the doctor toward that discovery?

32. What is the symbolic relationship of the groom to the doctor's frustration, the doctor's impotence, the doctor's selfishness, and the doctor's need for power?

33. What alternatives did the groom's asking whether or not to yoke up offer the doctor?

34. What is revealed by the doctor's never answering the groom's question except to tell Rose to "Give him a hand"?

35. In each instance where one or both horses are mentioned, with what action or decision of the doctor does their appearance coincide?

36. What is the power relation between the horses and the doctor?

37. Precisely what do the horses symbolize?

38. Item by item and person by person, how well did the doctor know what, including himself, was in his own house?

39. As a story that illustrates a relationship of man to God, what does the parable of the woodsman teach about the knowledge man can have of God?

40. What is the relationship of the doctor's assuming omnipotence to his belief that he does his duty at all costs?

41. What keeps the doctor from realizing the irony of his lying to the boy about the reality of the parable?

42. Why is it ironic that a reader who can respond sympathetically to "A Country Doctor" probably recognizes modern anxiety in the

face of meaninglessness but may have almost no acquaintance with biblical allusions?

43. How does the wound function as the unifying symbol of the story?

44. How are the central irony, the central symbol, and the central paradox of "A Country Doctor" related?

45. What complexity does the doctor eliminate from the reasons why he has no horse? From his accepting the services of the groom? From his examination of the patient? From his telling of the parable? From his consideration of why he wanders astray?

Index

action, 12
  in allegory, 256
  antecedent, 16
  climax, 19
  complicating, 17
  deliberative, 33
  differentiating of kinds, 37, 47
  existential freedom of, 290
  expected, 32, 33
  expository, 15
  habit of, 119
  inciting, 15, 33, 34–35
  internal, 12, 33–34, 60, 62
  major, 17–18
  objective summary of, 10, 12
  protagonist's response, 15, 33–35
  resolving, 19, 39, 47, 72
  selection of for short story, 1, 2
  speech as, 16
  as symbol, 195
  unexpected, 16, 33, 34–35
action line, 12, 13
  as index to details, 12
  major actions of conflict on, 34
  omissions from, 12
  as record of character, 19–20
  as summary of external conflict, 14–19
  use of to verify interpretation, 48
Aesop, 253
allegory, 254, 256
  contrast with fable and parable, 254–256
  and "A Country Doctor," 255, 297–299
  as instruction, 254
  "Other Side of the Hedge, The," as, 272–276
allusion, 255, 261, 262, 276
  in "A Country Doctor," 306–312
  as symbol, 128, 200
  usefulness of, 262
analysis
  effect of, 48
  see also reader, critical and creative, techniques of study, understanding the short story
antagonist, 14
  blind, 47
  climax, 19
  comic, 48–49
  crisis, 18–19, 33–34
  inciting action of, 14–15, 33, 34–37
antecedent action (flashbacks), 16
  in episodic formal plot, 229
  purpose of, 2
atmosphere, 138–143

"Bartleby," 77–115
"Beggar, The," 53–58
biological traits, 31
  see also traits

"Champion of the World, The," 203–228
character
  assertion about, 3, 18, 31, 33, 35, 60
  complexity of, 34, 38, 41, 119, 125, 194
  consistency of, 47
  contribution of to atmosphere, 142

319

INDEX

character *(continued)*
 development of, 2, 3, 13
 see also traits
characters
 in allegory, 256
 in comedy, 48–49
 in fable, 255
 minor, 2, 118–120
 in parable, 256
 in tragedy, 19, 48
Chekov, Anton, 53
climax, 18–19, 39
Coleridge, Samuel Taylor, 45, 140
comedy
 nature of, 48–50
 protagonist and antagonist in, 48
 see also humor
conflict
 action line as summary of, 13
 complication of, 17, 18, 33
 contributions of, to atmosphere, 142–143
 defined in action, 15, 34–37
 identification of protagonist in, 50–51
 importance of deliberation and emotion to, 33
 inner dramatized by outer, 62, 64
 parts of the formal, 14–19
 of protagonist, antagonist, 66–67
 protagonist identified in, 50–51
 in radial plot, 230
 relation of character to, 14, 34
 setting and, 139
 similarity of major actions in, 66
 as structure for most short stories, 2
 universal, 14
Conrad, Joseph, 149, 192, 193–195
contract with reader, 245
 Conrad's, 192
 effectiveness of style and, 248
 Thomas', 248
conventions, *see* antagonist, humor, narration, and protagonist
"Country Doctor, A," 277–283
 action in, 283–284
 as allegory, 297–299
 allusions in, 306–312
 atmosphere of, 293–294
 central symbol of, 312–313

character traits in, 284–292
conflict of, 302–304
effect of, 294, 313
fable, parable, allegory, and, 253, 255
irony of structure in, 298–299
parable in, 304–305
paradox, 295, 311–312
plot of, 230, 299, 312–314
point of view in, 284
recognition in, 295, 313–314
resolution and blind narrator of, 299
setting in, 292–293
style and tone of, 295–297
symbols in, 299–302
theme of, 314
"Couriers," 263
 in biographical frame, 254
 comparison to "Prodigal Son," 253
 as parable, 265
crisis, 18–19, 39, 47
 as frustration of emotion, 33–34
 shared by protagonist, 38
"Crumbs of One Man's Year, The," 232–237

Dahl, Roald, 203
Dante Alighieri, 253, 254
deliberation, 32
 comic, 48
 expedient, 32, 34, 255
 habitual, 125
 importance to conflict, 33
 importance to resolution, 34
 moral, 32–34
 recognition of consequences of, 123
deliberative traits, 32
 comic, 49
 frustration of emotion and, 32, 125
 as revelation of basic character, 31
 tragic, 19
diction, 242
 see also linguistic clues
Divine Comedy, The, 253–254

effect, 139, 143
 contributions to, of atmosphere, conflict, intellect, realistic detail, 140–143
 duality of, 143–144

INDEX

and reader's recognition, 143
suspension of disbelief and, 45, 140
emotional traits, 32
  as bar to recognition, 35–36
  complication, crisis, inciting action, and protagonist's response as, 33–40
  revelation of basic character of protagonist in resolution, 39–40
  validity of assertions about, 69
episode, *see* plot
existentialism, 289–291
  anxiety distinguished from fear, 289
  existential freedom of action, commitment, courage, and religious faith, 289–291
  religious and false faith, 289–290
expository actions, *see* contents of exposition
exposition, 15
  in complex story, 195–196
  contents of, 15, 139–140
  focus on protagonist in, 50
  as resolution, *see* "Bartleby," 132
  symbol collection in, 141

fable
  beast, 253
  and "A Country Doctor," 255
  differentiation from allegory and parable, 255–256
  as instruction, 253, 255
  history of moral in, 253
  "The Unicorn in the Garden," 253
fiction, 1; *see also* narration
foreshadowing, *see* antecedent action
formal short story, *see* plot
Forster, E. M., 253, 255, 262, 266

habit, *see* natural and habitual traits
Hawthorne, Nathaniel, 134
  ambiguity in style of, 145–146
  recurrent themes in writing of, 147
  "Hollow of the Three Hills, The," 134–138
"Hop-Frog," 21–30
humor
  "Champion of the World, The," 231
  conventions of, 49
  objectivity of, 48–49
  see also comedy

inciting action, 15, 46
  for identification of conflict, 34–37
  similarity of, to climax, 66–67
  tests for, 16–17
  as unexpected action, 33
incongruity, *see* humor, irony, style
internal action, 12
  and choice of narrator, 60–62
  crisis as example, 18–19
  proportion of, to external action, 64
irony, 71
  character's acceptance of, 128–129
  of duplication, 49, 119, 130–131
  as key to universal emotion, 241
  in present and retrospective narration, 63
  reader's awareness of, 71–72, 121, 127
  of structure, 298–299
  verbal, 71

Kafka, Franz, 252, 263, 265, 277

linguistic clues
  to atmosphere and effect, 141
  to bias, 70
  to character, 119, 125
  to collection of symbols, 141
  to identification of symbols, 193
  to interpretation by omnipresent narrator, 61
  for objective summary, 11
  to person of narrator, 59–63
  to point of view, 60
  to protagonist, 50
  in stream-of-consciousness, 230, 242–244, 247
Luke, 257

Melville, Herman, 77
metaphorical, 274
  difference from symbolic, 274–275
misinterpretation, causes of
  accepting narrator's bias, 60–63, 68
  confusing action, emotion, 43, 64, 67
  failing to test conclusions, 44
  failing to verify stated emotions, 144

INDEX

misinterpretation, causes of *(cont.)*
  missing dual effect, 139, 144
  mistaking the meaning of action, 43
  mistaking multiplicity of symbols for fragmentation, 230
  oversimplifying characterization, 11
  reading too few levels, 192
  reading parables as general, 253–254
  substituting opinion for fact, 11
  thinking fables are moral, 253
Munro, H. H., 5

narrators
  as author's creation, 58–59
  first person, 59, 61–62, 63
    major, 62, 63, 67
    minor, 62, 63, 67
    at second-hand, 62, 63, 67
  third person, 60–61, 67–68
    limited-omniscient, 60, 62–63, 67–68
    omnipresent, 61, 63, 67
    omniscient, 59–60, 63, 67
    truth of assertions by, 60–62, 68–69
narration, conventions of, 58–63
narrative, 1, 31
natural and habitual traits, 32, 37, 46
  break in habitual patterns, 37, 46
  deepest revelation in resolution, 39
  expected actions and, 33
  repetition as clue to, 44

objective summary, 10, 11–12
objectivity
  of narrator, 69–71
  pose of, 125
Odyssey, The, 255, 276
"Other Side of the Hedge, The," 253, 254, 266–272

parable, 253–256
  characters in, 256
  in "A Country Doctor," 255
  and "Couriers," 254
  and "Prodigal Son, The," 254
  purpose of, 253, 256
paradox, 295, 311–313

physical traits, 31–32
  expected actions and, 33
"Piece of News, A," 61
plot, 228
  formal, 229
    episodic, 116, 145, 229–230
  radial, 229–230
  stream-of-consciousness, 229–230
  structural peculiarities of, 115–116
Poe, Edgar Allan, 1, 21, 33, 245
point of view, 63
"Prodigal Son, The," 257–258
  comparison to "Couriers," 253
  in historical, religious frame, 254
  teachings of, 260–261
  used as allusion, 261
protagonist
  blind, 51
  comic, 48, 49
  insight of, vs. antagonist's, 38
  resolution by, 19, 34
  resolving actions possible by, 39
  response to inciting action, 15, 33, 35–37, 46
  symbols in setting as key to problems of, 142, 299
  tests for, 50–51, applied, 116
  tragic, 19

reader, critical and creative
  application of fiction to life by, 40
  attending to detail, 3
  author's contract with, 245
  entering mind of character, 37, 139
  evaluating asserted motives, 68–71
  extending action by logic, 44
  generalization of recognition, 139
  humor as a source of objectivity, 48
  inferring motive from action and deliberation, 70, 123, 127
  interpreting ambiguity, 145–146
  keeping levels of relationship, 194
  learning context of parables, 254
  learning from comedy, 49–50
  objectivity with empathy, 38, 121
  personal experience of, 39–40, 46, 143, 240
    as key to symbol, 45
    as proof of universality, 146
  reading biased narration, 61–62